Bitten by the Red Sox Baseball Bug

About the Author

Bill Nowlin was one of the first fans on the field when Jim Lonborg clinched a tie for the American League pennant in 1967, but his membership in Red Sox Nation dates back to the 1950s and includes many lean years when there was little to cheer about beyond the heroics of his hero, Ted Williams.

Bill has specialized in Red Sox research since he turned to writing in the late 1990s. He is the author or co-author of dozens of books on the Red Sox and Red Sox players, including seven on Ted Williams. Bill has written more than 1000 articles for SABR and edited or co-edited more than 100 books in all.

Bill was elected as SABR's Vice President in 2004 and re-elected for five more terms before stepping down in 2016, when he was elected as a Director. Bill was the 2011 winner of the Bob Davids Award, SABR's highest honor.

He is also co-founder of Rounder Records of Cambridge, Massachusetts, and his development of and work for that company and its success resulted in his gaining membership in the International Bluegrass Music Hall of Fame.

Bill has also traveled widely, visiting more than 125 countries to date, and has occasionally taught courses at Boston-area universities on "Baseball and Politics" and "Sportswriting." He lives in Cambridge, Massachusetts.

Bitten by the Red Sox Baseball Bug

A Fan's Lifelong Passion

by Bill Nowlin

SUMMER
GAME
BOOKS

Contents

1   Birth of a Red Sox Fan 3

2   Dawn of the Red Sox and Early Glory 13

3   Two Dark Decades and the Arrival of "The Kid".................... 35

4   The Impossible Dream and a World of Possibilities 51

5   Postseason Pain Tempered by Accomplishment at
Rounder Records 75

6   Entrenched in the October Losing Habit 99

7   Writing About the Red Sox and the Deepening Curse 121

8   No Better Way to Break a Curse.....................................139

9   Dejection Is Replaced by...Expectation? 157

10 Another Decade and Two More Titles 181

11 More Writing About the Red Sox 215

Selected Bibliography 231

Notes 237

Bitten by the Red Sox Baseball Bug

1

Birth of a Red Sox Fan

If my brain hemorrhage had proved fatal, I never would have seen the Red Sox finally win a World Series. On Opening Day of the 2003 season (the home opener, on April 12), I had a sub-arachnoid hemorrhage and was rushed to Massachusetts General Hospital. I spent the next 28 days at Mass General and then the Spaulding Rehabilitation Hospital.

The doctors and staff at MGH saved my life, and then between MGH and Spaulding helped me "learn" to walk again and to climb stairs. How damaged I might be mentally is for others to decide. I don't seem to have come out of it any worse for the wear. There was no Pan-Mass Challenge for me that year, though – a 192-mile bicycle ride to raise money to fight cancer in children. [There are shorter rides, which I have done after reaching a more advanced age.] The beneficiary of the PMC is the Jimmy Fund, which has been a principal charity of the Red Sox since 1953. My first year was 1994. The 2023 ride alone raised $72,000,000, for a total to date just $28 million short of one billion dollars. The PMC annually raises more money for charity than any other single athletic event in the country.

I was one of the lucky ones. Among other things, I was lucky to live only a few miles from Mass General, one of America's premier hospitals.

I was also lucky in that in October 2004 I was able to experience something that many New Englanders never did – seeing the Boston Red Sox win a World Series.

It was, as is well-known, the first time in 86 years that the Red Sox had won one. There were a generation or two of Sox fans, some of whom were born and then died without that ultimate experience.

Many of us thought we never would. Fate was against us. Perhaps the team was even cursed. It might sound silly to believe in curses, but was there any better explanation for how many times the team came so close, only to fall short each and every time?

When they finally did win, it was in the most improbable way possible. Several of us mused at the time that had a Hollywood screenwriter come up with a script outlining how it all played out, they would have been turned down.[1]

It seemed surreal. It was hard to believe it really happened. For days, and even weeks afterward, some of us questioned whether this had really occurred. The 2004 Red Sox had won the World Series? Really?

The brain hemorrhage didn't get me, but I had already borne another affliction: I'd been bitten by the bug of Red Sox baseball.

What's so special about me?

Nothing, really. I am representative of tens of thousands of Red Sox fans from across New England, and around the world. Geography is part of it. But there also was something of a bond that developed between some fans and the team that either found a way to always lose at the last minute – or was just bad to begin with (as in much of the 1920s and 1950s). The phrases "long-suffering" and "Red Sox fan" seemed inseparable. In American pop-ular culture, there is something of a strain of rooting for the underdog. Maybe at some level some of us even felt we were being more heroic in pas-sionate loyalty to a team that so often came so close…but lost every time.

Red Sox fans sometimes tend to be obsessed. That might be one of the kinder ways that non-Sox fans would describe us. I would argue that it's obsessed in a good way, though. One could even pat one's self on the back and describe the team as a cultural institution, one that has become rooted in tradition over time, one that is worthy of documentation.

First let's look at what Mr. Red Sox Fan was born into, and then what things were like over the next years. And years. And years.

My goal here is to, from time to time, offer some of my story – representative in some ways but, as with any one person, individualized as well – in the context of a look at the Red Sox in postseason baseball.

A little family history

I was born on Valentine's Day in 1945. The Second World War was still under-way. Hitler was alive for another 2½ months (until April 30). The A-bombs hadn't been tested yet – nor used. The first test was on July 16, 1945. Many years ago, I suggested that everyone born after then is a mutant of one sort or another...but that's not nice. Sometimes it seems like Hitler was ancient history, like Genghis Khan. No, he was alive in my lifetime. There remain some Holocaust survivors that fortunately were liberated in time. I've had the opportunity to visit Dachau and Auschwitz. They were real. The threat of anti-Semitism and other manifestations of racism and hatred remain with us.

I was born in the city of Boston, at Faulkner Hospital in the part of the city known as Jamaica Plain. The hospital is 4.0 miles from Fenway Park. The second-floor walkup apartment in which my parents lived was half a mile closer to the park.

I was spared the trauma of the 1946 World Series, since I was just a year and a half old at the time – but, who knows? Maybe some mystical mental virus of the day surreptitiously crept into my being.

I can't remember not being a Red Sox fan, but I don't know when and how it developed.

I do know my father had a Red Sox connection, of sorts. He worked two seasons at Fenway Park. In 1937 and 1938, well before I was born and while he was still a teenager, age 15 in 1937, he and a friend decided they wanted to go to the planned 1939 New York World's Fair so they both got jobs working for Harry M. Stevens, the concessionaire, selling soft drinks and hot dogs at Fenway. They did pretty well, he told me. He said he could make as much as $40 on a Sunday, and that was for selling hot dogs for 25 cents apiece. In 2024 dollars, that $40 would be a lot!

When I interviewed him for the book *Fenway Lives*, he told me that when I was in first or second grade, a teacher asked me in class what my father did and I said he sold hot dogs at Fenway Park. Having heard that had clearly made an impression on me. I distinctly recall thinking that this work was on a par — or better — with being President of the United States.

When I interviewed him in 1999 or 2000, he told me, "I probably went to four or five games a year before I started working there. My father was a big baseball fan and even though we didn't have the money, he'd take me. We listened to games at home, too. We were living in Somerville then, and there was a trolley car that ran into Lechmere Station, and then you got a train to Fenway Park."[2]

How was I born in February 1945 while the war was still going on? My father had, after going to the World's Fair, entered Northeastern University, where he met my mother Betty Binkley (a native of Denver), but had then entered military service and been placed in the Army Air Intelligence Corps. He was, I was told, stationed on an island off the coast of Yugoslavia with a cryptography unit dedicated to capturing and trying to decipher German codes. After a stretch there, some in the unit were flown to Cairo, given a week's R&R. He got to see the Pyramids, the Sphinx, and all. When their time was up, they boarded the transport plane to head back to work — but the plane crashed while leaving Cairo.

My mother had told me never to ask him about the war. And I didn't, for years and years. All I knew was that something traumatic had happened in North Africa sometime in 1943. I knew he was in intelligence work. That's all I knew. In my imagination, he was a spy someplace in, perhaps, Algeria, and had to sneak up behind Nazis and strangle them to death with piano wire. (I have no idea where that speculation came from.) Long after my mother was gone (of cancer before she reached 50), and when I was in my 50s, I finally asked. What had happened was the plane crash. He said the last memory he had was the brains of his best friend being blown across him – and then waking up two months later in the Fifth Army Hospital in Casablanca. He had suffered two broken arms and two broken legs and been in a coma for two months. He said he was the only one in his group that survived.

The doctors apparently did a good job on him – and he was incredibly lucky. I had never detected any deficits in his walking or arm movements. He did later develop an alcohol problem, but that hadn't held him back from a successful marriage, three children, moving from Jamaica Plain out to the suburbs (Lexington, Massachusetts in 1950) and raising the three of us there.

I learned one lesson of life early on. I was William Gerard Nowlin Jr. My father had the same name. And his father was named William, too, but William Aloysius. My grandfather been born in Boston in 1881, to Frederick Mortimer Nowlin, a teamster (later a baker, and Lizzie (Sullivan) Nowlin. Grandfather William became a clerk in a drug store and later managed a pharmacy. I never met him. When I was around 10 or 11, I remember looking him up in the phone book, and seeing that he lived in the Roslindale neighborhood. I never called, never met him, and he died a couple of months before I turned 12. That was the only time I ever met my grandmother. She came for dinner – once – to our family's house in Lexington the evening of his funeral in December 1956. She died five years later. I only saw her the once. My father had a sister who died young. He had no other siblings and I know no way of learning more about him – for instance, why his father was a Red Sox fan as my father told me he had been. I'd say my father was a kind of passive fan. I don't even remember him watching games on TV – once we got a TV. I never asked enough questions about his growing up, or about his father as a Sox fan. I do know that my paternal grandfather was born in October 1881 and died in 1956. This means that he turned 22 the month that Boston's American League team won the first World Series ever held. And he turned 31 in 1912, 34 in 1915, 35 in 1916, and 37 in 1918. That might well cement you as a Red Sox fan. But the Boston Beaneaters had won pennants in 1891,1892, 1893, 1897, and 1898. Surely he must have been impressed by those teams. Did he ever go to the South End Grounds? Probably – but I can't know. Did he change his allegiance to the new A.L. team? I can't know that, either.

The two sides of the family were clearly different. My maternal grandparents – Russell and Ethel Binkley – actually lived in the same second-floor apartment as we did in Jamaica Plain. I entered the Boston Public Schools a year early, at age 5. I was only there for a few months, though, before the four adults moved to Lexington, getting me into one of the best public school systems in the state. The Binkleys lived with us for a few more years before returning to Denver. (They were natives of Goshen, Indiana, but lived many years in Denver, where my mother had been born and grew up.) My first time behind the wheel was driving on two-lane highways through Kansas. Driving back to Boston on one of the trips when we visited the extended family there. Russell Binkley had been an auditor for Armour, the meat packing firm.

Growing up in Lexington – "The Birthplace of American Liberty" – I learned early on about the first battle of the American Revolution that had taken place on April 19, 1775 on the Lexington Battle Green. There is an annual reenactment of the battle and a parade every Patriots Day; the parade passed by about a half-block from our house on Maple Street. Our family attended the Follen Church, which was literally next door to Adams School, where I finished first grade and the five that followed. It was known as the "Christmas Tree Church" because the church's founder Charles Follen had "brought the tradition of decorating an evergreen tree for the Christmas holiday to the U.S. from his native Germany in 1832."[3] Every year since 1952, when my father helped with the first sales, Follen Church has annually sold Christmas trees. I was active helping, through my teenage years. The church was a "community church" which drew its pastors from the Unitarian ministry.[4]

A mid-1950s family photo in Lexington, Red Sox cap in place.

What was the life lesson learned? My mother told us — my sisters Joyce and Lisa, and me — that while her parents lived with us, the reason was had never met our father's parents is that his mother (Mary Nowlin) had wanted him to become a Catholic priest. Not only did he fail to become a priest, he married a Unitarian. Without digging in deeply here, Unitarians are not trinitarians. Though believing that he was a great teacher, a model to emulate, they do not believe in Jesus as the son of God. One of the childhood texts I remember was *Jesus, the Carpenter's Son*. My father had married a non-Christian. He was essentially ostracized, primarily by his mother.

At some point, both Joyce and I recall being told that my father's older sister Mary Elizabeth – she was a little over six years older – had been in a bad car accident and remained in a vegetative state the rest of her life. There was clearly a lot of tragedy in that family.[5] The lesson I take from it is to try to be more forgiving.

I never asked enough about all this, but one time my father told me that his father was quite a nice guy (he must have been – taking him to a few games each year at Fenway Park!) but that his mother was unyielding. It must have been a very difficult experience seeing her that one time after the funeral in 1956.

But how did I become a Red Sox fan? Why did I start going to games myself – often alone, not always with friends, and hardly ever with family? I don't know. I just got the bug. I was infected at a relatively early age. By the time I was 12, I was going to at least a half a dozen games a year. I wish I could pin down how this all began, but it's probably simply unknowable.

Writing this reminds me of something that A. Bartlett Giamatti once said. Giamatti, the president of Yale University (1978-1986) and later Commissioner of Baseball. In August 1986, a front-page article in the *Boston Globe* began: "A fatalistic gloom hangs over Boston. It's August and the Red Sox are in first place."[6] Giamatti, born in Boston, and a Red Sox fan, recognized the phenomenon. He said, of his fellow New Englanders, "There's an almost Calvinist sense of guilt at success, that we must re-enact the Garden of Eden again and again. There's a sense that things will turn out poorly no matter how hard we work. Somehow the Sox fulfill the notion that we live in a fallen world. It's as though we assume they're here to provide us with more pain." In the same article, Harvard psychologist Richard Herrnstein said the Red Sox were still "expiating the guilt" for selling Babe Ruth.

Whatever it was that infected the souls of Red Sox fans, there was a stubborn belief that dashed hopes were the destiny of anyone who dared root for the Red Sox to win it all.

I was born into it. I can remember musing, even into the 2004 season, as to what would happen should the Red Sox ever win a World Series. It was so unfathomable that I didn't waste much time in speculation, but did wonder whether we could bear it.

The autographed photo of Ted Williams that my dad got for me in 1951
helped form the chain that has bonded me to the Red Sox my whole life.

2

Dawn of the Red Sox and Early Glory

For a team that famously went 86 years without winning a World Series, the Boston Red Sox were actually the first team to ever win one. They weren't named the Red Sox until 1908, but Boston's first team in the American League was launched in 1901. They attracted a few different nicknames in the press, but when the first World Series was held – in 1903 – it was the Boston Americans which prevailed.

Boston had had a National League team since 1876, and they had enjoyed remarkable success. In 1887 the Boston Red Stockings won the pennant by seven games over the second-place Louisville Grays. They won the National League pennant again the following year, by four games over the Cincinnati Reds.

They fell to second in 1879 and then to sixth place in 1880 and 1881. In 1882, they edged back up to third.

Under a new name, the Boston Beaneaters won the National League pennant again in 1883. They then dropped to the middle of the pack, or worse, through the rest of the 1880, until 1889, when they fell just one game short, outpaced by the New York Giants.

The Beaneaters won their next pennant in 1891, with a record of 87-51, which saw them finish 3½ games ahead of the Chicago Colts. They won the pennant three years in a row – in 1892, with an expanded season and a league that had grown from eight teams to 12, they posted a record of 102-48, 8½ games ahead of the Cleveland Spiders, and in 1893, they finished 8½ games ahead of the second-place Pittsburgh Pirates.

This was beginning to look something like a dynasty. This Boston team had even played what was called a World's Series in 1892, beating second-place Cleveland five games to none (with one tie) in postseason play.

The Beaneaters dropped back to the middle of the pack for the next three seasons, but then finished first again in 1897 and 1898 with 93 wins and then 102, edging the Baltimore Orioles both times.

They didn't finish first again until 1914, as the Boston Braves.

Come 1901, there was a new league formed and a new team in town – the Boston Americans. The new team poached a good number of Beaneaters, offering better pay. Of the 21 players on the 1900 Beaneaters, fully six of them switched teams: Jimmy Collins became the American League team manager, joined by outfielders Buck Freeman and Chick Stahl, and three pitchers: George Cuppy, Bill Dinneen, and Ted Lewis. The Boston Americans also enticed a pitcher from to come over from the St. Louis Cardinals: Cy Young, who won 33 games his first year in the American League.

The new A.L. team was more popular from the start – much more. In 1901, they outdrew the Beaneaters by almost double – 289,448 to 146,502. In 1902, their attendance was almost precisely triple that of the Beaneaters – 348,567 to 116,960. Over the course of the first decade (1901 through 1910), Boston's AL team outdrew the NL team by 4,863,094 to 1,641,780.

In 1903, there was an agreement reached that the pennant winners in the two rival leagues (National and American) would play each other in a best-of-nine World's Series. The Boston Americans won their first A.L. pennant, with a record of 91-47, finishing 14½ games ahead of the second-place Philadelphia Athletics. The Pittsburgh Pirates were National League champions.

The first World Series – 1903

Details of the eight games played in the 1903 World Series – it was a "best of nine" competition against the Pittsburgh Pirates – can be found in a number of places. Two that this author can recommend are the writeups of the individual games on SABR's Games Project at www.sabr.org and in the book *The Boston Red Sox World Series Encyclopedia [No Longer the World's Shortest Book]* written with co-author Jim Prime.[7] That book also contains summaries of Red Sox World Series games through the 2007 season. Other sources for 1903 are varied and include Roger I. Abrams' *The First World Series and the Baseball Fanatics of 1903* (Boston: Northeastern University Press, 2003). Bob Ryan's *When Boston Won the World Series* (Philadelphia: Running Press Books, 2003), Louis P. Masur's *Autumn Glory: Baseball's First World Series* (New York: Hill and Wang, 2003), and *The 1903 World Series* by Andy Dabilis and Nick Tsiotis (Jefferson, North Carolina: McFarland, 2004). There are, of course, numerous books that provide coverage of World Series play, and the Red Sox in particular.

The very first World Series game was played in Boston at the Huntington Avenue Baseball Grounds, and it got off to a bad start from a Boston perspective. The Pirates scored four runs in the top of the first inning.

The playoffs between the Pirates (champions of the National League) and the Boston Americans (champions of the three-year old American League) hadn't been mentioned in newspapers of the day until September 1 of that year, just a month before the very first game. There was a bit of "on-again/off again" to the possibility because, among other things, the contracts for Boston's players expired on September 30. A compromise was finally worked out on September 25 and a World's Series was announced. Ticket prices ranged as high as one dollar.

Cy Young started for Boston; he'd led the AL with 28 wins. But, as noted, Pittsburgh scored four runs on him in the first, adding single runs in the third, fourth, and seventh. Deacon Phillippe threw six scoreless innings for Pittsburgh, before Boston got to him for two in the seventh and a third run in the bottom of the ninth.

Was it possible that the game was thrown? Glenn Stout and Richard A. Johnson wrote that it was "in all likelihood thrown by Boston."[8] They provided some context. Gambling on baseball was not unusual at the time. Neither team's players had been all that happy with the financial arrangements. The World Series was by no means an institution; these were seen as "glorified exhibition games," and there was a benefit to a series that ran to eight or nine games. There was speculation in some of the newspapers.

In Game Two the following day, Boston's Bill Dinneen (a 21-game winner) shut out the Pirates on three hits, a 3-0 win over Sam Leever (25-7). Boston left fielder Patsy Dougherty hit two home runs in the game – thus the first two homers in World Series history. And Game Three drew more people than the previous two together. It was played on Saturday, yes, before an overflow crowd. There was every indication that the World's Series had captured the imagination of the public. Pittsburgh won Game Three, 4-2, Phillippe pitching on just one day's rest. Tom Hughes gave up the first three runs; Cy Young threw seven innings of one-run relief. (He had helped by serving as a ticket taker before the game.)

The Series shifted to Pittsburgh for the next four games. Famously, Boston's Royal Rooters – more than 100 of them – took the train to Pittsburgh for the games, and were demonstrative in their passionate cheering for their team, accompanied by a hired brass band and the song "Tessie" which they played and sang with gusto (and with lyrics derisive of the Pirates.) Indeed, Pittsburgh third baseman Tommy Leach later said, "I think those Boston fans won the Series…We beat them three out of four games, and then they started singing that damn Tessie song…Sort of got on your nerves after a while. And before we knew what happened, we'd lost the series."[9]

Left fielder Patsy Dougherty, who hit the first two home
runs in Red Sox postseason franchise history, both in
Game Two of the 1903 World Series (Boston Red Sox).

The Pirates survived a three-run Boston rally in the top of the ninth and
won Game Four, 5-4. Deacon Phillippe was already 3-0 in the Series after
just four games. Dinneen was the losing pitcher.

Boston claimed its second victory in Game Five, with Cy Young facing off
against Brickyard Kennedy. The game was scoreless through five, but then
the Bostons exploded for six runs in the top of the sixth, two of them on a
triple down the left-field line by pitcher Young. They added four more runs
in the seventh (Young collected another RBI). The final score was 11-2.

Boston drew even with a 6-3 win in Game Six. Leever and Dinneen both
gave up 10 hits. Boston scored three in the third inning, Dinneen kicking

things off with a single to left. After 6½, it was 6-0, Boston. The Pirates scored three times in the bottom of the seventh, but no more.

Game Seven was the final one in Pittsburgh, and saw Boston take the lead in the Series with a 7-3 victory credited to Cy Young and a loss borne by Phillippe. Back-to-back triples by Jimmy Collins and Chick Stahl helped give Boston a 2-0 lead in the top of the first. Triples by Buck Freeman and Hobe Ferris helped set up two more runs in the third. They added a fifth and sixth run in the top of the sixth. The Pirates scored lone runs in the fourth, sixth, and ninth. Both teams took the 25-hour train trip back to Boston.

Cy Young, 2-1 in the first World Series, with an ERA
of 1.85. In his years with Boston, he was 192-111
(2.00 ERA), with 275 complete games and
38 shutouts (Library of Congress).

Game Eight was on October 13 and featured the more-rested Dinneen against Phillippe, who had won all three of Pittsburgh's games and then lost Game Seven. Dinneen threw a four-hit 3-0 shutout, despite his pitching hand being hit by a Jimmy Sebring line drive in the third inning. Baseballs Dinneen threw for the rest of the contest were stained with his blood, but he hung in there. The Americans scored their first two on a triple by Freeman. Parent reached on an error, Freeman holding at third. Parent was sacrificed to second, and then both runners scored on a single to center by Hobe Ferris. Second baseman Ferris drove in the third (and final) run in the sixth with a single that followed a triple by Candy LaChance. Boston played errorless ball, as they had in Game Two, the only other game in which either side was error-free. In all there were 25 triples hit in the series (several of them due to ground rules required to address overflow crowds spilling onto the outfield.)

Boston's American League team – the team that before long was called the Red Sox – had won the first World Series.

Another pennant in 1904

The Boston Americans won the pennant again in 1904, edging out the New York Highlanders (later known as the Yankees) by just 1½ games. There was no World Series, though. The National League champions were the 106-47 New York Giants, led by John McGraw. His team finished 13 games ahead of the second-place Chicago Cubs. The Giants manager was still upset at the upstart American League, and in particular with A.L. president Ban Johnson, who had arranged the move of the Baltimore club into New York (the Highlanders) before the 1903 season. McGraw announced as early as July that the Giants – who had a substantial lead in the N.L. – would under no circumstances play the A.L. champions, regardless of who they might be.[10]

The question was raised repeatedly as the season wore on, but McGraw never wavered. On October 10, after Boston had won the pennant, owner John I.

Taylor sent a message to McGraw, reading in part, "I challenge your club to play for the championship of the world. Of course, if you refuse to play, we get the title by default, but I should prefer to win it on the diamond."[11]

Indeed, though McGraw would not have seen it this way, Boston Americans remained the reigning world champions.

1905-1911

The World Series resumed in 1905 and became an annual event. McGraw's Giants did play the Philadelphia Athletics, winning four of five games in which every game remarkably ended in a shutout for one team or the other.

The 1905 Boston Americans had a winning record (78-74), but not by much and only good for a fourth-place finish. Fair enough. No team is going to win the pennant every year. In 1906, though, things fully fell apart. The team lost 105 games and only won 49. Losing more than two-thirds of their games plunged them into the cellar – they finished 45½ games behind the Chicago White Sox. Not until 1925 did they lose more than 100 games again.

After finishing in seventh place in 1907, the team was renamed the Boston Red Sox. They are found in the middle of league standings for the years 1907 through 1911. In 1912, they won the pennant once more.

Were the Red Sox the league's first dynasty?

Indeed, the Red Sox won both the pennant and the World Series again in 1912. They won again in 1915, 1916, and in 1918. As of that year – 1918 – the franchise had taken part in five World Series and won every one of them. That totaled one-third (five of the 15) World Series ever played to that point in time.[12]

After their fifth world championship, it was a mere 86 years until they won another in the year 2004 – in the next century. But who's counting? Well, Red Sox fans were. And so were those who loved to mock them. The year they had last won – the year itself – became a sing-song chant with New York Yankees fans loved to chant to taunt Red Sox fans ("19…18").

But this truly was a dynasty – the first in the American League. It was a stretch worth savoring.

1912-1918: Four World Series Wins in a Seven-Year Stretch

The 1912 World Series – first season in Fenway Park

In 1912, the Red Sox won the pennant by a big margin – 14 games over the second-place Washington Senators. Save for 1903, it was by far the largest margin of victory they ever enjoyed. In 1904, it had been 1½. The closest they ever came again was in 1946 (12 games) and 2018 (8 games). By the time wild card play came around, it was possible to come in second and still win out. We can note that the 2004 Red Sox finished second in the A.L. East, three games behind the Yankees.

Win they did, in 1912, and they faced the New York Giants in the World Series. The Giants had won the 1905 Series, which had then become a best-of-seven playoff, winning four and only losing one. They made the Series again in 1911, with a 99-win team that had beaten the Chicago Cubs by 7½ games, but been beaten in the World Series by Connie Mack's Philadelphia Athletics, four games to two.

Game One, at the Polo Grounds, featured New York's Jeff Tesreau (17-7, 1.96) against 34-game winner (!) Smoky Joe Wood, who was 34-5, 1.91. Wood had 10 shutouts on the season and had thrown 35 complete games, both of which (like his wins total) led the majors. The Giants had won 103 games, the Red Sox 105, and the Giants had scored 823 runs with a team ERA of 2.58 to Boston's 799 runs (2.76 ERA). John McGraw was still team manager. Right fielder Red Murray drove in two runs for the Giants in the bottom of the third. Tesreau no-hit the Red Sox through five, but Tris Speaker tripled in the top of the sixth and scored on an infield grounder. They added three more in the seventh on back-to-back one-out doubles by Heinie Wagner and Hick Cady. Harry Hooper doubled over first base and drove in Wagner. Shortstop Steve Yerkes singled both runners home, to take a 4-2 lead. They scored one more in the bottom of the ninth.

Game Two was at brand-new Fenway Park the next day and ended as a 6-6 tie after 11 innings, Ray Collins starting for the Red Sox against Christy Mathewson of the Giants. The Red Sox scored first, taking a 3-0 lead in the first, and led 4-2 after seven, but New York got three in the eighth, with Boston tying it in the bottom of the eighth. Each team scored once in the 10th. Night baseball at Fenway was more than 30 years in the future; the game was called on account of darkness.

The Giants took Game Three, 2-1, Rube Marquard against Buck O'Brien, with Boston scoring its one run in the bottom of the ninth. With two on and two outs, it looked as though Cady had hit a game-winning drive to deep right-center but Giants right fielder Josh Devore (who stood 5-feet-6) ran it down and made the catch, arguably one of the greatest in World Series history. After three hard-fought games, the *New York Times* said if the rest of the games were anything like the first three, the two cities would "fill all the nerve sanitariums with their citizens."[13]

Game Four was back in New York, matching up Tesreau against Wood. Larry Gardner's second-inning triple was followed by a wild pitch, and Boston took a 1-0 lead. The Sox added another on a walk, two outs, and then a single from Cady. The Giants got one back in the bottom of the seventh, and would have tied it but for a runner thrown out at the plate. Wood knocked in a third run in the top of the ninth.

Gave Five, back in Boston, was a 2-1 win for the home team, Hugh Bedient against Mathewson. Bedient (20-9, 2.92 in the regular season) allowed just three base hits and one seventh-inning run. The Red Sox got their two runs on back-to-back triples by Harry Hooper and Steve Yerkes, and a run-producing groundout by Speaker.

"Smoky" Joe Wood compiled one of the greatest seasons for a pitcher in baseball history in 1912, winning 34 games (against only 5 losses) and three more in the World Series (Library of Congress).

The sixth game was a 5-2 win at home for New York. In the very first inning, Buck O'Brien gave up five runs on six hits. Collins threw seven scoreless innings after that, but the Red Sox were unable to score more than the two they got in the top of the second, with two on and two outs. Manager Jake Stahl pulled O'Brien for pinch-hitter Hack Engle, who doubled off the left-field wall. Marquard improved to 2-0.

Game Seven was in Boston, Tesreau finally beating Wood, thanks to seven hits and two stolen bases all off Wood. Charley Hall relieved Wood in the second inning and promptly gave up the first of five additional runs spread out over the eight innings he worked. It was a leadoff homer by Gardner, their only home run in the 1912 Series.

The deciding Game Eight was played on October 16 and it went 10 innings – Hugh Bedient starting against Christy Mathewson. Devore drew a leadoff walk in the third, advanced on consecutive groundouts, then scored when Red Murray doubled to center. They held the 1-0 lead until the bottom of the seventh. With runners on first and second and two outs, Stahl had Olaf Henriksen pinch-hit for Bedient. Still the only native of Denmark to play major-league baseball, Henriksen doubled off the third-base bag and into left field, tying the game.

Joe Wood took over pitching, having worked just the one inning the day before. The game was tied 1-1 after nine. Red Murray hit a ball into temporary seating in left-center but it was a ground-rule double, the seating indeed being temporary. He scored the go-ahead run, nonetheless, on a single by Fred Merkle.

Hack Engle pinch-hit for Wood in the bottom of the 10th. The ball landed in center fielder Fred Snodgrass's glove, but then popped out (the legendary "Snodgrass's muff"). Engle was safe on second. After a flyout and then a walk to Yerkes, Tris Speaker tied the game with a single to right. On an unsuccessful throw to the plate, Yerkes took third base and Speaker took second. McGraw had Mathewson intentionally walk Duffy Lewis and pitch to Larry Gardner. Gardner flied out to Devore in right but on a ball hit deep enough that Yerkes could tag and score the winning run.

The Red Sox had won the 1912 World Series, and beaten John McGraw on the diamond.

1915 World Series

In 1913, the Philadelphia Athletics easily beat the Giants, winning the World Series in just five games. In 1914, the National League's "Miracle

Braves" – the Boston Braves – swept the Series from the Athletics. The Braves had dominated in the latter years of the 19th century but had finished in last place for four years in a row (1919 through 1912). They finished fifth in 1913, but were in last place again from May 8 through July 18, 1914. Before the first week of September was up, the Braves had claimed first place. They played their home games at the larger-capacity Fenway Park in the 1914 Series and won all four games.

The Red Sox, now under new ownership (Joseph J. Lannin), saw Bill Carrigan take over as manager in midseason, but finished in fourth place. In 1914, they finished second but a full 8½ games behind the Athletics.

In 1915, in an odd twist, it was Boston against Philadelphia once more in the World Series, but this time it was the 101-win Red Sox against the Philadelphia Phillies, and the Boston home games were played at the freshly-opened Braves Field, which offered more seating than Fenway.

The Phillies won the first game, 3-1, at Baker Bowl, Pete Alexander (with a terrific 31-11, 1.22 record) winning over Ernie Shore, who had been 19-8 with a 1.64 ERA.

Game Two featured the other 19-game winner on the Red Sox (Rube Foster – who had been 19-8, 2.11). He held the Phillies to three hits. Harry Hooper led off against Erskine Mayer with a base on balls, then went first to third when Speaker singled with one out. With runners on first and third, they attempted a delayed double steal but would both have been thrown out had catcher Ed Burns not let the ball get away from him at the plate. One run scored. The Phillies tied it on back-to-back doubles leading off the fifth. It remained 1-1 heading into the ninth. Larry Gardner singled to lead off. After one out, Gardner took second as Mayer fielded a ball hit back to him, which he had to throw to first. The next batter was Foster himself, and he singled to center, scoring Gardner. Foster had three of Boston's 10 hits off Mayer. He retired the Phillies in the bottom of the ninth on two outfield flies sandwiched around a strikeout.

Game Three was in Boston, another 2-1 win for the Red Sox and another game resolved in the ninth. Dutch Leonard threw his own three-hitter for the win. The Phillies scored first on a leadoff single, a bunt on which Boston's Dick Hoblitzell bungled third baseman Gardner's toss, another bunt which advanced both baserunners, and then a one-run single to center by Dave Bancroft. From that point on, Leonard retired 20 consecutive batters. In the bottom of the fourth, Speaker tripled over first base. Hoblitzell lifted a fly to center field, deep enough that there was no throw home. The game was tied. In the bottom of the ninth, Hooper singled to right and was sacrificed to second. Speaker was walked intentionally. Hoblitzell grounded out, both runners moving up. Duffy Lewis singled over shortstop and drove in the winning run.

The fourth game was the third consecutive 2-1 Red Sox win. Ernie Shore got the win; George Chambers took the loss. After two scoreless innings, second baseman Jack Barry drew a walk in the bottom of the third. Cady bunted to first, for a hit. Shore laid down a sacrifice bunt, and both runners moved up. Hooper reached on an "ugly bounder" – an infield single batted down by the second baseman, Barry scoring. They got their second run in the sixth, on Hoblitzell's one-out single to center and Duffy Lewis's double that rolled to the wall in left-center. In the top of the eighth, a two-out triple and a single gave the Phillies their one run.

Game Five was back at Baker Bowl. The Phillies grabbed a 2-0 lead in the bottom of the first. Rube Foster hit leadoff batter Milt Stock, then gave up back-to-back singles. The bases were loaded with nobody out. Foster almost escaped scoreless when right fielder Gavvy Cravath (his 24 homers in 1915 were 10 more than the entire Red Sox team) hit into a 1-2-3 double play. First baseman Fred Luderus doubled to left-center, though, and two runs scored. Facing Mayer, Boston got one back in the second (on a two-out triple by Gardner and single by Barry) and then tied the game with another in the third, when Hooper led off with a solo home run, a bounce homer to center. Today, it would have been a ground-rule double. Luderus homered in the bottom of the fourth, the first of two runs for the Phillies. Eppa Rixey had relieved Mayer back in the third.

He'd only given up a couple of singles until a single and a Duffy Lewis home run tied the game for Boston in the top of the eighth. In the top of the ninth, Harry Hooper homered, too – his second home run of the game, another bounce homer to right-center. That gave the Red Sox a 5-4 edge. Foster struck out the first Phil, and then induced two groundouts. The Red Sox had won the World Series.

It was the fourth game decided by just one run.

Oddly, rookie Babe Ruth was an 18-game winner for Boston (18-8, 2.44) and despite only working in 32 games had twice as many homers as anyone else on the team (four homers). Yet he only appeared once in the entire World Series, as a pinch-hitter in the first game. He grounded out to first base. Leigh Montville has written, "Carrigan said years later that he never pitched Ruth because he simply had other, better pitchers at the time. He preferred right-handed pitchers against the slugging Cravath of the Phillies."[14]

1916 World Series

The very next year, the Red Sox repeated as pennant winners and World Series champions. They beat out the White Sox by two games and the Tigers by four. Their winningest pitcher was Babe Ruth (23-12, with a league-leading 1.75 ERA). He had nine shutouts to his credit. He had only hit three homers, however, matched by Del Gainer and Tillie Walker.

The National League pennant was won by Brooklyn, by 2½ games over the Phillies.

Game One – at Braves Field again – matched Ernie Shore (16-10, 2.63) against Rube Marquard (13-6, 1.58), the same Marquard who had faced them as a New York Giant in 1912 and beaten them twice. The Red Sox scored first, on Hoblitzell's third-inning triple and a double by Duffy Lewis. Brooklyn promptly responded with one of their own on Casey Stengel's single and Zack Wheat's triple. Walker singled in Hooper in the fifth, but Boston's big inning was the seventh when they took a 5-1 lead with three runs on one hit, a leadoff double by Hal Janvrin. There followed back-to-back errors, a sacrifice, a fielder's choice, and a sacrifice fly. A sixth run, also unearned due to another error, gave them the 6-1 lead they needed when Brooklyn scored four times in the top of the ninth thanks to a pair of walks, a hit by pitch, an error, and three singles, the last one off reliever Carl Mays. The Robins left the bases loaded. It was, nonetheless, a Red Sox win.

Game Two was also a one-run game, but a much better-played one. Ruth got the start and gave up one run in the top of the first on an inside-the-park home run by center fielder Hy Myers. Red Sox shortstop Everett Scott tripled to left-center off Brooklyn's Sherry Smith (14-10, 2.34), leading off Boston's third. He scored on Babe Ruth's groundout hit to second base. There were other scoring opportunities for both sides, but neither managed another run. Both teams saw a runner thrown out at the plate, the Robins in the top of the eighth and the Red Sox in the bottom of the ninth. Both Ruth and Smith stayed on as pitchers through the 10th, 11th, 12th, and 13th, Ruth throwing hitless ball and Smith giving up just one single in the 10th. Darkness threatened to limit the game to just one more inning. Ruth retired the Robins in order in the top of the 14th. Smith walked leadoff batter Hoblitzell. Lewis bunted to sacrifice him to second. Del Gainer pinch-hit for Gardner, and singled in the winning run.

The Series reconvened the next afternoon at Ebbets Field. Jack Coombs (13-8, 2.66) started for Brooklyn and Carl Mays (18-13, 2.39) for Boston. Brooklyn built a lead with one run in the third, on three singles. They added another in the fourth, on a single, sacrifice, and another single. The Robins took a 4-0 lead in the fifth on two walks and a triple by shortstop Ivy Olson. The Red Sox got on the board with a one-out walk in the sixth, followed by Harry Hooper's triple and — after a popup to short — a single by Chick Shorten. Larry Gardner hit a solo homer in the top of the seventh, but manager Wilbert Robinson called on Jack Pfeffer to relieve and Pfeffer retired the eight batters needed to close out the game. Rube Foster had thrown the final three innings for Boston.

Dating back to 1915, the Red Sox had now played seven consecutive one-run World Series games, losing only this one.

Game Four was a 6-2 win for Boston's left-hander Dutch Leonard (18-12, 2.36) against Marquard. Right fielder Jimmy Johnston hit Leonard's first pitch for a triple, scoring on Myers' single. A walk, wild pitch, and an error allowed in a second run. In the top of the second, the Red Sox took the lead on a four-pitch walk, Duffy Lewis' double off the wall in right, and an inside-the-park home run to right-center by Larry Gardner. With two outs in the fourth, Bill Carrigan singled in Lewis. The Sox added a run in the fifth off reliever Larry Cheney and another in the seventh, both on base hits by Dick Hoblitzell. a double and then an infield single, the latter thanks to a throwing error by Cheney.

Game Five was back in Boston, Shore against Pfeffer. Brooklyn scored first, in the second, without a hit. A four-pitch base on balls was followed by a sacrifice bunt, a groundout, and then a passed ball. Duffy Lewis lined a triple down the left-field line in the bottom of the second, then tagged and scored on Gardner's fly to left. In the third, a single, walk, and error allowed one run to score. A caught stealing was followed by Shorten's single producing another run. The Red Sox added a fourth run in the fifth on a two-out single by Hooper and Hal Janvrin's double to center. The game seemed such a mismatch that the *New York Times* said it "resembled a tug of war between an elephant and a gold fish."[15]

The Red Sox had won their fourth World Series.

1917 Red Sox

Harry Frazee purchased the team from Lannin shortly after the 1916 World Series. Bill Carrigan retired as manager. The Red Sox finished second, nine games behind the Chicago White Sox. The first World War had begun and, right after the season ended, eight Red Sox entered military service.

1918 World Series

Ed Barrow became the new manager of the Red Sox and, in a season shortened by war, led the Red Sox to yet another pennant. The season's final games were played on September 2, Boston finishing with a record of 75-51, 2½ games ahead of the Cleveland Indians. The National League pennant was won by the Chicago Cubs, finishing a full 10½ games ahead of the second-place Giants.

Babe Ruth hit a total of 49 homers for his first team, the Red Sox, and was 89-46 (2.19) as a pitcher (Library of Congress).

It was an astonishing season in which the Red Sox won 26 games in which the other team never scored – that's right, more than one-third of their 75 wins were shutouts. And eight of the shutouts were 1-0 wins. They had started the season 11-2, which included the first two 1-0 wins. They were themselves shut out 13 times. They'd had a losing record (6-11) against the Yankees, though were never shut out by them. The team ERA was 2.31 which helped make up for a team batting average of .249.

It was perhaps fitting in some respects that Game One of the World Series was a 1-0 shutout of the Cubs at larger-capacity Comiskey Park. Babe Ruth (13-7, 2.22) pitched for the Red Sox against Hippo Vaughn of the Cubs. Barrow had wisely used Ruth in games other than as pitcher; in 95 regular-season games, Ruth hit 11 of Boston's 15 team homers. Oddly, he never hit one in a game he won, and didn't hit any at all after June 30. Despite a .300 batting average for the season, Ruth was 0-for-3 in this game. He allowed six hits and walked one, but shut out the Cubs. The only run of the game came off Vaughn in the top of the fourth. Dave Shean walked. Amos Strunk tried to bunt him to second but popped out to Vaughn. Left fielder George Whiteman singled to left, Shean to second. First baseman Stuffy McInnis singled to left on a hit-and-run play, and Shean slid across the plate just ahead of the throw. Vaughn didn't allow another hit the rest of the game, but that one run was sufficient.

The Cubs evened things up the next day, winning Game Two 3-1, Lefty Tyler over Bullet Joe Bush. All three of their runs came in the bottom of the second. A walk, a bunt single, an out, then a double by Bill Killefer followed by a two-run single by pitcher Tyler. Boston's lone run came in the top of the ninth inning on back-to-back leadoff triples by Amos Strunk and George Whiteman. Whiteman was stranded on third as Tyler got the final three outs.

The first three games were played in Chicago; any remaining games were to be played in Boston. The Red Sox took Game Three, 2-1. Both Carl Mays and Hippo Vaughn threw seven-hitters. Vaughn walked seven batters, but that isn't what did him in. With one out in the top of the fourth, Vaughn hit Whiteman with a pitch. There followed four successive singles. The ones by McInnis, Wally Schang, and Everett Scott produced two runs. Fred Thomas's single to right resulted in Schang being thrown out at the plate. Mays then lined out to end the inning. Chicago's lone run came in the bottom of the fifth. Second baseman Charlie Pick led off with a double. After one out, catcher Killefer singled him home with a hit to left field.

The Red Sox played their 1918 games at Fenway Park. Because attendance was down due to wartime, the Red Sox recognized they didn't need the larger Braves Field. They won Game Four, 2-1, Ruth against Tyler. The Red Sox scored first, with a pair of runs in the fourth, and both were driven in by the pitcher, Babe Ruth. With runners on first and second and two outs, Ruth tripled over the right fielder's head with a ball that rolled almost to the seats in right-center. In the top of the eighth, though, the Cubs tied it after a walk, single, and wild pitch. The first run scored on a groundout, second to first. Les Mann then singled to left for the second run. The runs off Ruth broke his World Series scoreless innings streak after 29⅔ innings. The Red Sox responded right away against reliever Phil Douglas. Pinch-hitter Wally Schang singled. He took second on a passed ball. Hooper bunted to try to move him to third. Douglas fielded the ball, but threw it away and Schang scored the go-ahead run. After Ruth allowed the first two Cubs to reach in the top of the ninth, Joe Bush took over (Ruth moved to left field). A bunt was fielded by McInnis at first base, who threw to third for the first out. The next batter hit into a 6-4-3 double play.

Game Five was a shutout for Hippo Vaughn. He held Red Sox batters to five base hits, while Sad Sam Jones (his 16-5 winning percentage was the best in the majors) gave up a run in the third (walk, stolen base, Les Mann double) and a two-run double by Dode Paskert to left-center in the eighth.

With a three-games-to-two lead for the Red Sox, Game Six again presented the possibility of a World win. Carl Mays started for them, Tyler for the Cubs. Seeing only four pitches, Mays drew a base on balls leading off the bottom of the third. He took second on Hooper's bunt. Another walk put Dave Shean on first. Strunk grounded out, but both runners moved up 90 feet. George Whiteman hit a ball to Flack in right, a fly ball that he let glance off his glove and both runners scored. The Cubs got one back right away, in the fourth, Flack leading off with a single. He took second on a groundout to first. Mays then hit batter Les Mann. Catcher Schang, though, picked Mann off first base. Mays walked the batter, then saw Flack steal third base, and Fred Merkle single Flack home. That was, though, the only run the Cubs got all game long. Mays threw a three-hitter. The game ended 2-1, Red Sox. They had won the World Series.

And they had won it at Fenway Park. It was 95 years before the Red Sox won another World Series at Fenway.

There had been 15 World Series played to this point and Boston's American League team had won five of them – as well as the pennant in 1904 when John McGraw declined Boston's invitation to play a World Series.

3

Two Dark Decades and the Arrival of "The Kid"

After the war – and the beginning of The Curse?

The first World War ended with Armistice Day on November 11, 1918. The 1919 Red Sox plunged from first place to sixth place in the A.L. standings, and this despite scoring 91 more runs than the year before. The pitching staff's earned run average was almost precisely a full run more, though – 3.30 in 1919 compared to 2.31 the year before. Carl Mays had won 21 games in 1918, but only won 5 in 1919. This isn't the place to delve into all that went wrong; several other teams improved and the Red Sox did not. The Red Sox did have one standout performance – Babe Ruth drove in 113 runs and hit 29 homers. In 1918, admittedly in a somewhat shorter season, he'd hit 11 and driven in 61.

In 1920, Ruth began playing for the New York Yankees, where he nearly doubled his home run total yet again – from 29 to 54. He drove in 135 runs. Even the 11 homers he had hit in 1918 had led the league – tied with Philadelphia's Tillie Walker (who had himself been on the 1916 World Champion Red Sox) – and five more than anyone else in the league. The 29 he hit in 1919 were almost triple the second-place batters. Likewise, in 1920 – second-place George Sisler hit 19 to Ruth's 54.

The Red Sox had sold Babe Ruth's contract to the Yankees.

Even with Ruth, the Yankees finished third in 1920, but they made it to the World Series in 1921, 1922, and won their first one in 1923.

This is where some denizen of the "fellowship of the miserable" could note that the Yankees made it to the World Series in 1921, 1922, 1923, 1926, 1927, 1928, 1932, 1936, 1937, 1938, 1939, 1941, 1942, and 1943 (winning all but two of them, from 1923 on).

The Red Sox made it to the World Series again in 1946. And lost. We'll visit that year in a moment.

After 1946, the Yankees were the American League team in the World Series in 1947, 1949, 1950, 1951, 1953, 1953, 1955, 1956, 1957, 1958, 1960, 1961, 1962, 1963, and 1964. It was quite a run. They won the world championship five years in a row, from 1949 through 1953, and all in all, one could say they did quite well.

Red Sox fans, perhaps born in – say, 1900 – had seen the Red Sox dynasty during their teenage years but that must have come to seem like nothing compared to this, particularly as the memories faded. There were other things in the world, like radio, the growth of the film industry, the Great Depression, and the onset of the Second World War.

How had the Red Sox done in those years, 1919 through the war? There were eight teams in the league. The Red Sox finished 6th, 5th, 5th, 8th, 7th, 8th, 8th, 8th, 8th, 8th, 8th, 6th, 8th, 7th, 4th, 4th, 6th, 5th, 2nd, 2nd, 7th, 4th, and 7th. One might suggest that something had changed.

Was it the Curse of the Bambino? The Red Sox were cursed because they had sold off their popular star?

Dan Shaughnessy's book of that title – *The Curse of the Bambino* – was published in 1990. The book was incredibly popular and well-received. The title resonated perfectly. Everyone with any awareness that Babe Ruth had been an early Red Sox star sold off to the Yankees knew immediately what it meant. It seemed to suit the times perfectly – just a very few years after yet another Red Sox team had lost yet another World Series to a different New York team (the Mets), at the last moment and even after congratulations to the Red Sox had momentarily been flashed on the Shea Stadium message board.[16] More on the 1986 season later.

Dan Shaughnessy by no means claimed to have authored the phrase, Indeed, he credited it to high school teacher John McKeon, who had sold 1,000 16-page booklets on Opening Day in 1987.[17] Shaughnessy later wrote that the title – and the idea for his book came from an editor for Dutton named Meg Blackstone, and she said the phrase came to her from her maternal grandfather.[18] Perhaps several others came up with a similar phrase at various times. Perhaps that's why it had such immediate resonance. Every longstanding Red Sox fan knew exactly what it meant. These, after all, were what the film *Fever Pitch* called "one of God's most pathetic creatures – a Red Sox fan."

This is what I was born into?

The 1946 pennant race and World Series

OK, I was one year old in 1946, but something truly special happened, for the first time in 28 years: The Red Sox did win the American League pennant and did make it to the World Series. And they looked pretty formidable. After a seventh-place finish in 1945, they won their first five games of 1946 and – with a 15-game winning streak – completed the first two-dozen games with a record of 21-3.

It was a time of new hopes. The Second World War was over, both in Europe and the Pacific, with America victorious. The Great Depression was a memory for those who had endured it. The many ballplayers who had served in wartime were back with their teams. The Red Sox didn't lose their 10th game until June 12; they were 41-10. A month after that – on July 14 – their lead in the league increased to double digits, and never dropped below that. They finished the season 104-50, a full 12 games ahead of second-place Detroit. The Yankees were third, 17 games behind.

It really hadn't been *that* long – not 86 years! The entire nation had been through terrible times and emerged stronger than ever, ascendant as a true world leader. Red Sox fans had been through tough times, too – for instance, those eight last-place finishes.

The race in the National League was a tighter one, so tight that the Brooklyn Dodgers and St. Louis Cardinals were tied for first place on the final Friday, Saturday, and Sunday of the season. That necessitated the two teams squaring off in a best-of-three playoff for the pennant. The Red Sox hadn't really had to stay in fighting shape. Manager Joe Cronin had even given vacations (!) to some of the players in the final weeks.[19] That may have been a mistake. The Cardinals, who won both of the first two games of the playoff, were well-honed and sharp.

Ted Williams and Dom DiMaggio, at the May 18, 1986 Old Timers Game (Kathy Borchers Photojournalism Collection).

To try and keep in some kind of shape, the Red Sox prevailed on a number of "all-star" players from other teams to come to Fenway for a series of three tune-up games. Among them were Joe DiMaggio from the Yankees (his brother Dom was the Sox center fielder, whose .316 average only trailed Williams' .342 and Johnny Pesky's .335), Luke Appling, Stan Spence, Cecil Travis, and Hank Greenberg. There was a tragic incident in the fifth inning of the first game (October 1) when Ted Williams — later voted American League MVP on the basis of a majors-leading 158 RBIs and .667 slugging percentage — was hit on the elbow by a pitch by Mickey

Haefner of the Washington Senators. He was removed from the game. X-rays proved negative but it was badly swollen – the Associated Press described "swelling about the size of an egg" – and it clearly hampered Ted throughout the Series.[20] He hit .200, just 5-for-25 and not a single extra-base hit. In seven World Series games, he drove in a total of one run.

Even with the setback, the Red Sox won three of the first five games and only needed a win in Game Six or Gave Seven to become World Champions. They lost Game Six but were tied 3-3 after the top of the eighth inning in Game Seven. With Enos Slaughter on first base and two outs, Harry Walker dropped a double into left-center. Dom DiMaggio had had to leave the game with a pulled muscle and Leon Culberson wasn't nearly as adept a fielder. He played the ball a bit casually and threw in to Pesky at short, while Slaughter went all out with a "mad dash" attempting to score all the way from first on a ball that truly had dropped in. Did Pesky "hold the ball" while Slaughter scored? Veteran St. Louis sportswriter Bob Broeg didn't think so. It had seemed like a routine single. Broeg believed that Slaughter's daring and speed should be credited. [21]

The Cardinals won the game and thus the World Series. There was disappointment, of course, among Red Sox fandom but no suggestion of anything like a curse.

1947–1950

The Red Sox finished strong in three of the next four seasons. They finished third in 1947, but in both 1948 and 1949, they battled right to the final day. In 1948, the Cleveland Indians and Red Sox were tied at 96-58 when the regular season ended. That necessitated a single-game playoff for the pennant, held at Fenway Park. Denny Galehouse couldn't hold back the Indians, and lost, 8-3.

In 1949, the Red Sox had a one-game lead over the second-place Yankees with two games to play. The two games were both in New York. Despite an early 4-0 lead, the Sox lost the first one – which

Ted Williams, 1947 (Leslie Jones).

would have clinched the pennant – by a 5-4 score. The final, decisive game saw New York take a 1-0 lead in the first inning and add four more in the eighth. A last-gasp three Red Sox runs in the top of the ninth left them two runs short. All they had had to do was win one of the two. Instead, they dropped them both. That made it three seasons out of four that the Red Sox had been eliminated in the final game they played. This time, it was to the Yankees.

They battled in 1950, scoring 1027 runs – which remains a team record despite the season adding eight more games after the 1960 season. They were as close as one game out of first place as late as September 18 but couldn't close the gap. They wound up four games out. One of the reasons was, as in 1946, an injury to Ted Williams. This one was a broken radius suffered during the All-Star Game as he successfully caught a Ralph Kiner drive but slammed into the outfield wall in doing so. He played out the full game but required surgery and missed two months. By July 7, Williams already had 25 home runs on the season and 83 RBIs. Had he kept going at that pace, he might well have doubled each figure. It was bad luck, but bad luck was Boston's fate.

The 1950s – a decade of mediocrity, the excellence of Ted Williams

The decade was one of mediocrity for the Red Sox. The best they finished was in third place; the worst was sixth. After 1950 itself, they never finished closer than 11 games to first place (1951) but plunged below 20 – way below, to 42 games behind in 1954 – only once. That one year dragged the average down to 17 games out of first place. How does one become, or remain, a Red Sox fan at times like that? There was always something – but one constant throughout (for the teenager I was becoming) was Ted Williams. In early 1952, he departed to fly Marine combat missions during the Korean War.[22] But from 1954 through 1958, he was among the best hitters in baseball with yearly batting averages of .345, .356, .345, .388, and .328. His most impressive year was arguably 1957 – the year he turned 39 (and the year I turned 12), when he logged that .388 mark and with six more base hits would have hit .400.

That was the year I started making my way to Fenway Park fairly often. It was relatively easy for me. I rode my bike about a mile to Arlington Heights station, took a bus to Harvard Square, transferred via Park Street to Kenmore Square and walked to the park. Being under 14, total cost each way was 5 cents at the time. A ticket to the bleachers was 50 cents. I never bought anything at the park, but I would occasionally get a couple of hot dogs at Joe & Nemo's (they were 15 cents apiece or two for a quarter). So for less than a dollar, I could take in a Red Sox game. I went to about 10 games a year.

I thought Ted Williams was going to hit a home run every time up. He didn't – but he did get on base about half the time. We didn't study this stat at the time, but he had an on-base percentage of .513 in 1954, .496 in 1955, .479 in 1956, and .526 in 1957.

I also knew he represented the Jimmy Fund, the charity that raised money for kinds with cancer. Ted Williams was the celebrity face of the Jimmy Fund for many, many years. That was another thing that helped make him a hero in my mind.[23]

We had no reason to expect the Red Sox to win, but we weren't scarred by the losses. It was exciting when they won, but there was no long history of near-victories, not the sense of Sisyphean shortcomings that came to build in later decades. The Yankees won all the time. It was just the way it was. Those my age were too young to have known about the late 1940s. We came to know that the Red Sox had once been great, but that was decades in the past. There were other things in life, too. Television had come in; I know our family was the second in the neighborhood to get one and kids from other houses came over to watch *Howdy Doody* and the like.

A statue of a Lexington Minuteman – musket ready – at the Lexington Battle Green (Public Domain).

And we played baseball, too. Neighborhood kids all did that then. I remember no such thing as a basketball hoop anywhere around. I guess they played football in high school but not in our neighborhood. Mr. Duffy lived two houses from ours on Maple Street and he had a back field he let us mow and level out enough to play baseball. That's what the kids did. I was pretty good, regularly hitting over .900 (we didn't count errors, so if a ball that was fielded poorly or thrown away, I had a hit.)

I wasn't really that good. I never really made it in Little League, though I did get a double once – the one year I played it. We had more fun playing out back.

I also started in "media" at the time, and Stan Brown and I started a newspaper, the *Maple Street Mumbles*. We produced it on a hectograph – maybe a dozen copies at a time, and sold it for a penny. It was a one-page paper at first but then I became the "sports editor" and we printed on both sides! I had the back page which was called "The Fast Ball" and there I commented on the Red Sox, and our neighborhood games.

Maybe some of the interest in newspapers came from the many years I had an afternoon newspaper route. I worked as a paper boy from around age 11 through 16. It was while on my route that I heard Ted Williams hit his last home run, in September 1960. I was on top of the wooden bridge – Pierce's Bridge – about five doors away on Maple Street, listening on my transistor radio. I should have gone to the game. I'm still beating myself up about that.

I started another job when I was 14 – as an Official Historic Guide in Lexington. I learned about the idea from Harold Michelson, who ran Michelson's Shoes on Massachusetts Avenue in Lexington Center. One of his sons had done it and he suggested I try it out – for whatever reason. I guess he had a sense I'd be good at it. I took a test on the history of the Battles of Lexington and Concord and the start of the American Revolution and earned a license (a metal badge) from the Town of Lexington. Other than that, I was on my own. I wore a tricorn hat to which I affixed the badge; that was my "uniform." There was no National Historic Park in those days. When a car of tourists pulled up alongside the Battle Green, I approached them. I told them I was an Official Historic Guide and that if they had 5 minutes, or 10, or 20, I'd like to tell them the "true story of the Battle of Lexington" (a bit of a hook there.) I said, "There is no set fee for my services. After I'm finished, you can pay me whatever you thought it was worth, and if it wasn't worth anything at all, don't pay me anything."

I had pretty good luck, and was sincere about wanting to tell the story – I'd usually get a dollar if it was for 5 minutes or for 20, but the nascent teacher in me appreciated the longer talks because I got to explain more. Sometimes I'd take tourists into the old burying ground behind a nearby church, and talk a little more about town history. Maybe once a day a car would hire me to take them out the Battle Road to Concord to see the Old North Bridge where the battle there took place. That usually took a couple of hours in all. I took this seriously. It was an important story and I wanted people to appreciate just how incredible it was that the farmers and tavernkeepers (all British subjects at the time) in the area rose up in a struggle for self-rule against their own government, and achieved independence.

It was rewarding to be able to tell the story and I would often make $10 to $20 on a weekend day. It was good enough income that I did it for seven summers – all the way through high school and college, too.

Race and the Red Sox

There was something else about the 1950s and the Red Sox. The team did not field a Black ballplayer until midseason 1959. They had the opportunity to be the first team in either league to do so, and accorded a tryout to Jackie Robinson as early as 1945. Pressed to do so by Boston City Councilman Isadore Muchnick, the Red Sox held an unpublicized "tryout" on April 16. Three Black ballplayers tried out – Jackie Robinson, Sam Jethroe, and Marvin Williams. The word "tryout" has been placed in quotation marks here because most agree – at least in retrospect – that it was something of a sham. According to those conducting the tryout, all three performed creditably – but not one of them ever received a follow-up call from the Red Sox, not even a "thanks for coming in."[24]

And yet they were demonstrably good players. Just two years later, Jackie Robinson was the 1947 Rookie of the Year at a time when there was just one player denoted as such across both the American and National

Leagues. In 1950, Sam Jethroe was named National League Rookie of the Year – playing, perhaps ironically, for the Boston Braves, and being quite well received by the fan base of the team that played at Braves Field, about a mile from Fenway Park. In three years of Negro Leagues play (1943-45), Marvin Williams batted a combined .370. In 1945, he hit .383.

Robinson played for the Kansas City Monarchs in 1945, then for the Brooklyn Dodgers from 1947-1956, with a career .313 batting average, eight times finishing in the top 15 in the MVP voting and winning the award in 1949. Think he might have been able to help the Red Sox?

Fifteen years later, every other team in the NL and AL had fielded one, or many, Black ballplayers. The Boston Red Sox had still not done so. Not once. I can recall being embarrassed – as a Red Sox fan – that the team I rooted for had still not signed a Black man to play for the team.

Growing up in Lexington the 1950s, I hadn't known many Black people. One of my Sunday School teachers. One kid in class at LHS (Lexington High School). That was it. But I was aware of the history of Boston being one of the centers of the Abolitionist movement in years gone by. Massachusetts was supposedly a progressive state, though it wasn't difficult to see racial issues debated in the news. The Civil Rights movement was in full swing by the end of the decade. The landmark *Brown vs. Board of Education* decision of the U.S. Supreme Court had been handed down in 1954. The Red Sox still didn't have a Black ballplayer.

Eight authors contributed to this book of essays on Pumpsie Green, the "reluctant pioneer" who was the first Black ballplayer on the Boston Red Sox.

One personal family moment made an impression on me. It was around 1955, I'd guess. My parents drove to Washington, taking my sisters and me to visit Our Nation's Capital. The interstate highway – Route 95 – hadn't yet been built; that happened in 1956. It was summer, and it was hot, and most cars still didn't have air conditioning. Ours certainly didn't. We were driving through rural Maryland, getting much closer to D.C. and getting hungrier and thirstier. There was a long stretch without a gas station, or anything. Finally, up ahead on the left we saw a restaurant of some kind, set back maybe 50 feet, and we all let out a cheer. We bustled out of the car, got to the door, and then my father said, "Everyone get back in the car." I remember being a little bewildered. He didn't say anything, but just pointed to a sign by the door to the restaurant: "Whites only." We could have gone in, but he would not. I take pride in remembering that.

Fortunately, it wasn't far at all until we came to another place we could stop for food and refreshment.

And, though they were last, the Red Sox finally did field a Black ballplayer – Pumpsie Green, who debuted on July 21, 1959. A week later, he was joined by pitcher Earl Wilson. In the summer of 1963, Wilson became the first Black pitcher in the American League to throw a no-hitter.

The 1960s – a decade that turned things around with the Impossible Dream

Ted Williams did retire at the end of the 1960 season.[25] I never met him back them. I did meet Jimmy Piersall once – at an event at Michelson's Shoes. He's the only ballplayer I had ever met, but he was a Red Sox player![26] I didn't hang around after games. But I followed the team, mostly via Curt Gowdy on radio. They won enough to maintain the interest, and besides, they were "our team!" The 1960s weren't very good years, though, for the most part. In fact, they were pretty bad: starting with 1960 itself, the annual standings tell the story: 7th, 6th, 8th, 7th, 8th, 9th, and 9th.

The league had expanded to a 10-team league starting in 1961, so the Red Sox weren't the worst team in the league. In each one of the first five of those years, the New York Yankees finished first. Is it any wonder that Red Sox fans weren't exactly fond of the Yankees? Besides, the saying went, rooting for the Yankees was like rooting for General Motors – the number one automobile manufacturer. What does it say about someone who only roots for the team destined to win?

The ninth-place finish of the Red Sox in 1966, though, was accompanied by something remarkable – they finished just a half-game ahead of the Yankees, who finished dead last. The Yankees hadn't finished last since 1912. Climbing into ninth place in 1967, the Yankees haven't finished last since. The Red Sox have.

College years

I graduated high school in June 1962. The summer before, I took my first trip away from home on my own – with my friend Stan Brown. We decided we wanted to see the reenactment of the 100th anniversary of the first Battle of Bull Run, in the Civil War. It was pretty adventurous of us, for age 16. We took a bus from Boston to Washington, with our three-speed bicycles in the baggage hold. We disembarked there and rode to Manassas, Virginia, about 32 miles away.

Some 45,000-50,000 people turned out for the two-day reenactment. Our plan was to go to the first day, then travel by bike to Harpers Ferry, West Virginia, and Gettysburg, Pennsylvania, taking a bus back to Boston from there. The temperatures were in the 90s the first day of the reenactment. Over 2000 soldiers took part in the event.

We hadn't really thought about booking a place to stay, perhaps not having any comprehension just how many people would be visiting the area. We had looked on a map and seen what we thought was a town set off by itself, at a distance from Manassas. That's where we figured we'd spent the night – at Gilbert's Corner, Virginia. It was about 21 miles away, to the northwest.

We got there late in the day and saw a gas station. There was a crossroads. And on one of the corners, a gas station. Owned by someone named Gilbert. There was so little in the area that someone placed it on a map. There was no place to stay there, so we pedaled on to Leesburg. There, I had an idea. We went to the police station and said we had no place to stay and asked if we could just stay in jail for the night. This was apparently against their policy. They said we had to commit a crime to be jailed. I asked what was a small crime that might count, but instead they called a local minister who invited us to stay at his house, with him and his wife. We had a home-cooked breakfast the next morning and went on our way.

We did make it to Harpers Ferry, to Gettysburg, and home.

This maybe set me up for another adventure six years later. I went to college a few miles from home, at Tufts University in Medford and Somerville, Massachusetts. I did stay in the dorm, but sometimes went home for dinner on the weekend. My freshman roommate was Ken Irwin, from New York. A Dodgers fan. We found a mutual interest in music and by February of that first year became "campus representatives" for the Folklore Concert Series and the Theatre Company of Boston. Basically, we put up flyers on the Tufts campus and each earned two free tickets to concerts and theater shows. Our first concerts included Odetta, Ramblin' Jack Elliott, and the Greenbriar Boys. Our first theater shows included actors such as Dustin Hoffman and Paul Benedict, who were both just starting out and playing to small repertory audiences of maybe 30 or 40 people.

We saw a lot of music, often spending three nights a week at Club 47 in Harvard Square or other local places. One time we saw a guy named Bob Dylan at Café Yana, more or less next door to Fenway Park. After his show had to end because of a 1:00 A.M. city ordinance, he had the club pull down the shades in the windows and played another 20-30 minutes.

By our junior year, we had gotten adventurous enough that we hitch-hiked to Union Grove, North Carolina to take in the Old-Time Fiddlers Convention there. Hitching was a thing; we thought nothing on going back and forth to New York to maybe buy a couple of 33-rpm records at Sam Goody's or one of the less-expensive record stores there.

It was a few years after we graduated in June 1966 that we started Rounder Records with Marian Leighton and launched the record company that became our life's work. Over the course of the next 50 years, we released over 3,000 albums and built a significant business, largely in the area of folk and "roots" music.

In time, we saw a lot of great music, won some awards (the pinnacle was one of our albums winning the Grammy Award for both the 2008 Record of the Year and the 2008 Album of the Year, with the album *Raising Sand* by Alison Krauss and Robert Plant.)

Mostly, we enjoyed it and knew we were doing good and valuable work, exposing music that might otherwise not be heard or preserved.

4

The Impossible Dream and a World of Possibilities

After Tufts, I went to graduate school at the University of Chicago, pursuing my major in political science. The first year (September 1966-June 1967) was a tough one. I didn't know anyone there. And I had to work really hard to keep up. I shared an apartment just south of the Midway with a couple of students in love with each other, with me just helping with the rent. I studied hard and won an award given to a first-year overachiever who had not come in with any financial aid at all. That covered my tuition for the rest of my time at U.C.

The summer of 1967 was quite a summer, both for me and the Red Sox. When I had graduated from Tufts in 1966, my father told me as a graduation gift he would give me $1,000, with the stipulation I spend it on travel. In the summer of 1967, I flew to Europe and spent 10 weeks hitchhiking from London to Scotland, through Wales, to the Netherlands, to Belgium, through France to Italy, all the way to the tip of the boot then back north to Venice, and then to my first "Communist" country, Yugoslavia. I was surprised to be just waved across the border; it hardly seemed like I was behind the "Iron Curtain." From there to Greece, and to the Greek Islands. On Crete I met a guy named Bill Kornrich, and through happenstance ran into him again in the Covered Bazaar in Istanbul. He was going to be going to University of Chicago in the fall so we decided to room together. I stayed for a while at the home of Neside Akyoruk in Istanbul; she had been a foreign exchange student who lived with the Nowlin family for a year in Lexington and my sister Joyce had lived with her family for several months.[27]

Everywhere I went, people were asking me what the United States was doing fighting in Vietnam. I hadn't really thought about it a whole lot – which was admittedly odd, given that my field was political science. I then hitched north through Bulgaria (one youth hostel said it was only for Communist youths, so I said, "OK, I'm a Communist" – but that wasn't good enough. You had to be the sort of Communist in favor with the regime in Bulgaria.) I headed north and eventually into Germany, where Dachau was my first stop. I made my way back to Paris and then home. I'd mostly slept in dollar-a-night hostels, hitched, and sometimes just slept on park benches. After 10 weeks, I'd spent $700 and came home with the other $300. It was – literally – Europe on $10 a day (but that included the airfare!)

Naturally, I tried to follow the Red Sox while I was traveling but these were different times. If someone had talked about a cell phone, I would have thought they were describing a prisoner having the opportunity to make an allotted daily call. Mostly I relied on such coverage as there was in the *International Herald Tribune*, when I was able to find a copy. Not a single hostel I stayed in had anything like television, and keep in mind that television of the day was itself not what it is today. Boston did have 11 television channels in 1967, a dramatic increase over the three channels I remember from earlier times. Even had I been at home, not all ballgames were on television. On Monday night, the 21st, were I in Greater Boston, I could have listened to the game on WHDH radio (AM radio), but that was the only broadcast medium available.

Working on this book, I looked back to August 20, a little more than a week and a half before I returned home. The Red Sox played a double-header at Fenway Park that Sunday afternoon, beating the California Angels 12-2 in the first game (Reggie Smith had five RBIs and Yaz had three), then winning the second game, 9-8, overcoming an early 6-0 deficit. Yaz drove in three more runs in the second game. The Red Sox had been three games out of first place before the day began, and 1 ½ games back at day's end. I might well have gone to the game had I not been traveling from Belgrade to Munich at the time. When did I learn about it? I can't say for sure – probably while working on this book. I wouldn't have learned much about individual games at the time. On the 20th, I was on the train. I'd met some guy named Martin and he taught me some of the ways to ride for free. At one point, he hid in the toilet for two hours. Yes, I still have my journal; that isn't something I particularly remember. We eventually arrived. After spending the evening of the 20th at the Hofbrauhaus, it was indeed on August 21 when I visited Dachau.

When games were on TV, color TV was an option for those who could afford one. Sears offered color TVs that were as large as 23 inches, measured diagonally, for $499 – or a bit over $4,500 in 2024 dollars. Median income in those days was, of course, much lower than in 2024. The U.S. Census Bureau reported that median income for men was $5,600.[28] Symptomatic of the times, it was reported that median income for non-white men was $3,400, and for women only $1,800.

There was radio. There was television. There were no cellphones. There was really no such thing as email for public use until nearly 30 years later – the mid-1990s.[29] There was no Ballpark App. You couldn't look up sports scores on Yahoo; Yahoo wasn't launched until 1995. I couldn't go to an internet café and check the scores; such places didn't exist until the 1990s. So many things that people take for granted in the 2020s simply didn't exist, or were only being developed. We did have electricity. That we had. But following baseball while hitching around Europe wasn't really anything I could do, other than to look at line scores and standings in the *IHT*.

I landed back in the US on August 30. The Red Sox were in first place! And had been for four days. This was the year of the Impossible Dream!

I'd missed out on much of the season, but I was home for all of September and went to a few games. Journals were something I only kept for travel, so I really have no way to track which games I went to. I did go to the final four home games, the last games of the season.

Carl Yastrzemski was electrifying as the Sox clinched the
pennant on the final day of 1967, with Yaz driving in nine
runs in the final four home games (Boston Red Sox).

As noted, they only finished a half-game out of *last* place in 1966. Las
Vegas bookmakers reportedly offered 100-1 odds on the 1967 team winning the pennant.[30] No one would have predicted they had any shot at a
pennant in 1967. But there they were. The Red Sox put together a strong
season, never as much as two games out of first place from August 19 on.
Carl Yastrzemski came up big-time at the end. In the final 12 games, Yaz
went 23-for-44 (.523) with 16 RBIs and 14 runs scored. In the last two
games, both of which Boston had to win to secure the pennant, he was
7-for-8, with 5 RBIs.

The University of Chicago was on the quarter system, so classes at
Chicago started much later than at many schools. That worked out nicely

for me. On September 27, the Red Sox were one game behind the Minnesota Twins and only a few percentage points ahead of the Detroit Tigers in the standings. They went head-to-head with the Twins at Fenway Park on Saturday, the 30th. They won, 6-4, putting them in a tie. They were to play the Twins for the pennant on Sunday, October 1.

I don't know why, but I went with my sister Lisa to Sunday's game. She was 15. We had standing room only, but kept creeping closer as the game went on. People were sitting in the aisles on the third-base side. The Twins were leading 2-0 through five innings but the Red Sox scored five runs in the bottom of the sixth. Jim Lonborg went the distance and held the Twins off. Lisa and I crept closer to the field, and squeezed into the aisles in the lower box seats when Rico Petrocelli backpedaled and caught a popup for the final out. Whatever security there was may have been watching the game. It had, after all, been 21 years since the Red Sox had won a pennant. I jumped onto the field and made it to the mound (along with a couple of dozen others) in time to pat Lonborg on the back before everyone realized that there were hundreds – even thousands – of others starting to pour out of the stands. It was, in the words of broadcaster Ned Martin, "pandemonium on the field" – fans surrounding some of the players, tearing signs off the scoreboard as souvenirs, climbing the netting behind home plate up toward where the radio team was broadcasting. Lonborg had his shirt nearly torn off by enthusiastic fans. I realized I did have a responsibility to my sister, so we got out of there, got home, and that very evening I was on my way to Chicago. I watched the World Series games there in the student union building, mostly surrounded by Cardinals fans.

It was a euphoric time. I don't recall anyone talking about curses. There was no doom and gloom. This was so unexpected that everyone was simply thrilled, and then a bit disappointed.

It had been a magical season. As noted, finishing a half-game out of last place in 1966, no one really had any reason to expect anything like this. It truly did unfold like an impossible dream.

Fenway Park had come alive again. Just two years earlier, I had seen Dave Morehead throw a no-hitter at Fenway on September 16, 1965 – me and just 1,246 other fans.[31] Despite a no-hitter having happened less than two weeks later, the total attendance for an entire homestand against the California Angels (admittedly just a two-game one) drew a combined total of 870.

In 1967, fans had turned out – and not just at Fenway Park. After a 10-game road winning streak ended on July 23, an estimated 10,000 fans turned up at Boston's Logan Airport to welcome the team home. That was more than had come out to greet The Beatles. Annual attendance leapt from 811,172 in 1966 to more than double that amount: 1,727,832 in 1967. They never dipped below 1,481,000 again in a 162-game season. It truly was the birth of what later became known as Red Sox Nation.

1967 World Series

It had been 21 years since the Red Sox had last been in a World Series, and they faced the same team that had beaten them in seven games back in 1946 – the St. Louis Cardinals. The Cards had won 101 games and cruised to the pennant, 10½ games ahead of the second-place San Francisco Giants.

Game One featured Cardinals ace Bob Gibson who, despite missing six weeks due to a broken leg in July, was 13-7 and had finished strong. Manager Dick Williams went with Jose Santiago (12-4) since Lonborg had just pitched the clinching game. Santiago went seven innings, allowing only two runs – one in the third and one in the seventh, both of them on groundouts hit by Roger Maris. Gibson, though, went the distance, allowing just one run – a solo homer by Santiago in the bottom of the third, into the netting atop the wall in left-center. He only homered one other time.

Jim Lonborg threw a one-hitter, a shutout, in Game Two. It had been a perfect game through six, and a no-hitter through seven. Julian Javier's double in the eighth was the only hit of the game. Dick Hughes (16-6, 2.67) pitched for Red Schoendienst's Cardinals. He gave up a lead-off home run to Yastrzemski in the bottom of the fourth, hit into the right-field stands near the foul pole. After a couple of walks and an error filled the bases in the sixth, Ron Willis relieved Hughes. Rico Petrocelli's sacrifice fly made it 2-0. Yaz hit a three-run homer over the bullpen in right-center in the seventh, as the first batter facing reliever Joe Hoerner. Boston won, 5-0. Yaz said that after he hit the first homer, he had told Lonborg, "You have enough, big guy. Go get 'em."[32]

The Series shifted to Busch Stadium in St. Louis and the Cardinals won Game Three and Game Four. They jumped out to a 3-0 lead off Boston's Gary Bell on a leadoff triple by Lou Brock followed by an RBI single by Curt Flood and then a two-run Mike Shannon homer in the second inning. Nelson Briles threw a complete game, allowing just two runs — the first on a sixth-inning single by Dalton Jones and the second on a leadoff homer in the seventh by Reggie Smith. Maris singled in a fourth St. Louis run and Orlando Cepeda doubled in their fifth. The final: 5-2, Cardinals.

In Game Four, Bob Gibson shut out the Red Sox on five hits. Santiago didn't even finish the first, hammered for four runs on six base hits. The Cards added two more off reliever Jerry Stephenson in the third inning and coasted to a 6-0 victory.

Lonborg worked Game Five at Busch and threw a three-hitter, winning 3-1. The only run the Cardinals scored came with two outs in the bottom of the ninth on a home run by Roger Maris. Steve Carlton was the starter for St. Louis. After a Joe Foy single and an error that allowed Foy to reach second, Ken Harrelson singled in Foy. It was Harrelson who the Sox had signed after Tony Conigliaro had been badly beaned in August. Jack Lamabe was St. Louis's fourth pitcher of the game, coming in facing a bases-loaded situation in the top of the ninth, the game still 1-0, Boston. Elston Howard singled and drove in two, both unearned due to an error by the right fielder.

It was back to Boston for Game Six, again a must-win game for the Red Sox to stay alive. Rookie Gary Waslewski got the start, only his ninth start in the majors (he was 2-2, 3.21). Hughes started for the Cardinals. Before the game was over, St. Louis had used eight pitchers and Boston three. The first run came on Petrocelli's solo homer in the second inning. Third-inning RBI singles by Brock and Flood tilted it in favor of St. Louis, 2-1. Yaz led off the Boston fourth with a homer to tie it and, before Hughes was removed, both Reggie Smith and Rico Petrocelli had hit solo shots, too. A two-run homer by Brock off Red Sox reliever John Wyatt tied it, 4-4, in the top of the seventh. The Cards burned through four pitchers in the bottom of the seventh as the Red Sox scored four times, with one RBI apiece for Joe Foy, Mike Andrews, Jerry Adair, and Reggie Smith. The final score was 8-4, with Wyatt getting the win.

Once again, it was the Cardinals against the Red Sox in a final Game Seven. This time it was in Boston. Both teams were able to go with the aces – as it happens, the Cy Young Award winners in the two leagues. Lonborg was 2-0 in the World Series and so was Bob Gibson. Lonborg, though, was pitching on just two days' rest. Gibson allowed just three hits and two runs. Lonborg gave up two on the third (the second on a wild pitch) and two more in the fifth (the first of those on a Gibson home run). After George Scott tripled to lead off Boston's bottom of the fifth, scoring on an error, Julian Javier hit a three-run homer to make it 7-1, Cardinals, in the sixth. The Red Sox scored once more, in the eighth, but lost, 7-2.

As in 1946, it was the Cardinals who won the World Series. The Red Sox, however, had enjoyed a great season. There were no goats, no recriminations. They gave it their best shot and came up just short. There was reason to have hope for future years.

Glenn Stout summed up the season nicely in an article titled "When Defeat is Not a Loss – The 1967 World Series." In couple of sentences near the end, he wrote, "Over the course of a remarkable season the Red Sox had won something more important. After all the ups and downs, in the end, they had won their city back."[33]

Even with the loss, hope was in the air. And it had, after all, only been 49 years since their last World Series win. There were a good number of people still living who had experienced the win in 1918.

The team had several stars. There was every reason for optimism. And, as it happens, twice in the next eight years, and three times in the next 11, the Red Sox came very close.

Right after the 1967 Series – a personal evolution

Nine days after the 1967 World Series, I was in Washington along with about 100,000 others who marched on the Pentagon. My conversion from a conservative Republican to a radical was almost instantaneous.

As mentioned, while hitching around Europe everyone was asking me about the US presence in Vietnam. I really hadn't been thinking about it, but my two roommates at Chicago (Bill Kornrich and Bob Greenberg) were ready to go to Washington, so I went along pretty much just for the experience. Becoming part of the counter-culture wasn't difficult; I fit in with much of my generation in the way I was dressing, the music I was listening to, and all. But I wasn't really firmly against the war – until I was. I tended to believe in the "domino theory" – that Communism was expanding like dominoes, and we had to put a stop to it or be overrun. But when we got to the Pentagon, sides were drawn by the firm presence of the U.S. marshals there. All of a sudden, when there was some pushing and shoving, it was "us" vs. "them."

I was on one side, with all the marchers, and the other side was "them."

Six months later, when my plane landed in Chicago after a week's vacation in Mexico, I learned that Rev. Martin Luther King Jr. had been assassinated at the Lorraine Motel in Memphis. Bill, Bob, and I lived at 65th and Cottage Grove, the only White people in an all-Black neighborhood a few

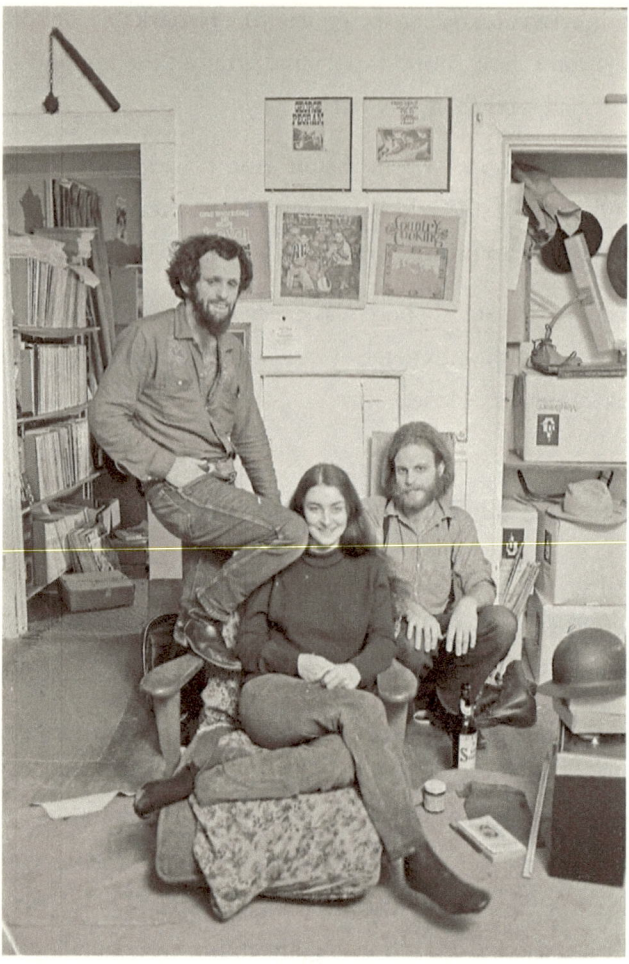

"The Rounder Founders" in their no-bedroom apartment
in Somerville, with their first 5 albums on the wall: L to
R: Ken Irwin, Marian Leighton, Bill Nowlin (courtesy Carl
Fleschhauer).

blocks south of the university. By the time I got back from the airport,
there were National Guard troops up and down the block in front of our
house and they didn't want to let us in. That we lived over a storefront
with Malcolm X posters in the windows might have made them question why we were even there. We had to feint and then run by them to
get into our apartment. With rioting all around, we decided to leave the
area for a few days. It was a day or two later that we joined some others

who had the genius idea to go and surround the National Guard armory in downtown Chicago. Fortunately, I had on a heavy leather jacket; the bayonet that pierced it drew a few drops of blood but I didn't require any hospitalization or treatment. The prodding worked but, as one might gather, I had become radicalized.

From mid-May to June 24, I lived in a plywood shanty on The Mall in Washington as part of the Poor People's Campaign. A few hundred of us built these shanties and lived there for six weeks until the authorities finally tired of us and bulldozed "Resurrection City." I went back home to Boston, dropped out of my Ph.D. program (eventually writing a master's thesis on the Poor People's Campaign, which served as something akin to a consolation prize), and took in some baseball games.

The next summer, I was off to California, in a driveaway car (driving someone's car to California for them, in exchange for the free transport accorded by the vehicle.)

I'd been hoping to meet my girlfriend Janie there – she was supposed to fly across the country, but at the last minute decided not to. I did see my college roommate Ken, who was living in a crash pad on Haight-Ashbury with his friend Marian Leighton. They hitchhiked back and forth across the US that summer. A year later, the three of us formed Rounder Records. That notion hadn't even crossed our minds at the time. In Berkeley, at People's Park, there was a demonstration in solidarity with students who were revolting in France. For two nights, there were clashes between police and demonstrators. A local Bank of America branch was set on fire. I got chased into someone's apartment the first night, and spent the night there. The next night I was arrested and spent the night in the Santa Rita Correctional facility.

I was released the next day, "borrowed" a prison shirt on my way out, left California, went back East – and moved to New York City, where Janie was. (Nothing developed on that front.) For the fall months, I worked nights as a "supervisor" in the toy department at Macy's (basically cleaning up the place and getting it ready for the next day), and then driving a taxi. You don't always know who you're picking up but the two fares I was most aware of were both of a musical nature: Martha and one of the Vandellas at one point and Peter Townsend and Roger Daltrey of The Who another time. I picked The Who guys up outside the Criminal Courts building after they had been at a hearing following an incident some time before at the Fillmore East, where they had pushed a policeman off the stage. I'd been at that concert.

In the summer of 1969, I moved back to Massachusetts, got a second-floor apartment in Somerville, entered a Ph.D. program back at Tufts, worked as a t.a. (teaching assistant) for a year. Starting in September 1970, I joined the faculty at what is now the University of Massachusetts Lowell. I was a political science professor. It was then called the Lowell Technological Institute (there was no major in political science; it was an elective.) After merging with Lowell State Teachers College, it became the University of Lowell, and finally U Mass Lowell.

The very next month – October 1970 – Rounder Records released our first two albums. The first was of George Pegram, a banjo player from North Carolina, and the second by The Spark Gap Wonder Boys, an old-time music band from the Cambridge/Boston area. Three books tell the story of Rounder Records more fully that I would want to burden Red Sox fans with here. Two are more objective: see 2013's *The Never-Ending Revival: Rounder Records and the Folk Alliance* by Michael F. Scully (University of Illinois Press) and 2023's *Oh, Didn't They Ramble – Rounder Records and the Transformation of American Roots Music* by David Menconi (University of North Carolina Press.) The third is the story as told by myself: *Vinyl Ventures: My Fifty Years at Rounder Records* (Equinox Publishing, 2021).

I was living in a second-floor apartment on Somerville Avenue in Somerville, near Porter Square. Ken and Marian moved in and we started the company as what we called an "anti-profit collective." About four years later, it had become enough of an enterprise – with a number of musicians counting on us for at least some of their income – that we realized we probably ought to prepare and file tax returns and the like. In October 1971, we released three more albums. Then in 1972 we released 19!

We had apparently started Rounder at the right time. There were a lot of others like us, wanting to have recordings of the musicians we enjoyed, and everything just came together. We had started with $1,000 – and that's all. My teaching salary helped for the first year or two; both Ken and Marian worked at other jobs. We pooled such money as we had, spent as little as we could on other things, and worked around the clock.

We knew that we were in a special moment in history. Many of the musicians we were recording were true "folk" musicians – having learned their repertoire and to play their instruments from others, face to face, and not through a medium such as television. Much of the music was "home-grown" and we knew that, as the years passed, there would be less and less of it. In one month alone – June 1972 – we released five albums. In each of the next two, we released three. The encouragement we received from so many was crucial – not just customers buying the records. We had photographers donating images, a designer who designed our first several albums for free, people writing notes without a thought of pay. People could see we weren't in it for the money and the three of were seen spending many nights sleeping in a VW van. They saw our dedication and were happy to help with the "mission" we were on – and that's how we felt about it. We were on a mission.

Returning to the Red Sox

The Red Sox did not contend again in 1968. They did win more than they lost (87-76) but placed fourth in the American League. The A.L was then a 10-team league so at least they finished higher up than some (for instance, the fifth-place Yankees), but they were 17 games behind the Detroit Tigers in league standings.

In 1969, they finished third in the new six-team American League's East Division. In 1970 and 1971, they finished third again both years.

The 1972 season – one game too few

The first few days of the 1972 season were never played; the start was delayed by a players' strike and the Red Sox season began on April 15 in Detroit, with a 3-2 loss to the Tigers. After the strike was resolved, the plan was for each team to simply play out what remained of the originally-announced schedule. This resulted in teams playing an uneven unequal number of games. There was divisional play now. In the AL East, the Tigers played 156 games, as did the Indians and Brewers. The Red Sox played 155, as did the Red Sox and Yankees. The Orioles played 154.

The Red Sox got off to a slow start, but took first place on September 7 and were still in first through October 1. Playing three games against the Tigers, they lost the first two and then won the final. It left them at 85-70 and a half-game behind Detroit (86-70). Had they been able to play one more game – equaling the number of games the Tigers played – and won, the two teams would have been tied, and forcing a final tiebreaker – as happened six years later, with the Yankees, in 1978.

1973 and 1974

It was second place again in 1973, with 89 wins but eight games behind the Baltimore Orioles. In 1974, they were in first place much of the season, and through Labor Day, but were 11-18 in September and dropped to third, finishing seven games behind the O's. Each year, though, they drew quite well. The desultory Red Sox of 1961-66 (in which home attendance was under a million each year) was a thing of the past. The Impossible Dream team had truly revived the franchise.

The 1975 Postseason

The Red Sox won the pennant again in 1975. Both Jim Rice and Fred Lynn enjoyed their first full seasons with the team – and placed first (Lynn, .331 with 105 RBIs) and second (Rice, .309 with 102 RBIs) in Rookie of the Year voting. Lynn was named league MVP and Rice placed third. It was the first time in major-league history that the same person had been both ROY and MVP. Rice and Lynn were dubbed the "Gold Dust Twins." Catcher Carlton Fisk (.331) was essentially the team leader. They had no 20-game winners on the pitching staff, but Rick Wise won 19, Luis Tiant won 18, and Bill Lee won 17. Roger Moret won 14 and Reggie Cleveland 13. There were a true team and won 95 games, with no drama in the final games as there had been in 1967 and 1972. They had been in first place from June 29 on and finished 4 ½ games ahead of Baltimore.[34]

Under manager Darrell Johnson, the Red Sox played their first-ever American League Championship Series, against the Oakland Athletics who – with 98 wins – had won the A.L. West, seven games ahead of the Kansas City Royals. It was a best-of-five ALCS, and the Red Sox swept it in three.

They did so without future Hall of Famer Jim Rice, who – like Ted Williams in 1946 – had a serious injury shortly before postseason play. In Rice's case, he was hit by a pitch and suffered a broken left hand in the game of September 21. He missed both the ALCS and the World Series, and one can only wonder how the World Series would have turned out had Rice been able to play. He was the team leader in home runs (and tied for the lead in stolen bases), and one suspects he might have been first in RBIs had he been able to play the final 5 ½ games.

How many games had I gone to? I don't specifically remember going to Fenway Park during these years. No games really stand out in memory. I didn't keep a Red Sox journal of any sort. And we were doing a lot of traveling for Rounder. In the early 1970s, we took a lot of road trips – which sometimes lasted for weeks, taking in fiddlers' conventions and early bluegrass festivals in the southeast. I had a Volkswagen van, and then another, and the three of us slept in the van, wherever we could. I don't know when we first took a hotel room, but certainly not for the first 5 or 6 years. We were definitely a bare-bones outfit, wanting to put every dollar we could back into building the business. I didn't go to as many games as I had, partly because we were out of town so much and partly because when we were home we were literally working around the clock.

We released 21 albums in 1973, 18 in 1974, and then 29 in 1975. By year's end, we had a catalog of 92 albums.

Rounder 0044 (1975), nearly 50 years later voted overwhelmingly "All-Time Favorite Album" in a readers' poll of *Bluegrass Unlimited* magazine.

I was doing other things than follow the Red Sox and work at Rounder. For one thing, I was working on my dissertation. Being in political science, and having been radicalized, I chose to write about the life and ideas of Alexander Berkman. His fellow anarchist Emma Goldman had received a lot of attention but he himself had not. In August 1974, right after the National Folk Festival in Washington, I took a trip to Europe to visit the home of the Berkman papers in Amsterdam and spent a week at the International Instituut voor Sociale Geschiedenis (International Institute of Social History). On the same trip, I also visited another archive in Lausanne, Switzerland – the Centre International de Recherches sur l'Anarchisme. I was also able to visit two friends of Goldman and Berkman, Augustine Souchy in Munich, and Nikolai Lazarewitch in Paris.

I did ultimately get my doctorate in 1980, from Tufts. Years later, Stuart Christie published my book based on the dissertation: *Alexander Berkman, Anarchist: Life, Work, Ideas* (Read and Noir, 2014).

I took advantage of being in Europe again to reprise some of my hitch-hiking exploits of 1967 – returning again to Istanbul to stay with the Akyoruk family there for a few days, traveling through Hungary and Romania to get there. I then headed further east, all the way across Turkey to Iran (the Shah was still in power) and visited an American family in Teheran, the Walters. I then traveled south across Iran to Abadan, crossed to Kuwait, and then went on to Lebanon, Syria, and Egypt. I flew to Paris and then traveled a bit more, including a visit to East Berlin. Yes, I was gone a long time – August 6 to December 4. Thanks to Ken and Marian for putting up with this long absence. Weirdly, in a Brussels bar the night before heading home, there was some bluegrass on the radio – I made a note of hearing the Bill Monroe classic "Uncle Pen." I guess it was time to head back to Rounder. Sorry, Red Sox, I didn't get to any games the last couple of months of the 1974 season.

It was in 1975 that Rounder first filed tax returns and registered as a business. We even hired our first employee. The work was just too much for us alone. That summer – in August – we released Rounder 0044, by J.D. Crowe and The New South. It was a path-breaking album of contemporary bluegrass that became more widely known by its catalog number ("Rounder 0044") that by any other handle. It was such a landmark album that in 2023, in the Reader's Poll conducted by *Bluegrass Unlimited* magazine, this release from nearly 50 years before was voted "Favorite All-Time Album," which the magazine reported won "by a wide margin – almost as many votes were cast for J.D.'s album as all of the other top five albums combined."

The 1975 ALCS

Luis Tiant threw a three-hitter in Game One at Fenway. It was a 7-1 win, the Red Sox already having scored their seven before the A's got one in the eighth, thanks to a double and an error. The first two runs the Red Sox got were in the first inning, and both of those scored on errors, too.

They then scored five runs on five hits in the seventh, driving starter Ken Holtzman from the mound as well as relievers Jim Todd (who only faced one batter) and Paul Lindblad. The A's committed four errors in the game, and only two of the seven runs were earned runs.

Reggie Cleveland squared off against Vida Blue in Game Two. They each gave up three runs. Blue was gone after three innings, Cleveland after five. The A's scored two in the top of the first (on a two-run Reggie Jackson home run) and a third run in the fourth. Yastrzemski hit a two-run homer in the bottom of the fourth; a third run scored on a subsequent double play, tying the score. In the sixth, Yaz doubled and Fisk singled him home for the go-ahead run. Petrocelli's leadoff homer in the seventh made it 5-3. In the eighth, Juan Beniquez singled and, with two outs, Lynn singled him home. The final was 6-3.

Game Three was at the Coliseum, Holtzman against Rick Wise. Boston scored first, in the top of the fourth, on a two-out RBI single by Petrocelli. They added three more runs in the top of the fifth. After two outs, Denny Doyle got an RBI with a single. Yaz singled, and then Fisk singled, driving in Doyle. On a wild pitch, Yaz scored. The Athletics got a run in the sixth, but Cecil Cooper singled in a fifth run for Boston in the eighth. Sal Bando and Reggie Jackson each drove in a run in the eighth, but the 5-3 score held and Boston prepared to play the World Series against Cincinnati's Big Red Machine.

The 1975 World Series – and the Fisk home run that gave fans hope

It had been eight years since 1967, but the Red Sox were back in the World Series. The Cincinnati Reds had dominated in the N.L. West, with 108 wins and with the second-place Los Angeles Dodgers a full 20 games behind them in the standings. They then swept the Pittsburgh Pirates in the NLCS by scores of 8-3, 6-1, and then (after the Pirates had tied it in the bottom of the ninth), a 10-inning 5-3 win in Pittsburgh. Ken Griffey and Tony Perez each had four RBIs. Pitcher Don Gullett had three.

The World Series was a tight one, with five of the games being decided by just one run, and with two of those in extra innings (one win in extras for each team).

Game One was a Tiant vs. Gullett pitchers' duel for the first six innings. The Red Sox almost scored in the first but Dwight Evans was thrown out at the plate. In the bottom of the seventh, the Red Sox exploded for six runs. It started with Tiant singling to left. Evans reached on a sacrifice bunt. Doyle singled, loading the bases, and Yastrzemski singled, scoring Tiant with the first run of the game. Clay Carroll relieved Gullett and walked Fisk on six pitches, forcing in a second run. Will McEnaney relieved Carroll. He struck out Fred Lynn, but Petrocelli drove in two with a single to left and Rick Burleson singled to drive in Fisk. The sixth and final run came on a Cecil Cooper sacrifice fly. Tiant faced six batters in the eighth and ninth and retired each one. It was a special night for Tiant because his father Luis Sr. – a great pitcher in both Cuban and Negro League baseball history – had been flown in before the game and the two were reunited.[35]

The second game was a tight one right to the end. Starting pitchers were Bill Lee for the Red Sox and Jack Billingham for the Reds. Boston scored first, in the bottom of the first, when Cecil Cooper led off with a double and went to third on an infield single from Doyle. Yaz hit into a double play that included Cooper being trapped in a rundown between third and home. Yaz made it to second and scored on a single by Fisk. In the fourth, the Reds tied it on a walk to Joe Morgan, single by Johnny Bench that sent Morgan to third, and a force play at second on which Morgan scored. A sixth-inning single, error, and a single by Petrocelli gave Boston a 2-1 lead. When Bench doubled off Lee to lead off the ninth,

Dick Drago relieved "The Spaceman." After two outs, Bench scored on Dave Concepcion's infield single, tying the game. Concepcion stole second, then scored the go-ahead run on a Ken Griffey double. It was all they needed to win Game Two since Rawly Eastwick retired the last three Boston batters.

Games Three, Four, and Five were at Riverfront Stadium in Cincinnati. Fisk led off the second with a solo homer off started Gary Nolan, but Rick Wise (after throwing three hitless innings) gave up a two-run homer to Bench in the fourth, and then fifth-inning leadoff homers to Concepcion and Cesar Geronimo. Morgan's sacrifice fly later in the inning provided a 5-1 Cincinnati lead, but the Red Sox responded. Lynn's sacrifice fly in the sixth made it 5-2. Bernie Carbo hit a solo homer in the seventh to make it 5-3. In the top of ninth, Evans hit a two-run homer off Eastwick to tie the game. In the bottom of the 10th, Geronimo singled off Jim Willoughby. Ed Armbrister bunted and Fisk was charged with an error (despite what many Red Sox fans believed was interference by the batter). Plate umpire Larry Barnett ruled it unintentional contact. With runners on second and third and nobody out, Moret was brought in. He intentionally walked Pete Rose, which loaded the bases. He struck out the next batter, but Joe Morgan singled to center and the game was over.

The Red Sox evened matters at two wins apiece, with a 5-4 win in Game Four. It was Fred Norman vs. Tiant. The Reds didn't wait to score. Pete Rose singled to center. On the next pitch, Griffey doubled to left-center and scored Rose. Griffey had tried to take third but was thrown out. Joe Morgan walked, advanced to second on a groundout to short, and then scored when Bench doubled to right. The 2-0 score stood until the Red Sox upended it with five runs in the top of the fourth. Fisk and Lynn hit back-to-back singles. After one out, Evans tripled to right. Burleson doubled and scored Evans. Pedro Borbon relieved Norman. Tiant singled. Beniquez reached on an error at first base as Burleson scored. With two outs, Yastrzemski singled Tiant home. In the bottom of the fourth, the

Reds got back two of the runs on a two-out single, double, and Geronimo triple, but that was it for scoring. Over the final five innings, Tiant gave up three singles and walked three batters, but threw a complete game, in excess of 150 pitches, without giving up another run. He improved to 3-0 in the postseason.

The Reds took a three-games-to-two lead in Game Five, outscoring Boston 6-2, Gullett getting the win and Reggie Cleveland the loss. A first-inning run on a triple and sacrifice fly and a second run in the top of the ninth on two singles and a Fred Lynn double was all Boston could manage. A three-run homer by Tony Perez was the biggest blow off Cleveland. The two teams traveled back to Boston, with Cincinnati only needing to win either of the two games to win the World Series.

Game Six proved to be one of the most notable games in Red Sox history. I'd gotten in line around 2 A.M. and gotten tickets for both Games Six and the possible Game Seven – standing room for Game Six but actual seats for Game Seven. The matchup was Tiant against Gary Nolan, Tiant able to pitch again because of three days of rain. It could hardly have started more nicely than with a first-inning three-run homer into the right-center field bleachers by Fred Lynn. After four, it was still 3-0, Red Sox, but in the top of the seventh, Tiant put a couple of batters on base, then saw Ken Griffey triple them home, and Johnny Bench single in Griffey. The score was tied. A couple of singles and a two-run George Foster double gave the Reds a 5-3 lead, and Geronimo homered to lead off the eighth. It was 6-3, Cincinnati. Moret replaced Tiant on the mound.

Fred Lynn swung at Borbon's first pitch in the bottom of the eighth and reached on an infield single. Petrocelli walked. Eastwick came in from the bullpen and got outs from both Evans and Burleson. Bernie Carbo pinch-hit for Moret – and homered into the center-field bleachers, tying the game 6-6. Drago threw the top of the ninth for Boston

Atop the Green Monster next to the Carlton Fisk Pole.

and retired the Reds in order. The Red Sox got the first two runners on; Eastwick came in and intentionally walked Fisk. The bases were loaded with nobody out. But Lynn flied out to left field, the throw to the plate getting Doyle out for a double play. Petrocelli grounded out and the game went into extra innings.

Some of us in standing room moved down and sat in the aisles between sections; I sat on the concrete in the aisle between Sections 17 and 18 – my view looking directly down the left-field line.

In both the 10th and the 12th, the Reds got a runner in scoring position but could not score. Pat Darcy – the eighth pitcher of the game for Cincinnati – retired the Red Sox in order in both the 10th and 11th. On a 1-0 count, his second pitch of the 12th, Darcy threw the ball over the plate and Carlton Fisk hit it high and deep. The only question was whether it would stay fair. It did. The Red Sox won, and survived to play another World Series Game Seven. The video of Fisk "waving" the ball fair as he leapt down the first-base line, hoping to be able to get into a home-run trot, has become iconic. One could not have had a better vantage point than I did, given where I was seated. The ball did stay fair. The Red Sox did win the game.

There was still hope – and exultation – throughout New England and the diaspora of Red Sox fandom.

Bill Lee started Game Seven for the Red Sox and Don Gullett did for the Reds. We had splurged and got grandstand seats; Bill Kornrich and I took our fathers to the game. Nearly half a century later, Bill recalls sitting in front of some very loud and drunken people, one of whom fell forward and broke Bill's father's glasses. Naturally, there was hope in the air. Lee was touched for three singles, but no runs, over the first three frames. The Red Sox scored three times in the bottom of the third, and Red Sox fandom – still high from Game Six – couldn't have been much happier. Yaz drove in the first run after a walk and single preceded him. Fisk was walked intentionally (Yaz had advanced to second on the throw to third) Lynn struck out, but then Gullett issued bases-loaded walks to both Rico Petrocelli and Rick Burleson.

In the top of the sixth, Tony Perez hit a two-run homer to bring Cincinnati to within a run. With one out in the seventh, Lee walked Griffey. Moret came on in relief, got a second out, but then – after Griffey stole second – walked Armbrister. Pete Rose singled and the game was tied. Jim Willoughby got the third out. It remained tied, 3-3, as the ninth inning began. Jim Burton came in from the pen. He walked Griffey. Geronimo sacrificed him to second. On a groundout, Griffey took third base. Joe Morgan dropped a single into right-center field, the Reds took a 4-3 lead, and the Red Sox couldn't match it. For their third World Series in a row, the Red Sox had taken it to Game Seven, but once again had lost.

The feeling after Game Seven somewhat echoed Glenn Stout's "when a defeat is not a loss" phrase regarding the 1967 Series. Yes, the Red Sox had lost, but Game Six was SO magical, so exhilarating, that in some respects it (almost) seemed not to matter a great deal that the Red Sox had come up a run short against the Big Red Machine. There was, arguably, not yet a true market for a book on the Curse of the Bambino. That would come, after agonizing losses in 1978 and again in 1986.

5

Postseason Pain Tempered by Accomplishment at Rounder Records

---

The 163rd game in 1978 – a one-game Yankees vs. Red Sox tiebreaker for the pennant

The Yankees won the East in 1976, 15½ games ahead of the third-place Red Sox. They won the pennant, but then were swept by Cincinnati in the World Series – Red Sox fans perhaps took some degree of satisfaction in that the Red Sox had pushed the Reds to the ninth inning of a seventh game while the Yankees had lost four in a row, only one of them a particularly close game.

In 1977, the Red Sox won 97 games, but so did the Baltimore Orioles, and – perhaps more significantly – the Yankees won 100. Both Baltimore and Boston tied for second place, 1½ games behind New York. Head to head, the Red Sox had won more games from the Yankees and Orioles than they lost. This time, the Yankees played the Los Angeles Dodgers in the World Series and came out on top, four games to two. It was the Yankees' 20th world championship.

As September began, the Yankees were 6 ½ games out of first place in the A.L. East. The Red Sox were in first. They had been in first place since May 20, and by as many as 10 games in early July. They had been 11½ games ahead of the third-place Yankees at the All-Star Break. Milwaukee was in second place, nine games behind Boston.

New York was gaining on them, and a fateful four games in September saw them snatch four games off Boston's lead. At Fenway Park, from September 7 through 10, the Yankees beat the Red Sox by scores of 15-3, 13-2, 7-0, and 7-4. It was another "Boston Massacre." There was little solace for Red Sox fans. They had a four-game lead before the four-game stretch. After the game on the 10th, the two teams were tied for first place. The *Globe*'s Peter Gammons ascribed Boston's slippage to over-reliance on some of the starters in the lineup – such as Fisk, Lynn, Scott, and Yastrzemski, forcing them to play more games without adequate rest, likely producing some injuries.[36]

By the 13th, they had lost 11 of their last 14 and dropped to second place. They fought to get back and actually won the last eight games on the schedule, the final one a 5-0 Luis Tiant shutout of Toronto. Indeed, four of those eight victories were shutout victories. That's what it took to achieve a tie with the Yankees on October 1, that plus New York losing to Cleveland, 9-2. Both teams had records of 99-63. A single-game tiebreaker would be needed to determine who would truly win the A.L. East.

After the game on October 1, I left my seat in the bleachers and immediately got in line at the Red Sox ticket office. Earlier in the month, it had been announced that any tiebreaker would be at Fenway Park the very next day.[37]

Some recalled the only other tiebreaker in league history, also held at Fenway Park, back in 1948, when Cleveland had beaten Boston, 8-3.

Manager Don Zimmer's starter was Mike Torrez (16-12, 3.92) and Lemon's was Ron Guidry (with an astonishing record of 24-3, and a 1.72 ERA). Guidry led the league in both categories, as he did with nine shutouts.

Torrez had won two games for the Yankees in the 1977 World Series, both of them complete-game wins – Game Three and the clinching Game Six. Now he was with the Red Sox, pitching against them in another equally big game.

This game was not a shutout. Carl Yastrzemski drew first blood with a leadoff home run down the right-field line off Guidry in the bottom of the second inning. George Scott led off the third inning with a double off the center-field wall. A sacrifice sent him to third, with one out, but the Sox couldn't get him home. Peter Gammons wrote that 24 times in the final month Boston had gotten a runner on third base and not scored him; in five of those games they lost by one run. [38]

They still had the lead. At the end of five innings, the score still stood at 1-0, Red Sox. Torrez set down the Yankees in order in the top of the sixth. Rick Burleson doubled, leading off Boston's half of the sixth. Jerry Remy laid down a sacrifice bunt and Burleson took third base, scoring when Jim Rice singled to center. It was 2-0, Red Sox.

Zimmer stuck with Torrez, who had only allowed two base hits and two bases on balls. After he got the first out of the seventh, both Chris Chambliss and Roy White singled. After the second out, the unthinkable happened; shortstop Bucky Dent homered into the screen above the left-field wall. Suddenly the Yankees had a 3-2 lead. Dent was hardly known as a homer hitter. He only had four on the year, fewer than any other regular on the team save Willie Randolph. He had a .243 batting average. He was the ninth batter in the order. In the more refined, or at least more polite, Boston circles, he was known forever after as Bucky Bleeping Dent.

After Torrez walked the next batter, Mickey Rivers, Zimmer called on Bob Stanley to relieve. Rivers then stole second and scored on Thurman Munson's single to center. It was 4-2, Yankees.

The Sox failed to score against Guidry and then Rich Gossage, in the eighth. And the Yankees added a fifth run in the top of the eighth on a leadoff homer by Reggie Jackson.

In the bottom of the eighth, the Red Sox closed the gap to a run – 5-4 – when Jerry Remy led off with a double and Yaz singled him home. Fisk followed with a single, and so did Lynn, driving in Yastrzemski. But that's where it ended – the game and the season. They got two on with just one out in the bottom of the ninth but couldn't produce a tying run.

I did watch all this from my seat in the bleachers. I hadn't gone with anyone. I was there by myself. There was no one in particular to commiserate with – just some 32,924 others, mostly Red Sox fans, with our hopes dashed again. By the Yankees.

The Yankees played the Dodgers again in the World Series, and won again, in six games.

It was not until 2021 – a mere 43 years later – that the Red Sox finally exorcised this particular loss, when they beat the Yankees in that year's Wild Card game.

In 1978, it was another crushing defeat, in a game that never would have been played had the Red Sox won any one of the previous 63 losses they had endured. But that hadn't, and this being a loss to the Yankees made the loss even more painful. It seemed to hurt worse than the Game Seven losses in 1967 and 1975. This was now perhaps the true beginning of the re-evaluation of Red Sox history since 1918 and the genesis of thinking there might be something supernatural going on here.

The years from 1979 through 1985

There was time for any such thoughts to fester. The Red Sox finished third in 1979 and fifth in 1980. The 1981 season was a weird one, with a work stoppage in the middle. With the two halves combined, it was a tight race in the A.L. East as witnessed by the fact that even though the Red Sox finished fifth (of seven teams), they were only 2 ½ games behind the leading Milwaukee Brewers. It wasn't any cause for celebration, though.

The team had been a winning team. From 1967 through 1980, they finished with a winning record 14 seasons in a row. In 1981, the streak was snapped. They rebounded to third place in 1982, six games behind, but they fell 20 games behind in 1983, 18 in 1984, and 18½ in 1985 with a record of 81-81. Playing .500 baseball was not inspiring. The way they played in 1986, however, was.

In the meantime, Rounder Records was growing. I retired from my position at the university. It was a secure position and in the earlier days had provided some useful startup money to help the three of us live while Rounder got going. But we released 29 albums in 1975 and then never released fewer than 32 from the years 1976 through 1982. In the middle 1970s, George Thorogood and the Destroyers became our biggest act – and we got our first gold record (sales of 500,000 units) with *Move It On Over*, which we had released in October 1978. As the decade ended, we had 22 employees in 1979. So I retired, at age 37, so I could work full-time for Rounder.

In 1980 we released 43 albums, with 40 more in 1981 and 43 again in 1982. That was more than three albums a month. We were busy. I realized the company needed more attention.

There was a baseball connection with George Thorogood and the Destroyers. They were big baseball fans, George in particular. When we had such a big hit with *Move It On Over*, MCA Records saw an opportunity to try and cash in. The company bought up some tapes the band had recorded, in pre-Rounder years – basically, demo tapes. They purchased them from an erstwhile friend of George's, but told George they would shelve them if he agreed to have the band record two new albums of material for them. Well, that wasn't going to happen. MCA proceeded to release an album in January 1979 provocatively titled *Better than the Rest*. They were not; these were demo tapes we had heard but declined to release, finding them falling short of the band's potential. Instead, we invited the band into the studio knowing they could do better.

George was appalled, and refused to keep the "tainted money" sent by MCA. The band hailed from Newark, Delaware. They made arrangements that all money which might otherwise come to them be redirected to help restore and upgrade a local baseball field for the citizens of Newark. We at Rounder kicked in $1,000 to the local VFW to help finance construction.[39] They called it Doubleday Field; in 2023, one sees it is named Leroy C. Hill, Jr. Park and is the home of the Newark American

Little League. Bassist Bill Blough wrote me in June 2023 saying, "Leroy Hill was instrumental in helping George and Jeff getting the league going."

Later in June, I spoke with George, a tremendous (and knowledgeable) baseball fan. Once I passed his opening test ("Who was the only player to ever pinch-hit for Ted Williams?"), he told me more of the story. George and drummer Jeff Simon often played catch at a field on Kells Avenue in Newark. Hill had been a professional baseball scout for the Pittsburgh Pirates and lived on Kells Avenue. They became friendly and spent a fair amount of time together in the middle 1970s. Mr. Hill had a couple of kids of his own who would play. George liked the idea of starting a team called Kells Angels. There was a lot on which some folks played ball – mostly softball – but one had to get a permit to play there and it was kind of a hassle to turn up at the civic center offices at 9 A.M. to secure a permit for later in the day. George conceived the idea of buying a vacant lot and turning into a baseball field for the city. It is now the home of Newark American Little League baseball.

The 6.3-acre park is now named after Leroy Hill. George says, "He threw out the first pitch there, by the way. Opening Day of Doubleday Park. It's a real small town. Everybody knows everybody. He was a cool cat. He knew a little bit about blues music, too." [40]

Speaking of The Destroyers, on October 23, 1981, they launched an ambitious tour that no other artists have ever tried – and they pulled it off: "50 States in 50 Dates – No Nights Off." They played The Wave in Honolulu on the 23rd, flew to Anchorage and played at the International Banquet House on the 24th, then flew to Portland, Oregon and played the Paramount Theater on October 25. The rest of the tour was all by land, with the band traveling in a Checker cab they had purchased. They hit every one of the 50 states, without a night off, taking them to Pasadena on December 11. They pulled it off. They didn't want to discriminate against Washington DC, so on November 25, they played both a show in Catonsville, Maryland and the Capitol Theatre in DC. One or another of the three Rounder Founders was with them for many of the dates.

Of necessity, in arranging the routing, booking agent Mike Kappus had them playing a number of rather small venues. On November 2, they played to 400 people at The Gaiety in Mandan, North Dakota. This was smaller than the 100,000 I'd seen them play to at the Los Angeles Coliseum on October 9 and 11, when they opened for The Rolling Stones. They had had the opportunity to open that year's Stones tour, and did indeed play the opening night show in Philadelphia, but they had already committed to the 50/50 tour, so they had to decline the full tour. There was one date that worked – Mike was able to book them into opening for The Stones at the Superdome in New Orleans as their Louisiana stop on December 5. After the tour wrapped up, they took off all of one night – and then joined The Stones for some final shows, in Tempe on December 13, Kansas City on the 14th and 15th, and then in Hampton, Virginia on the 18th and 19th. I still have my "Keith Richards birthday" T-shirt from the night of the 18th. The following summer the Destroyers opened a number of Stones shows in England, Ireland, France, etc.

George and the Destroyers weren't the only artists with whom there was a baseball connection. Way back when, the man who more or less singlehandedly created bluegrass music as a genre – Bill Monroe – used to select some of the members of his band with an eye toward their abilities to play baseball. His band traveled throughout the southeastern states, from his native Kentucky though Ohio, Indiana, and more to play music – but also to take on local teams at baseball. As Don Cusic notes in his book *Baseball and Country Music,* an advertisement in *Billboard* magazine back in April 1949 announced, "Bill Monroe will carry a baseball team with him again this summer in conjunction with his personal appearance tour. Monroe intends to line up fifteen players, some of whom will double in his show, to play all comers on afternoon dates, with his show set for the evening."[41] Monroe pitched some and played first base. The following year, in his 1950 songbook *Bill Monroe's Blue Grass Country Songs*, he claimed the team had a record of 80-50 for the 1949 season.[42]

Among 21st century bluegrass musicians who share an interest in following today's baseball are Danny Paisley (Rounder had released an album featuring his father Bob Paisley back in August 1973) and David Davis of the Warrior River Boys.

Naturally it works the other way around, too. Major-league umpire Tripp Gibson, a native of Mayfield, Kentucky who worked his first big-league game in 2013, plays banjo. Any number of major-league umpires play instruments of one sort or another. In *The SABR Book of Umpires and Umpiring*, which I co-edited with Larry Gerlach, I envisioned "The Umpire Band" which featured Gibson on banjo, Dan Iassogna on bagpipes, Brian Knight on guitar, Quinn Wolcott on euphonium, and Mike Everitt on trumpet.[43] Vocalists could include Joe West – who holds the record for the most major-league games ever worked by an umpire (5,460). "Cowboy Joe" West has two country music albums to his credit: *Diamond Dreams* on the Good and Western Records label and *Blue Cowboy* on the Blue Cowboy label.

In his passion for baseball, George Thorogood excels. When he and California native Marla Raderman married in 1985, it was on July 16 – the date of the major-league All-Star Game, which was played in Minnesota that year. They made arrangements and married at Jackie Robinson Stadium in Los Angeles. The stadium is the home field of the UCLA Bruins baseball team. George and Marla got married in front of a bronze statue of Robinson which had been installed that April. "Jackie Robinson could arguably be the most important figure in baseball history. We kind of used the statue as an altar. We stood in front of there with a judge. There's a plaque of Jack Roosevelt Robinson and we got our picture taken. Years later we showed it to Jackie Robinson's widow."[44]

At Rounder, we released our first reggae album in December 1981, launching Heartbeat Records, so there were trips to Jamaica that I needed to take – once with Duncan Browne and several times with our head Heartbeat man, Chris Wilson. Over time, we released more than 300 albums on Heartbeat.

In 1985, the Philo label from Vermont was financially unable to continue, so we took on that as well. Compact discs began to come into play. This required learning additional ways of preserving and marketing music. In 1989, working with the Smithsonian Institution, we started releasing compact discs on the Folkways label for a few years until they took this on fully themselves. From 1983 on, for the next 10 years, Rounder averaged just over 70 album releases per year. As I contemplate it while writing this in 2023, it's difficult to conceive how we managed to do all this, but we were *busy*. We also had a dedicated and growing staff.

Some thought we were crazy to jump into CDs the way we did, even cutting our own personal salaries to help fund expansion into offering the additional format. We'd started with vinyl LPs, then added cassettes, and a number of 8-tracks, but this was a whole different thing.

There was also some personal things doing on at this time. I turned 40 in February. In the days before we started Rounder, my college girl-friend had been Janie Julianelli. In the 1970s, there was a romance with Diane Della Vella, who was a bass player in a Boston area bluegrass band. A more serious one developed in 1985. It wasn't romance that I had in mind, when I told myself that I really should get to know some of our musicians better. Ken and Marian spent more time in the studio and with musicians, while I was performing backroom functions – like dealing with royalties or building our international distribution net-work. I met Mimi Farina when she came through Cambridge earlier in 1985. She lived in Mill Valley, California and I stopped by to see her for a couple of days as I returned from a trade show in China. Her 40th birthday was in April so for our "second date" we agreed to meet at the Grand Canyon. We spent three days, hiking down to Phantom Ranch on the canyon floor for one night and then two days hiking back up, camp-ing at the halfway point.

This kicked off a bicoastal relationship that lasted about a year and included visits to the Newport Folk Festival, a performance for prisoners at San Quentin that was arranged by the nonprofit she headed, Bread and Roses, and a trip to Haiti. Yes, she was Joan Baez's sister, but there was only once or twice that we met Joan (Newport was one such time.) I don't think Mimi and I ever went to a baseball game together. Does that prove the relationship was doomed? I doubt that was it, but it did end. Her album on our Philo label, *Solo*, was released that November.

The 1986 season

Dwight Evans hit the very first pitch of the season for a home run. The Red Sox lost the game, 6-5.

They played competitive ball, though, and after 30 games (on May 11) took first place. Dropping two out of three to the Angels, they fell out briefly but from May 14 on never left first place, never let it slip away from them.

At the end of May, they had a 2 ½ game lead. It was an eight-game lead at the end of June. That lead had eroded to four games at the end of July, but they still held first place. It was 3 ½ games at the end of August, but they built that up to a 10-game lead by September 17. Even after going 5-9 over the last couple of weeks, including losing every one of the four final games to the Yankees, they still wound up 5 ½ games ahead of the second-place Yankees.

The 1986 ALCS

The ALCS was against the California Angels. The two teams seemed fairly evenly matched. The Angels had finished five games ahead of the Texas Rangers in the A.L West, and they were thirsty for their first opportunity to reach the World Series. Since their first season in 1961, they had reached the ALCS twice before, losing to the Orioles in 1979 and the Brewers in 1982. This was their third shot.

The first game was at Fenway, with Roger Clemens going for the Red Sox. Clemens had the best won/loss record in the majors (24-4, with a league-leaguing 2.48 ERA). I had been fortunate to see him throw a

20-strikeout game in Boston on April 29. As July began, his record was 14-0. Results had not been announced yet, but Clemens won his first Cy Young Award (of seven) for his work in the 1986 season, and also won the A.L. Most Valuable Player award.

Opposing Clemens was Mike Witt (18-10, 2.84). He'd lost three of his last four decisions. But it was Witt who pitched, by far, the better game as the ALCS got underway, a com-plete-game 8-1 win, holding the Red Sox to just five hits. In the top of the second, the Angels scored four runs after Clemens had struck out the first two batters. There fol-lowed two walks, a single, dou-ble, and a single. The Angels

Roger Clemens set a major-league record striking out 20 batters on April 29, 1986 in front of me and 13,413 other fans at Fenway (Jerry Buckley/ Boston Red Sox).

upped their lead to 5-0 in the third. Boston's lone run was on a Marty Barrett single in the bottom of the sixth.

The Red Sox evened things up in Game Two with a 9-2 win, Bruce Hurst going all the way for the Red Sox. Hurst had been 13-8 (2.99) in the reg-ular season. Kirk McCaskill had been 17-10 for the Angels, with a 3.36 ERA. He worked seven innings. Barrett doubled in Wade Boggs, who had tripled to lead off the first inning. In the second inning, Barrett drove in the second Sox run, hitting the last of four singles. Dick Schofield singled in a run for the Angels in the fourth and Wally Joyner hit a solo home run to tie it, 2-2, in the top of the fifth. Boston edged ahead in the bottom of the fifth, when Dwight Evans singled in Bill Buckner.

In the seventh, plagued by two errors by Angels infielders, the Red Sox scored three unearned runs on one base hit and took a 6-2 lead. They added three more in the eighth off relievers Gary Nolan and Doug

Corbett. Buckner drove in one with a sacrifice fly and Rice homered for the other two.

The Series shifted to Anaheim Stadium for Games Three, Four, and Five. The starters were John Candelaria (10-2, 2.55) and Dennis "Oil Can" Boyd (16-10, 3.78). The Red Sox scored one in the second, on a Rich Gedman single. The Angels scored one in the sixth on a walk, fielder's choice, and Reggie Jackson single. A solo home run by Schofield and a two-run homer by Gary Pettis gave the Angels a 4-1 lead in the seventh. The Sox got two back in the eighth on a balk and another Gedman single, but in the end the Angels won, 5-3.

Game Four went 11 innings. Don Sutton (15-11, 3.74) squared off against Clemens. The game was scoreless through five. Buckner doubled in Tony Armas for a 1-0 lead in the top of the sixth. They took a 3-0 lead in the eighth on Barrett's single off reliever Vern Ruhle and a passed ball and error that allowed Barrett to score during the next at-bat. Clemens took the mound in the bottom of the ninth with a 3-0 lead, but Doug DeCinces led off with a home run, and then Clemens gave up a pair of one-out singles. Calvin Schiraldi came on in relief. Pettis doubled and made it 3-2. With the bases loaded and two outs, Schiraldi hit Brian Downing with a pitch, tying the game. In the bottom of the 11th, a single by Jerry Narron, sacrifice, and intentional walk set things up for Bobby Grich, first-pitch swinging, to win the game for the Angels, 4-3.

The Angels now held a three-games-to-one edge.

Game Five also went 11 innings. Gedman's second-inning two-run homer off Witt gave Boston an early lead. Bob Boone hit a leadoff homer in the third off Hurst, and it was 2-1, Red Sox. A two-run homer by Grich in the sixth tipped the scales the other way, 3-2 Angels. The homer had actually hit in Dave Henderson's glove, but then popped out and over the fence. Henderson had come into the game in the fifth, replacing Armas for defensive purposes. They added two more in the seventh off Bob Stanley. The game went into the ninth inning with the Angels up, 5-2. Buckner singled. Jim Rice struck out. Don Baylor hit a two-run homer, pulling the Red Sox to within a run. With two outs, Gary Lucas came in to get the final out. Instead, his first pitch hit Rich Gedman. It was the only pitch he threw. Donnie Moore came in to pitch to Dave Henderson.

"Hendu" had come over to the Red Sox in a mid-August trade and in 54 plate appearances hit .196 with one homer and three runs batted in. He had come in two earlier ALCS games for late-inning defense and had one at-bat, a fly ball to center in Game Four. On a 2-2 count, he was facing what could be the final pitch of the year for the Red Sox. This time Henderson hit a two-run homer into the left-field seats, giving the Red Sox a 6-5 lead. Word was that a clubby had already uncorked at least a couple of bottles of champagne in the Angels clubhouse.

The Red Sox couldn't hold the lead, though. Boone singled off Stanley, pinch-runner Ruppert Jones was sacrificed to second, and scored when Joe Sambito relieved Stanley and Rob Wilfong singled Jones home.

A forceout and a double play helped Moore get though the 10th but in the top of the 11th, he hit Don Baylor and then gave up back-to-back singles to Dwight Evans and to Gedman. This brought up Dave Henderson again. He hit a sacrifice fly to center, giving the Red Sox a 7-6 lead. Schiraldi struck out Wilfong and Schofield and got Downing to pop up foul to first base. Needless to say, Dave Henderson became a Red Sox hero. He had kept the season alive, and forced at least a Game Six, back in Boston. More than one writer suggested it might have "topped even the sixth game of the '75 Series."[45]

Fans at Fenway welcomed the team back for Game Six and were rewarded. Though two-out doubles off Oil Can by Reggie Jackson and Doug DeCinces gave the Angels a 2-0 lead in the first, McCaskill walked the first two Red Sox and then saw them both score on a groundout, passed ball, and another groundout. The Red Sox then scored five runs in the third on four consecutive hits, a fielder's choice and two more hits, with an error mixed in. Henderson drove in their eighth run on a force play in the fifth. The Angels did get a couple of more runs, but so did the Red Sox and the game ended 10-4, setting up the decisive Game Seven.

It was Clemens against Candelaria, but Candelaria was gone before the end of the fourth. Gedman singled in one and Boggs singled in two in the bottom of the second. In the fourth, Spike Owen singled in their third run and Jim Rice ended the Angels starter's game with a three-run homer off the light tower atop the wall in left. Clemens got the win, the only postseason game he ever won for Boston.

"Yogi's quote gets better and better," said manager John McNamara. "It's still never over till it's over. It's a dream come true to get there."[46] "Magic. A team of magic," said Wade Boggs.[47] And the headline on Leigh Montville's piece had it right: "Next – A New York/Boston World Series."

The 1986 World Series – finding another way to lose

It wasn't the Yankees; they can never play the Red Sox in a World Series, but it was a New York team: the New York Mets. The last time the Red Sox had played a New York team in a World Series was in 1912, Fenway Park's first year. They beat the New York Giants. And, notably, it had been 68 years since the Red Sox last won a World Series. The Mets had won one in 1969.

The Mets were formidable. They had won 108 regular-season games, losing only 54, and had won the N.L. East by 21⅓ games over the second-place Phillies. From the 10th game of the season, they had been in first place. Davey Johnson was the manager. They lacked a 20-game winner but had six pitchers with 10 or more wins and a team ERA of 3.11. The two teams were matched pretty closely in batting average, runs driven in, and the like. The Mets had cruised to victory and were confident, if not outright cocky. It had taken them six games to beat the Astros in the NLCS, though, winning the final two games in 12 innings and then 16. The Red Sox had won a somewhat magical league championship series and were riding high.

The first two games were at Shea Stadium. Game One couldn't have been much tighter. Neither team scored for the first six innings. It was Ron Darling for New York and Bruce Hurst for Boston. Each team had three scattered singles through those first six frames. In the top of the seventh, Darling walked Jim Rice, who took second on a wild pitch, but then stayed put when Evans grounded out to Darling. Gedman hit the ball to second baseman Tim Teufel, who – on a fairly routine ground ball – committed the only error of the game for either side, letting the ball get through him as Rice scored from second base. It was the only run of the game. Henderson almost drove in another in the ninth with a single to left, but Evans was thrown out at the plate trying to score from second base. Schiraldi relieved Hurst, walked Darryl Strawberry, but then got three outs. It was a 1-0 win for the Red Sox.

Game Two was another Red Sox win, with a lead they built and built to a final of 9-3. The starters were Dwight Gooden and Roger Clemens. Gooden had been Rookie of the Year in 1984 and won the Cy Young Award in 1985, with a solid 17-6 (2.84) season in 1986. Both starters were gone by the sixth.

The Red Sox scored first, with three runs on a walk, three hits, and an error in the top of the third. Then Wade Boggs doubled, Marty Barrett singled, and Bill Buckner singled, each hit producing a run. The Mets got two back right away on singles by Rafael Santana and Gooden, Lenny Dykstra's sacrifice, and then an RBI single by Wally Backman and a run-producing groundout by Keith Hernandez. Boston's Dave Henderson made it 4-2 with a home run to lead off the fourth. Jim Rice singled and Dwight Evans homered in the fifth to make it 6-2. The Mets got a run in the fifth after Clemens put two on (he had walked four in all), and Steve Crawford relieved him. New York's Rick Aguilera got through a scoreless fifth, but gave up five consecutive singles to lead off the sixth. Two runs scored. That was enough for Aguilera. Boston got one more run in the top of the ninth on a pair of singles and Wade Boggs' two-base hit. The final was 9-3, Boston. The Red Sox had 18 hits in the game. And they had won both games at Shea Stadium.

The next games were at Fenway Park and in fact the Mets turned the tables by winning Game Three and Game Four. After the first four, not a single game had been won by the home team. The third game was Oil

Can Boyd against Bob Ojeda (who'd pitched for the Red Sox in 1985), and the Mets had a 4-0 lead before Ojeda ever took the mound. Lenny Dykstra led off with a home run. Backman singled, Hernandez singled, and Gary Carter doubled. Boyd got an out but then DH Danny Heep singled, driving in two. The Red Sox got their one and only run in the bottom of the third on Henderson's second single of the game, a walk to Boggs, and an RBI single by Marty Barrett. Two singles, a walk, and another single (by Carter) gave the Mets a 6-1 lead. They added a seventh and final run in the seventh off Joe Sambito; Strawberry singled, took second on a wild pitch, took third on a passed ball, and then trotted home on Ray Knight's double to left. 7-1, Mets.

Game Four also went the Mets' way. It wasn't a close one, either. Boston started Al Nipper, who had been 10-12 with a 5.86 ERA in the regular season but had the possible advantage of not being overworked. He'd last pitched 18 days earlier, and he did well for the first three innings, while Mets starter Ron Darling escaped a bases-loaded situation in the first and then settled down. In the fourth, Backman singled and, after an out, Carter homered. Strawberry doubled and Knight singled and the Mets led 3-0. They bumped the lead up to 5-0 in the top of the seventh on Dykstra's two-run homer off Crawford (and off Evans' glove). And to 6-0 in the eighth on Carter's second home run of the game over the Green Monster. Roger McDowell replaced Darling and gave up a couple of runs but the Red Sox were four runs shy and remained that way.

Game Five in Boston saw 22 base hits but only six runs. The Red Sox finally won at home, and thus took a three-games-to-two edge in the World Series. They had a rested Bruce Hurst pitching. Doc Gooden was pitching for the Mets. Gooden got out of a bases-loaded situation in the first without a run scoring, but Henderson tripled with one out in the second and then scored on a sac fly by Spike Owen. In the third, after an error, a walk, and two outs, Dwight Evans singled in Bill Buckner for another run. The Sox built a 4-0 lead in the fifth. Rice tripled, leading off. Baylor singled. Evans singled. Sid Fernandez came in from the bullpen. He struck out Gedman but Henderson doubled in Baylor. In the top of the eighth, Teufel hit a solo home run off Hurst. In the ninth, after two outs, Hurst gave up a double to Mookie Wilson and a single to Rafael Santana, but then got the third out, striking out Dykstra. Hurst improved to 3-0 in the postseason.

All the Red Sox needed to do was win Game Six or, if necessary, a Game Seven – and there would be no talk of curses and the like. That's all they needed to do.

Game Six was on a Saturday night at Shea Stadium. The Red Sox got off to a nice start against Ojeda with one run in the first (Evans doubled in Boggs) and one run in the second (Barrett singled in Spike Owen), while Roger Clemens struck out four. He walked one but didn't allow a hit. Clemens retired the side in order in the third and the fourth. As the game passed the halfway point, though, the Mets tied it up in the bottom of the fifth. Strawberry walked, stole second, and scored on Knight's single. Mookie Wilson singled, Knight going first to third on an error by Evans and then scoring on a 4-6-3 double play hit into by pinch-hitter Danny Heep.

After Roger McDowell replaced Ojeda, Boston was able to take a 3-2 lead in the seventh. Barrett was up first and walked, taking second on a groundout, third on an error, and scoring as Evans grounded out. Clemens retired the side in order, but in the eighth the Red Sox loaded the bases on Henderson's leadoff single and two bases on balls. They failed to score, in a situation where manager John McNamara had told Don Baylor to prepare to bat for Bill Buckner, but then let Buckner bat. Buckner swung at the first pitch and flied out.

In fairness, Buckner – though hobbling on subpar legs – had driven in 102 runs during the regular season, second only to Jim Rice's 110 for the 1986 Red Sox. They likely wouldn't have won the pennant without him. McNamara normally had Dave Stapleton replace Buckner in the later innings for defensive purposes. It was thought that sentiment played a role, that McNamara wanted to reward the veteran Buckner with being on the field as the Red Sox won the World Series. In any event, he flied out – and took the field again at first base.

The Mets then tied the game (off Calvin Schiraldi) in the home half of the eighth when Lee Mazzilli singled, took second on a bunt, third on a sacrifice bunt, and – after an intentional walk – scored on Gary Carter's sacrifice fly. Neither team scored in the ninth.

It looked like the Red Sox had put the game away in the top of the 10th. Dave Henderson led off with a home run off Aguilera. The next two batters struck out, but then Boggs doubled to left and Barrett provided an insurance run with a single to center. Schiraldi took the mound with a 4-2 lead, needing just three outs for the Red Sox to win the World Series. Backman flew out to left. Hernandez flew out to center. Had one more Met made an out in the inning, there would have been no talk linking curses to the Red Sox.

As noted, the Mets scoreboard operator had pushed the wrong button on a message that had been prepared and had inadvertently posted congratulations to the Red Sox, which had momentarily flashed on the Shea Stadium message board.

Clearly, fate took another turn. Gary Carter singled to left. Kevin Mitchell pinch-hit for Aguilera and he singled to center. But Boston still had a two-run lead. Schiraldi got two strikes on Knight, but then saw Knight single to right-center, driving in one run as Mitchell went first to third. Schiraldi had thrown 55 pitches at this point. John McNamara pulled the plug and beckoned in "The Steamer" – Bob Stanley, the team leader in saves. Left fielder Mookie Wilson was up. Stanley got two strikes on him, mixed with a couple of balls, and saw Wilson foul off three pitches with the Red Sox still just one strike away. Then, a wild pitch (or passed ball, depending on whether you go with the official scorer or prefer to blame catcher Gedman.) The tying run scored as Mitchell scampered home. Knight took second base.

Three pitches later, Wilson hit an "innocent looking ground ball" to first base, a slow hopper that took maybe four soft bounces – but then scooted through Buckner's legs and on into right field as Knight scored the winning run.

During the regular season, there had been 29 occasions on which Stapleton had replaced Buckner at first base for what was deemed a stronger defense. He handled 101 chances without ever once committing an error. In the ALCS, he had done so in four of the seven games and in the World Series he had done so in Games One, Two, and Five. In 18 postseason chances, he never committed an error. But he had been left on the bench in Game Six.[48]

The Mets had won and forced a Game Seven. It wasn't over yet; both teams had a chance to win Game Seven. But emotions on both sides were decidedly different. If there was one moment that solidified the notion of the Red Sox being cursed, Game Six was that moment.

One out away, after waiting 68 years, and the Red Sox had been denied a World Series win once again. At least for a day. The game had ended a little after 12:30 AM on the East Coast and this author decided to leave my home in Cambridge and go out for a walk. Ambling around for about 20 minutes, I encountered at least six or seven other men trudging along, alone, not one of them acknowledging each other.

However devastating the Game Six loss had been for the Red Sox and their fans, there was another opportunity to set things right. There was a Game Seven, two nights later (rain had forced postponement of the Sunday game and given Red Sox fans an additional 24 hours of suffering.) The starters were Darling and Hurst. Hurst was 3-0 in the postseason with a 1.69 ERA. He'd won Game One of the World Series and also Game Five. Darling had lost Game One, but won Game Four and had an almost-equally-superb ERA of 1.89. Momentum was clearly on the side of the Mets, but it was the Red Sox who scored first – and not just once. They scored three times in the top of the second inning. Dwight Evans led off the inning with a home run. Rich Gedman was the next better, and he homered, too. Henderson walked. A couple of outs followed, but Boggs singled in Henderson and it was 3-0, Red Sox. Boston fans dared to hope. At the end of five innings, Hurst had allowed one second-inning single by Knight, but otherwise not allowed a single

batter to reach. It was an official game. Had there been a divine inter-
vention of any kind, or something else, the Red Sox would have won,
3-0, both the game and their first World Series since 1918. Nothing of
the sort occurred.

Sid Fernandez had relieved Darling back in the fourth. The Mets scored
three runs off Hurst in the bottom of the sixth, on two one-out singles, a
walk, a single, and a groundout. The score was tied.

Roger McDowell took over for Fernandez. He retired the Red Sox in
order, and then was the beneficiary as his teammates scored another
three runs. Knight led off with a homer off Schiraldi. A single, wild pitch,
and a single produced the second run. After McDowell bunted a sacrifice, so the runner on first could get to second, McNamara called on Joe
Sambito to relieve Schiraldi. An intentional walk, an unintentional walk,
and a sacrifice fly by Hernandez brought in a sixth run.

That sixth run loomed a bit larger when Dwight Evans doubled in two
runs for the Red Sox in the top of the eighth. It was 6-5, Mets, but
Boston had Evans on second and still nobody out. Jesse Orosco relieved
McDowell and secured six outs in a row, all that were needed to stave off
the Red Sox and win the game. The Mets added a couple of runs in the
bottom of the eighth, and won, 8-5.

After Boston had won the first two games, they had lost four of the next
five and thus lost the World Series.

No more postmortems are necessary here. It feels like time for a break
from contemplating the sorry state of the Red Sox of the day. There is
more to come.

Happier times away from the diamond

At least there were other things going on in the world. And Rounder
Records was doing well. The two years — 1975 and 1986 — detailed
in some unfortunate length above each saw a signal moment for the

record company. In August 1975, Rounder released its 75ᵗʰ album –
J. D. Crowe and the New South (Rounder 0044), noted above. It was a
well-received album offering some new sounds in bluegrass music and
became a classic.

Rounder had hired employees and over the stretch from 1975 through
1986 issued an average of 38 albums per year. That will keep one busy –
busy enough that after 12 years of being a college professor, I had felt
that need to retire, to devote full time to the record business. It was an
overdue move.

Standing behind George Thorogood at a video shoot in Europe, with
Destroyers' drummer Jeff Simon to my left.

There had often been a "political" side to some of Rounder's releases.
Back in January 1973 we had released Rounder 4001, *Mountain Moving
Day*, the first album of the women's liberation movement. That November
we released *Come All You Coal Miners* (Rounder 4005), an album of songs
from the union struggle – later, an Academy Award winning movie,
Harlan County USA, drew heavily on this album for its soundtrack. In the
very same year, we had released an album of Irish rebel song and also
Negro Songs of Protest, drawn from Lawrence Gellert's field recordings of
the 1930s.

I had enjoyed the opportunity to travel a lot for Rounder, helping set up a distribution network in Europe, Japan, and Australia. We had our first gold record, thanks to George Thorogood and the Destroyers, and I'd toured with them in the US, France, England, Ireland, New Zealand, and Australia.

Rounder put out a wide array of roots music and its contemporary off-shoots, and – though I tended to spend less time in the studio, and more working on bookkeeping and royalties – I had gone on several recording trips to Cajun country, Appalachia, Cape Breton, and even (with friend Dan Kahn) to Togo in West Africa in July and August of 1977.

Earlier in 1986, one of our albums in which I took the most pride was released. A couple of years earlier, a cassette labeled "Beatles Songs" had arrived at Rounder, mailed to one of my partners from an American friend who had gone to South Africa to teach photography. This was a bit of a mystery. Why would Bob Denton be sending us a tape of Beatles songs? It wasn't that at all. The cassette contained some clandestine recordings he had made of broadcasts into South Africa from radio facilities in Zambia. They were, essentially, propaganda broadcast into the apartheid-run country of South Africa. We learned that even being caught listening to the "Radio Freedom" broadcast could earn a sentence of five years in prison. In 1983, a South African commando unit had attacked the broadcast facility in Madagascar. I reached out to some African National Congress representatives in Boston, and then in New York at the United Nations, and – after correspondence with Thabo Mbeki (who in 1999 became president of South Africa) – decided to travel to Zambia with Dan Kahn. We arrived in January 1985 and spent a few days in Lusaka and at a farmhouse on the outskirts of the city, where the recordings for the radio were being made. We put together a documentary album from recordings we made and it was released in March 1986 – *Radio Freedom – Voice of the African National Congress and the People's Army Umkhonto We Sizwe* (Rounder 4019).[49]

The year 1986 wasn't without some degree of distinction. In November, just a couple of weeks after the World Series ended, Rounder Records was presented the Blues Label of the Year award in Memphis by The Blues Foundation.

Thanks to my father's original graduation gift that had seen me hitch across Europe back in 1967, I got bit by the travel bug to the point that I eventually traveled to more than 120 countries on one adventure or another, including places that not long afterward became unsafe to visit (e.g., Yemen, Sudan).[50]

That said, for a few of my books, I provided a couple of autobiographical lines that essentially said that despite all my travel, Fenway Park felt like home.

That didn't prevent me from missing Opening Day in 1987, though. I was in Tibet. I'd gone to a trade show in China to see if I could drum up some business, opening up a new country to carry Rounder. That didn't work, but I took advantage of where I was and flew to Chengdu, and then traveled to Lhasa for a few days in Tibet. The altitude was difficult for me and I remember vomiting in the gutter outside the hotel to the amusement of some of the local children. A couple of days later, along the road heading to Kathmandu on April 7, we saw Mount Everest from a distance.

In July 1987, Rounder released our first album by Alison Krauss. Her albums went gold, and even platinum (one million copies sold). She won her first Grammy Award in 1991, and then won one after the other – even to the point of winning more Grammy Awards (27) than any other woman in history, at least until some upstart named Beyoncé edged her aside in the year 2021. Yes, we kept busy.

6

Entrenched in the October
Losing Habit

The Red Sox did not implode after 1986, though in 1987 they did finish fifth in the A.L. East, a full 20 games out of first place. There was no postseason for them that year. Adjustments were made in 1988 – among them, relieving manager John McNamara of his position after starting 43-42. Joe Morgan was named to run the team and "Morgan Magic" happened: the team won 12 games in a row and 19 of their first 20 under the new skipper. During that stretch, they rose in the standings from nine games behind to being tied for first place. They dipped back a bit but by Labor Day took first place and held it through the end of the season, finishing one game ahead of the Detroit Tigers. Their record was 89-73.

The Oakland Athletics finished 104-58, clearly dominating the A.L. West, topping the second-place Twins by a full 13 games.

The 1988 American League Championships Series was closer that it might appear at first glance. Oakland won all four games, but Game One at Fenway was just by one run – ironically, the deciding run came in the top of the eighth when former Red Sox third baseman Carney Lansford (he had been the league batting champion for Boston in 1981) doubled off Bruce Hurst and the former Red Sox star of the 1986 ALCS, Dave Henderson, singled him home.

Game Two was also a one-run game. Boston scored first, with two runs in the sixth, but in the top of the seventh, Henderson singled off Roger

Clemens and Jose Canseco homered. Later in the inning, Mark McGwire singled in Lansford for a third run. In the bottom of the seventh, Rich Gedman hit a solo home run, tying the game, but three singles off reliever Lee Smith in the top of the ninth gave Oakland the edge.

The Athletics won Game Three, 10-6, overcoming an early 5-0 lead the Red Sox built in the first two innings. Three homers off Boston starter Mike Boddicker gave them an edge. Henderson's two-run homer in the bottom of the eighth provided the final two runs. Henderson also drove in the run that made the difference in Game Four, a 4-1 win for the A's. The A's lost the World Series in five games to the Dodgers.

In 1989, Oakland won the pennant again and swept the crosstown Giants in a Bay Area World Series. Those of the Red Sox who cared watched on TV; they had finished third, six games behind Toronto.

The 1990 Red Sox postseason

Yleana Martinez and I had just returned from Albania in mid-September. It hadn't been a long trip, but we were privileged to have been among the first hundred or so Americans who were not of Albanian ancestry to be able to visit the country; it had just begun to open to U.S. tourists and we booked through a travel agency in Greece. It was like walking into another time and place. I can recall standing in Skanderbeg Square – the Times Square of the capital, Tirana – and seeing nothing in the way of automotive traffic for minutes on end. Occasionally, a car of some VIP or Communist Party official would pass by, but for the most part all one could hear was foot traffic, the "slapping of leather against stone as hundreds of Albanians made their way from one place to another."[51] There wasn't music being played by retail stores; no radios that we could hear. Not even animated conversation; one suspects the populace was subdued by a couple of generations of some of the most repressive rule on the planet. As I wrote, "It was like watching a movie from 1910, but being inside the movie at the same time."

There was no *International Herald-Tribune* and the Red Sox were not the talk of the town. Shortly after I got back, the team dropped briefly out of first place, but recovered.

The 1990 Red Sox (88-74) edged the Blue Jays by two games and won the East. Again, they faced the Athletics, who with a 103-49 record had beaten the second-place Chicago White Sox by nine games.

It was Athletics vs. Red Sox in the ALCS once again. The Red Sox had a shot at redemption. In four games, as they were being swept once more, they scored four runs – one in each game.

Game One at Fenway was a 9-1 loss, though the Red Sox had led until the seventh inning. Roger Clemens threw six shutout innings, leaving with a 1-0 lead courtesy of a solo home run by Wade Boggs in the bottom of the fourth. Clemens had thrown 97 pitches, 20 of them in the sixth inning alone. Morgan called on Larry Anderson in relief. Mark McGwire walked, but was then forced out at second on a Walt Weiss grounder. Weiss went first to third on a pinch-hit single by Jamie Quirk and then scored the tying run on Rickey Henderson's sacrifice fly. In the top of the eighth, the A's edged ahead when Canseco singled, was sacrificed to second by Harold Baines, and then stole third with Carney Lansford at the plate. Lansford singled and it was 2-1. Oakland's Dave Stewart only allowed four hits and the one run through eight innings. The Athletics exploded for seven runs in the top of the ninth, as the ballpark progressively emptied of fans, off three Boston pitchers – Jeff Gray, Dennis Lamp, and Rob Murphy. Oakland's Dennis Eckersley threw a scoreless bottom of the ninth.

Game Two was also in Boston and the Red Sox also began with a 1-0 lead, after shortstop Luis Rivera doubled to left, scoring two batters later on a sacrifice fly from Carlos Quintana. In the fourth, the Athletics tied it when Willie McGee led off with a double off Sox starter Dana Kiecker and Baines singled him home. Greg Harris relieved Kiecker in the sixth. Oakland took the lead in the top of the seventh after two leadoff singles and a bass-loaded groundout by Baines. It was 2-1, Oakland, bumped up in the top of the ninth on Baines' third RBI of the game and then an RBI single by McGwire. Bob Welch got the win, 4-1.

The margin narrowed in Game Three on the West Coast. For the third game in succession, the Sox took a 1-0 lead but then never scored again. That run was produced by Tom Brunansky's second-inning sacrifice fly off starter Mike Moore. In the bottom of the fourth, the A's scored twice off Boston's Mike Boddicker. The first run came on a Dave Henderson sac fly and the second on a Willie Randolph single. Randolph singled in their third run, too, in the sixth, with the fourth scoring as Terry Steinbach stole home, jarring the ball loose from Boston catcher Tony Pena.

The score in Game Four was the same as in Game Three, 3-1. All three of their runs came early, charged to Roger Clemens after a one-out single, another single, a fielder's choice, a base on balls, and then (off reliever Tom Bolton) a two-run double by Mike Gallego. Boston's run didn't come until the top of the ninth. when Ellis Burks doubled off starter Dave Stewart and then Jody Reed singled to right.

The Red Sox had been swept again by Oakland, twice in three years. There was another World Series sweep, but this time it was Oakland, swept in the World Series by Cincinnati.

After losing the final two games of the 1986 World Series, and being swept in the ALCS both in 1988 and 1990, the Red Sox had now lost 10 consecutive postseason games.

A four-year wait for another postseason experience

The Red Sox finished second in 1991, seven games behind the Toronto Blue Jays, but then plunged to last place in 1992 (seventh place, 23 games behind Toronto.) The Blue Jays won the division for the third consecutive year in 1993. The 80-82 Red Sox placed third, 15 games behind.

In 1994, the league was divided into three divisions – East, Central, and West – so the worst a team could do was finish fifth. The Red Sox finished fourth, but only one game out of last place. The New York Yankees finished first.

Something else happened in 1991. I had gotten married – to Yleana Martinez, in February 1989. We flew to Laredo, Texas – her hometown – for the wedding. Our honeymoon was India – the Taj Mahal. We later hosted a reception in a room at Fenway Park for those from the Boston area who couldn't make the trek to Laredo.

Our son Emmet Raul Nowlin was born on July 19, 1991. I didn't go to the game that night, which was just as well since (I looked it up while writing this) the Sox lost, 3-2, in 11 innings to the Minnesota Twins. It wasn't too long, though, before Emmet went to *his* first game.

Unlike my father, who couldn't remember when my first game was, I knew I needed to properly document the occasion. It was Wednesday night, September 4. Yleana and I took him. We didn't need an extra ticket, of course. He was 47 days old – almost seven weeks old. Joe Hesketh started and the Red Sox shut out the Angels, 2-0. For a full writeup of the game, see the account I wrote for SABR's Games Project. It is available at: https://sabr.org/gamesproj/game/september-4-1991-a-final-push-

Yleana Martinez with Emmet Nowlin.

at-fenway-park/. After telling the story of the game, I added a bit of other information: "At one point during the game, it was time for a diaper change and Bill Nowlin went to the first aid room under the grandstand to ask if they had a facility. Earlier that day, the first Fenway Park diaper changing station had been installed. This was the first diaper changed on the foldout platform. A visit in 2012 revealed that the station was subsequently removed in favor of family restrooms around the ballpark."

As it happens, Emmet did not inherit Red Sox fandom genes. I did take him to a number of other games over the years, but that diminished over time. We did go to one in September 2022, when my sister Joyce and her husband Walt were in town. The Red Sox won. He'd gone to a number of games with me maybe 20 years earlier and helped take a few photos for the book *Fenway Lives*, but that was really only because I gave him the camera and pointed out who I wanted a photo of – a certain ticket taker, for instance. I tried to get him into research, and we nominally co-edited the SABR book *20-Game Losers* published in 2017. If I have the TV on watching an away game – which I usually do – he hardly ever sits down to watch, even for just a few minutes. Were I to ask him to name three players on the current team, he probably couldn't. In fact, I just paused and tried it while writing this in June 2023. Nope. He can't. He does like to play video games, though, and has any number of active online friends.

Now, Rounder Records. Our 25th anniversary was in 1995. Hard to believe. Filmmaker Bob Mugge made a documentary film about us – *True Believers: The Musical Family of Rounder Records.* It's still available. The film showed us, in the warehouse, in the office, at work, but likely of more interest it featured music performances by Alison, Tish Hinojosa, Marcia Ball (shot in Austin), Little Jimmy King (shot in Memphis), Beau Jocque (shot in Lake Charles, Louisiana), the Johnson Mountain Boys, and others. The *New York Times* (ahem) said the film was "a testament to Rounder's clarity of vision and consistency of taste." Well, thank you. This was the year we had our first platinum record (one million copies sold). That was *Now That I've Found You*, by Alison Krauss. We knew it as "0325" – Rounder 0325. That success aside, it's worth reminding readers that most of our albums sold in the range of 4,000 to 5,000 copies, and we were pleased when they did.

The 1995 postseason

In 1995, the Red Sox climbed back into first place. They faced the Cleveland Indians in the postseason Division Series (with the three divisions, there were two sets of Division Series games in each league, the winners contending for the respective AL and NL pennants in the League Championship Series.)

In manager Kevin Kennedy's first year with the Red Sox, he saw the team win 86 games, enough to finish seven games ahead of the second-place Yankees. The 100-win Indians played the Red Sox, while the Yankees played (and lost in five games to) the Seattle Mariners. The season had only been 144 games long, its start delayed by the ongoing players' strike which had truncated the 1994 season. The 100 games were equivalent to a 112-plus wins in a 162-game season.

The first two games were at Jacobs Field, and the first one was close, taking 13 innings to resolve. Veteran 41-year-old righty Dennis Martinez (12-5, 3.08) started for the Indians and Roger Clemens for the Red Sox (10-5, 4.18). As it happens, it was Clemens' last game pitching for Boston.

John Valentin hit a two-run homer in the top of the third, giving Boston an early lead. In the bottom of the sixth, Cleveland got three runs off Clemens on a two-run double by Albert Belle and an RBI single by Eddie Murray. Sox second baseman Luis Alicea tied it in the eighth with a leadoff homer off reliever Julian Tavarez. Before the game was over, each team had used seven pitchers. In the 11th, Tim Naehring hit a solo home run off Jim Poole. Belle matched that with a leadoff homer off Rick Aguilera, and the game went on. Boston left two on in the 12th; Cleveland left the bases loaded. With two outs in the bottom of the 13th, the game was brought to an end at 1:45 A.M. when Tony Pena homered off Boston's Zane Smith for a 5-4 Indians win.

Clemens, of course, was long gone from the game by then, but it is perhaps of some interest that – after starting nine postseason games for the Red Sox, he had a total of just one win – Game Seven of the 1986 ALCS.

Game Two was the next evening, and Boston's Erik Hanson pitched a complete game. He had a 15-5 (4.24) record in the regular season and had been named to the All-Star team. He'd allowed a two-run double to Omar Vizquel in the fifth and a two-run homer to Eddie Murray in the bottom of the eighth. The four runs were more than enough since Cleveland's Orel Hershiser who allowed just three hits – all singles – over the first 7⅓ innings, and no runs, and three Indians relievers (who allowed no hits at all) helped bring the 4-0 shutout to its conclusion.

Fenway Park hosted Game Three. Tim Wakefield started for the Red Sox. Indians third baseman Jim Thome hit a two-run homer in the top of the second, then came up again in the third with two outs and the bases loaded after a single and two walks. Thome walked, too, forcing in Cleveland's third run. Charles Nagy was as generous with bases on balls – both starters walked five – but they were not at all as costly. The first run the Red Sox scored was in the bottom of the fourth, when catcher Mike Macfarlane followed three consecutive singles with a sacrifice fly on a liner to left. In the top of the sixth inning, the Indians put the game away with five runs on five hits, off Wakefield and reliever Rheal Cormier. The Red Sox only scored one more run, in the bottom of the eighth, again on an out after three consecutive singles. This time Tavarez was pitching and the out was a groundout to second base, as Naehring scored from third.

The 8-2 loss in Game Three ended the Red Sox season. They had now extended their postseason losing streak to 13 losses in a row – one after the other, game after game. They'd lost the last two in 1986, then been swept in four 1988 games, four 1990 games, and now in three 1995 games.

What did the Red Sox – and their fans – ever do to deserve this? This couldn't go on forever – could it? These were all teams good enough to make postseason play, but somehow unable to eke out even one win over a span of 10 years.

They hadn't all been lopsided losses. Two went to extra innings; two others were one-run losses. The Red Sox had scored 30 runs in the 10 games, and surrendered 71. There was just once they were shut out. There were six games in which they scored just one run. Once they scored six and twice they scored five; they still lost all 13.

Try again in the 1998 postseason?

They kept coming back, though. The Sox finished third in 1996 and fourth in 1997, but in 1998 they won 92 games and finished second in the AL East. Boston finished second to the Yankees, and by virtue of their 114 wins the Yankees finished 22 games ahead of the second-place Red Sox. One wouldn't think that a team finishing 22 games behind could make the postseason, but Boston's 92-70 record was still much better than the second-place finishers in the Central and West divisions. Accordingly, they were the fourth team in American League postseason play.

Should they win the Division Series, they'd be facing the Yankees. Those 114 wins were daunting; the figure still stands as the most the Yankees have ever won in regular-season play.

The ALDS matchup for the Red Sox was against Cleveland again – the same team that had swept them in 1995. (And, for that matter, won the tiebreaker back in 1948.) Was there any point in playing the games? Well, the Red Sox did have a different manager in Jimy Williams. They had a 19-game winner in Pedro Martinez, his first season with the Red Sox. He'd won the Cy Young Award the previous year, with Montreal. They had Nomar Garciaparra, Rookie of the Year in 1997, who drove in 122 runs in 1998. They had another 100-RBI hitter in Mo Vaughn, with 115 RBIs. He'd been AL MVP in 1995 (not that it had helped them in that year's postseason, when he went 0-for-14 without either a run scored or driven in). In head-to-head play, the '98 Red Sox had beaten the Indians in eight games and only lost three (they had been 6-7 in 1995). Four of their wins had been by one run, which could be taken as skimpy but also as gritty.

The Indians had been in first place from Opening Day and, from the second game on, never even shared first place for a day. They were only the seventh major-league team to be able to boast that. The Red Sox, however, had been 8-3 against them during the regular season and as a team, Cleveland had only been 39-38 in the second half of the season, one game over. 500.

The *Boston Globe* printed a 16-page playoff preview section on September 29. The paper acknowledged the 13 consecutive postseason losses, with a capsule describing each one in a sentence or two, but there was no sense of inevitable doom awaiting the hometown team. There was no sense of preordained defeatism. Had something gone wrong at the paper? Did they know something no one else did?

Game One was in Cleveland, Jaret Wright against Pedro Martinez. Their records might seem to have favored Pedro. Wright had been 12-10 (4.72) while Martinez was 19-7 (2.89) and had been named to his third All-Star squad. And the game started propitiously for the visiting Red Sox. Center fielder Darren Lewis led off with a single. Third baseman John Valentin singled. And then first baseman Mo Vaughn homered. Three batters, a 3-0 lead, nobody out. A good way to start any game.

It remained 3-0 through four innings, and then the Red Sox struck again. Lewis got hit by a pitch. Valentin walked. This time Vaughn went down on strikes, but Garciaparra swing at the first pitch he saw and hit a three-run homer. It was 6-0, Red Sox, and Pedro struck out all three batters he faced in the bottom of the fifth.

Doug Jones had taken over from Wright. In the sixth, the Hit Dog (Mo Vaughn) came up again, with Valentin on first base, and hit his second home run of the game. With a lead of 8-0 and Pedro Martinez on the mound, did Red Sox fans dare to hope they might actually win the game? There is no scientific poll to cite, but one suspects that many did – though perhaps even more figured they'd find a new way to lose a postseason game.

Kenny Lofton hit a two-run homer off Martinez in the bottom of the sixth. Jim Thome hit a solo home run off him in the seventh. He wasn't invulnerable.

But the Red Sox didn't fold. They faced a new pitcher, Steve Reed, in the top of the eighth. Reed walked the first batter he faced, hit the second, and then gave up a bases-loading single to Valentin. With Vaughn due up, Indians manager Mike Hargrove had seen enough and brought in Jim Poole. Vaughn doubled to right, driving in two more Red Sox runs and giving him seven RBIs in this Game One. Nomar made it 11-3 with a sacrifice fly. The score held. The Red Sox won.

And, for those who perhaps could not believe it, the next day's newspapers affirmed it – after an 0-for-13 streak, the Boston Red Sox had finally won a postseason game.

There was no particular wonderment in those papers the day after Game One. Pedro Martinez did say, though, "This one is the first. I don't believe in anything about Bambino or curses or any of that. All I believe in is smoke."[52] And Dan Shaughnessy himself – his famous book already a bestseller in New England – wrote, of the optimism that seemed to attach to the 1998 ballclub, "Suddenly, no one is nervous. No one is fretting, waiting for something bad to happen. The 1998 Red Sox weren't expected to go anywhere, and now that they're in the postseason, they're insulated from some of the forment (sic) that haunted their hardball forefathers. Let's dream."[53]

1998 ALDS Games Two, Three, and Four

Whatever grace the Red Sox were granted after Game One began to dissipate over the three that followed.

Game Two was Dwight Gooden against Tim Wakefield. After a lengthy career with the Mets and then a couple of years with the Yankees, this was Gooden's first year with Cleveland. He was 8-6 (3.76). Wakefield was in his fourth season with the Red Sox and had been 17-8, though with an ERA of 4.58. Only Pedro Martinez, with 19, had more wins for the team. The Red Sox got to Gooden in the top of the first. A walk, stolen base, walk, and Mo Vaughn strikeout was followed by a Nomar double, and it was 2-0, Boston. The lead didn't last long. Cleveland got one run in the bottom of the first on a sacrifice fly by David Justice, then added five more in the second. Sandy Alomar doubled in one, Kenny Lofton doubled in another. A quick hook removed Wakefield, but in the next three pitches, John Wasdin got an out and then gave up a three-run homer to David Justice. Each team scored once in the third. The Red Sox closed the gap to 7-5, in the sixth but the Indians upped it to 8-5. In the end, on a Tom Gordon wild pitch in the eighth, they led 9-5, the final score.

Game Three was at Fenway, and a one-run game, Bret Saberhagen against Cleveland's Charles Nagy. The Red Sox scored first, one run on a ground-out by Garciaparra. The Indians came back with three solo home runs, one each in the fifth, sixth, and seventh, by Thome, Lofton, and Manny Ramirez – who hit a second solo home run in the top of the ninth off Dennis Eckersley, now with the Red Sox. The 4-1 lead held despite Nomar's two-run homer in the bottom of the ninth.

The fourth game had Boston's Pete Schourek face Cleveland's Bartolo Colon (14-9, 3.71). Schourek had only appeared in 10 games for the Red Sox, his contract having been purchased from the Astros after the first week of August. He was 1-3 (4.30), maybe not the sort of stats a fan would hope to see from a pitcher in a possible elimination game. He pitched quite well, as it happens, allowing just two base hits and no runs in 5⅓ innings, though he did walk four. Colon allowed one run, in the fourth inning, a first-pitch leadoff home run by Nomar Garciaparra, who drove in 11 of Boston's 19 runs in the series. The score was still 1-0 after seven full innings. Derek Lowe had closed out the sixth and thrown a hitless seventh. The Indians were on their third pitcher by that point. Red Sox closer Tom "Flash" Gordon relieved Lowe in the eighth. He had led the American League with 46 saves in 1998. After one out, he gave up back-to-back singles, and then Justice hit a two-run double, giving Cleveland the lead. The Indians used four pitchers in the eighth and the ninth, but not one of them gave up a run. The final score was Cleveland 2, Boston 1.

Mr. Shaughnessy of the *Globe* began his front-page postmortem: "They are the Red Sox. Good turns into bad. Victory dissolves into defeat. Joy gives way to sadness. We go to the theater and enjoy the performances, but the script never changes. In the end, the Titanic sinks. Hamlet dies, and the Red Sox lose the last game that matters."[54] This wasn't him reciting a shtick; it was something of a fact of life.

Once again, the Red Sox had been eliminated. This time they'd won one game – the first game – and then lost the next three. Their season was over.

The Indians lost to the Yankees in the ALCS. The Yankees had won the World Series in 1996, lost to Cleveland in the ALCS, but now were back in the World Series. Indeed, they won the World Series in 1998, sweeping the San Diego Padres.

But the big news for Red Sox fans was: the Red Sox had won a postseason game! Now they could boast a record of 1-16, starting with the fateful Game Six of the 1986 World Series.

1999 postseason play The Division Series

The very next year, in 1999, the Red Sox finished second once again, but this time they *won* a postseason series! Against Cleveland. It was a five-game Division Series. It didn't start well; the Indians won the first game, 3-2, at Jacobs Field. It had been Bartolo Colon against Pedro Martinez (23-4 on the season, with a 2.07 ERA). Garciaparra homered in the second inning for one run. The Red Sox got another in the fourth inning when Nomar led off with a double, scoring two batters later on Mike Stanley's single. Pedro left the game after four innings, with a 1-0 lead, due to a strained back muscle. Jim Thome hit a two-run homer off reliever Derek Lowe in the bottom of the sixth. The game went to the bottom of the ninth inning, still tied 2-2. Lowe hit Indians leadoff batter Manny Ramirez with a pitch. A single off Rheal Cormier put another man on. A walk off Rich Garces loaded the bases. A Travis Fryman single drove in the winning run.

The Indians won Game Two as well, somewhat definitively. The Red Sox scored first, once, in the top of the third when Trot Nixon doubled off Nagy and Jose Offerman singled. But Bret Saberhagen gave up six runs on three hits in the bottom of the inning, on a two-run triple by Omar Vizquel, an RBI double by Roberto Alomar, and a three-run homer by Harold Baines. In the fourth, reliever John Wasdin watched Vizquel collect another RBI on a sac fly and then Jim Thome hit a grand slam into the right-field bleachers. Neither team scored in the second half of the game, but they didn't need to. It was over.

After the series shifted back to Boston, the Red Sox took a pair of lop-sided wins themselves, evening things up. Game Three featured Pedro's brother Ramon Martinez pitching for Boston (he'd only appeared in four games and been 2-1) and Dave Burba (15-9, 4.25) for Cleveland. There was some back-and-forth in the game. The Indians scored once in the top of the fourth, the Red Sox claimed a 2-1 lead on the bottom of the fifth. The Indians tied it in the sixth. John Valentin's leadoff homer in the bottom of the sixth gave the Red Sox the edge once more, but the Indians tied it off Lowe in the seventh on a single by Lofton, who moved up one base at a time until scoring on an error. Jaret Wright had taken over from Burba. After the seventh-inning stretch, he walked Lou Merloni and hit Jason Varitek. Ricardo Rincon came in from the pen, got a couple of outs, but then walked a batter, gave up a two-run double to Valentin and a three-run homer to Brian Daubach. The Red Sox got a sixth run later in the inning and wound up winning 9-3.

Game Four saw a relentless Red Sox onslaught. They won 23-7. They scored enough runs in just this one game to have won any one of the three entire series in which had been swept in the 1988-1995 stretch. Instead of losing all four games, 12 of those 23 runs could have given them a Red Sox sweep in 1988. Twenty could have given them a sweep in 1990. Fourteen runs could have given them a sweep in 1995.

Though Cleveland scored first, with one run off Kent Mercker in the top of the first, the Red Sox scored twice off Colon. Cleveland got one more run in the second, but the Red Sox responded with five. Trot Nixon doubled in two and Offerman hit a two-run homer. They added three more in the third, Valentin's two-run homer the big hit. In the fourth, they got five more runs, the final three on a bases-loaded Valentin double. The Indians scored four in the top of the fifth and for the fifth inning in succession the Red Sox scored, adding three more. A Varitek two-run homer brought in the last two. Boston got its final two runs in the eighth. By the end of the game, Valentin had seven RBIs, and Offerman and Nixon both had five. Garces got the win in relief.

Game Five was back in Cleveland, but Red Sox batters pounded out another dozen runs, though the game was actually tied 8-8 as late as the end of the sixth. Indeed, Sox starter Bret Saberhagen was pulled in the second inning, charged with five runs, four of them on two-run homers by Thome and Fryman. The Sox had two on a first-inning Garciaparra home run. Indians starter Charles Nagy gave up a third run and then a grand slam to Troy O'Leary in the third. Manny Ramirez doubled off reliever Lowe in the third and Thome followed with a two-run homer. That made it 8-7, Indians. The Red Sox tied it in the fourth. Pedro Martinez took over from Lowe and pitched six innings of no-hit relief. The game stayed tied until O'Leary hit a three-run homer off Paul Shuey in the seventh. Nomar doubled in their 12th run in the top of the ninth.

1999 – the League Championship Series

The Red Sox had won the best-of-five ALDS and for the first time since 1986 went into the second round of the postseason. This time they went head-to-head with the Yankees for the very first time in postseason play. There had been the losses to them at the end of the 1949 season, and the

Visiting a favorite quirky Fenway spot in 1999 – the one seat that
constitutes the first row of Section 28.

tiebreaker in 1978, but those were regular-season games. This was the
first time the two rivals had ever squared off in the postseason.

The first two games were one-run games. The Red Sox jumped out to a
3-0 lead in Game One, scoring twice in the first inning and once in the
second, both off "El Duque" – Orlando Hernandez. In the bottom of the
second, Scott Brosius hit a two-run homer off Sox starter Mercker. New
York finally tied it in the seventh, when Derek Jeter singled in Brosius
against reliever Derek Lowe. The game went into the 10th inning, but
the first batter Rod Beck faced was Bernie Williams, who homered. 4-3,
New York. Mariano Rivera had a majors-leading 45 saves in 1999; in this
game, he got the win.

Game Two featured David Cone against Ramon Martinez. Tino Martinez
(no relation) homered off Ramon in the fourth to make it 1-0, Yankees.
Garciaparra hit a two-run homer off Cone in the top of the fifth. New
York tied it on a seventh-inning Chuck Knoblauch doubled off Martinez,
who then departed. Two batters later, Paul O'Neill singled in Knoblauch.
The Yankees used four pitchers in the top of the eighth and saw Boston

load the bases with one out, but in came Ramiro Mendoza who struck out Butch Huskey and then got Offerman to fly out. Rivera pitched the ninth, gave up two singles, but no runs. It was 3-2, New York.

In Boston for Game Three, there was a highly-touted faceoff between Pedro Martinez, Boston's ace, and Roger Clemens, Boston's former ace, who had gone over to the Dark Side. Clemens had left the Red Sox after the 1996 season and won back-to-back Cy Young Awards with the Toronto Blue Jays in 1997 and 1998, then signed with the Yankees. It was far from his best year, 14-10 with a 4.60 ERA. Game Three was also far from his best game; Clemens gave up two runs in the first, two runs in the second, and saw the Sox score two runs in the third. Valentin hit a two-run homer in the first and drove in the third run, in the second. After former Yankee Mike Stanley singled to lead off the third, Clemens was gone and the first batter Hideki Irabu faced – Brian Daubach – hit a two-run homer. Darren Lewis and Valentin each drove in a run in the fifth. The Sox got a ninth run in the sixth, thanks to an error, and then added four more in the seventh – Valentin and Stanley each with RBI singles and a two-run homer from Nomar in between. It was 13-0 and Pedro Martinez left the game with a comfortable lead. He had allowed just two base hits, both singles. Brosius was the first batter to face Flash Gordon and he homered, but the Red Sox won the game, 13-1.

It was the only game they won. Saberhagen started Game Four and allowed three runs in six innings, a solo homer by Darryl Strawberry in the top of the second and two in the fourth, the tie-breaking run on an error. Facing Andy Pettitte, Boston had scored once in the second and once in the third. It was still 3-2, New York after eight innings. The Yankees got a fourth run on an error, a fourth on a Bernie Williams single, and then four more runs when, once again, the first Yankee Rod Beck faced homered. This time it was pinch-hitter Ricky Ledee, who hit a grand slam. Boston got a couple of hits off Rivera in the bottom of ninth, but lost 9-2.

Game Five matched Mercker against El Duque. New York scored twice in the top of the first, before Mercker got the first out. Knoblauch singled and Jeter homered. That was enough to win the game, but of course no one could know it yet. The Yankees got two more runs in the seventh, the first on an error, the second on a Tino Martinez single. Jason Varitek homered off Hernandez to lead off the bottom of the eighth. With one out, the Red Sox had the bases loaded, but as in Game Two, Ramiro Mendoza entered, struck out one batter and got the next to hit a foul popup to third base. The game ended a 6-1 Yankees win after Jorge Posada hit a two-run homer off Tom Gordon in the top of the ninth and Mendoza retired all three batters he faced.

The Yankees won the World Series again in 1999, sweeping the Atlanta Braves. And – for the third year in a row – then won the World Series in the year 2000, this time losing one game to the New York Mets. It was their 26th world championship.

The Red Sox had lost another playoff series. And the Yankees were ascendant again. What a way to end a century.

I enjoyed one notable moment in the year 2000, starting on the evening of July 24 and ending shortly after daybreak the next morning. Rob Neyer and I spent the night – all night – at Fenway. Rob was engaged in a marathon adventure – he went to every single Red Sox home game all year long. He was an ESPN.com columnist at the time and remains a highly-respected baseball journalist. He wrote a whole book about the year – *Feeding the Green Monster* (iPublish, 2001). At the time, the ownership of the Red Sox – the Yawkey Trust – was actively promoting the idea of replacing Fenway. Rob pulled off the self-assigned task – not missing a single game.

I did the same thing, though not as a writing project, in the year 2022. I made it to every game, including one on September 2 when I was in the emergency room until 6 P.M. See more on this below.

In September 2000, during one of two games
I worked inside Fenway Park's manual left-field
scoreboard.

Back to 2000, though, as we were talking about various Fenway Park adventures, I mentioned how I had worked inside the left-field scoreboard for a couple of games. While working on what become the book *Fenway Lives*, among the people I had interviewed was Michael Hardy, the supervisor of the night cleaning crew. He talked about how, once the park empties, his crew would clean the park and ready it for the next night's (or day's) game. I watched them for a while, then went home. But it stuck in my mind that after an hour or so, there was basically no one in the park except the cleaners – and me. Who was to say I couldn't have

When the Red Sox installed the new electronic center-
field message board in the year 2000, I couldn't help
but climb around inside for a look.

stayed? Who would even have known? I suggested to Rob that we think about giving it a try.

Trying to keep things low-profile, we picked a Monday night, not a week-end, settled on a team that was less than a "big draw" (the Twins, not the Yankees), and a time of year when the weather would probably be sufficiently warm. July 24. The Twins won, 4-2, but for us the adventure was just beginning. I went and found Michael, said hello, told him Rob was a journalist, and that we just wanted to stay for a while and observe. Sure. I had brought a toothbrush – mostly just for fun – but I didn't tell Michael that.

We watched the crew for a while. I took a few photos of them at work. Then we went exploring on our own, sitting in the dugout, visiting the bullpen, noting the paint room underneath the stands, seeing where they store the fertilizer for the field, and the giant ice machine still churning out bags of ice cubes. Basically, no one paid any attention to us. Not a single security person came by to ask what we were doing. In fact, at 2:45 A.M., wondering where security was, we sought out and found Mike McDonald – the sole overnight security guard. You can read my interview with him on pages 243-245 of *Fenway Lives*. And you can read Rob's account of the adventure on several pages in *Feeding the Green Monster* (pages 186-191.) We stayed until the sun came up, another crew came in, and it seemed like a good time for home.

7

Writing About the Red Sox and the Deepening Curse

It was as the 20th century wound down that I started to become active writing about the Red Sox. It began with Ted Williams. When I was younger, I always thought to myself that I would write a book when I grew up. I turned 50 in 1995, so maybe it was time to grow up?

I came across a book that was published that year – *Ted Williams' Hit List*, by Ted Williams with Jim Prime. It was "the ultimate ranking of baseball's greatest hitters by the last man to bat .400." It was published by Stoddart, in Toronto. I'd never heard of them, or Jim Prime. In the book, my childhood hero – Ted Williams – ranked the top 20 hitters in baseball history and gave his reasons why. Out of modesty, he did not rank himself, but using his criteria one can see that he would have ranked second, behind Babe Ruth and before Lou Gehrig and then Jimmie Foxx.

Why wasn't the book published by a U.S. publisher? And who was Jim Prime? The book said he lived in New Minas, Nova Scotia. I asked Ted's son John-Henry Williams and he said they'd love to have a U.S. edition, so I started asking around and coming up with nothing – but a month or so later, John-Henry told me that a company called Masters Press was going to print an American edition. I immediately got in touch with them and enthused so much about the book that they and Jim offered to include two pages that I wrote as part of an Afterword. Wow! Here I was, with something I had written, in a book by Ted Williams! I got hooked.

With author Jim Prime behind the batting
cage at Fenway Park in 2002.

I was envious of Jim – who I met at the Ted Williams Museum in Hernando, Florida (meeting Ted Williams at the same time!). I had met Ted
Williams briefly as a fan back in 1988, when I went to spring training for
a few days with friend Henry Horenstein, who was working on a book
with Red Sox hitting instructor Walt Hriniak. Henry was off doing his
thing and I was sort of wandering around. I was standing outside the Red
Sox clubhouse in Winter Haven and saw players emerge from time to
time to head down to the practice fields. I heard this loud voice inside,
and knew it was Ted Williams, so I hung around. He was one of the last
to emerge, came out, and there was a group of about 15 of us. He made
a beeline for the person in the wheelchair, chatted with him for a bit,
signed for a few people, then said, "Gotta go" and hopped onto a waiting electric golf cart to be driven to the fields, which were down a long
pathway. The rest of us followed. We hung around there, him signing for
one or two people, then watching a batter take a few pitches. Finally, I
guess he decided to get rid of the rest of us so he signed something for
each. I hung back and was about the last one. I said, "Mr. Williams, I just
want you to know that in 1951 when I was in the hospital for a tonsil-
lectomy, my father sent away for a picture of you, which you signed to
me, adding 'Your pal, Ted Williams' and I still have that at home on my
desk." He didn't even look up, but just grunted, "Uh." That was my first

conversation with Ted Williams. I wasn't the least bit offended. I remember thinking at the time how appropriate his response was. What was he supposed to do? Look up all bright-eyed and say, "I'm glad that I was able to help give you a little pleasure at a time like that." No, that was fine. I do still have that 1951 photo on my desk. [55]

But back to Jim Prime. What could be better than to have written a book with Ted Williams? We started talking about the idea of collaborating on another book, *about* Ted Williams, largely drawing on appreciations of him by those who knew him. Masters Press went for the idea and both Jim and I plunged into interviewing people who knew Ted Williams, from teammates to fans to fellow Marines to people who knew him through the Jimmy Fund. I did a 45-minute interview with John Glenn, who flew combat missions with Ted in Korea before becoming more famous as an American astronaut (and later U.S. Senator). We interviewed more than half the living members of the National Baseball Hall of Fame. In all, we interviewed well over 100 people. Jim secured a foreword for our book from Robert Redford. The book was published in 1997 as *Ted Williams: A Tribute*. After Ted died in July 2002, the company (which had become part of Sports Publishing) put out a new edition, as *Ted Williams: The Pursuit of Perfection*.

Other books followed.

I had started doing some writing for various publications around this same time. In 1996, I had my first article published in *Boston Red Sox Magazine*, the team's own magazine. Starting around 2000, I became a regular contributor for them, with occasional articles through 2015. I also wrote for a couple of fan publications sold outside the ballpark — *Boston Baseball*, from 1996-2002 and literally dozens of articles for *Diehard*, from 2001-2012 and becoming assistant editor for *Diehard*. The Ted Williams Museum started its own magazine, *Ted Williams Magazine*, and I served as volunteer editor from 2000 until 2003. I wrote occasional book reviews of baseball books for the *Boston Globe* from 2003-2015. By no means did I do this with dollars in mind. I enjoyed the research and the opportunities to talk to so many different people, and enjoyed seeing the final result.

Ted Williams commenting on my game-used Joe Jackson bat, which was
loaned to the Ted Williams Museum.

I did, in time, have the opportunity to meet Ted Williams on several occasions. Over the course of the years, I had a breakfast, a lunch, and a
dinner at his house in Hernando. I don't think he could have told you my
name, but he did know me as "the bat guy" because I had assembled a collection of game-used baseball bats which I loaned to the Museum. I had
bats that had been used by Shoeless Joe Jackson, Babe Ruth, Lou Gehrig,
and everyone who had hit .400 – my 1941 Ted Williams game-used bat
meant the most to me. He had particularly enjoyed holding the Joe Jackson bat. And once hosted an event in nearby Crystal River where a number of researchers called for the admission of Jackson into the National
Baseball Hall of Fame. The argument was that Jackson had been banned
for life, because of his involvement in the Black Sox scandal of 1919, but
now, of course, his life was over. John W. Henry was one of the owners
of the Marlins at the time and he came to the event in his own team bus.

I also hold the honor of having ghost-written Ted Williams' last written
words. Each year, for the Ted Williams *Magazine*, he (meaning me) wrote
an introduction to welcome folks who came for the annual Hitters' Hall

of Fame induction weekend. When I wrote the welcome in early 2002, I couldn't have known he would die that July, but indeed he did.

On July 22, there was a memorial tribute for Ted Williams at Fenway Park. It drew more than 20,000, and several of Ted's teammates attended, as did his Korean War squadron mate John Glenn. Former broadcasters such as Curt Gowdy and Ned Martin, and many more. I was pleased to meet his two nephews – Sam Williams and Ted Williams, both sons of his brother Danny. I met them again in 2003 in San Diego, and Ted and I later spent time in Mexico visiting the ancestral home of May Venzor, mother of the Hall of Fame ballplayer. See more on this below.

And in 2002, when the Society for American Baseball Research (SABR) held its annual convention in Boston, I wrote a few pieces for that year's publication and hosted a panel talking about Ted Williams. All work for SABR is volunteer work. At the time of the convention, Cecilia Tan and I came up with the idea of asking convention attendees to all contribute articles about what it was like attending the Red Sox game that was one of the centerpieces of the convention, including even such things as an appreciation of the City of Boston while walking from the hotel to the ballpark. That was published as *The Fenway Project* by Rounder Books.[56]

Yes, Rounder Books. My partners indulged me by allowing me to start up a book division of Rounder. Surprise, surprise – we did a fair number of Red Sox books. We also published some music books, among them the book *Everything Grows* by children's artist Raffi and *Roadshow* as one of the books by Neal Peart, drummer for the band Rush.

The next couple of books off the press were a fond look at Fenway Park Entitled *Fenway Saved,* co-authored with Jim Prime and Mike Ross (Sports Publishing, 1999), and *Tales from the Red Sox Dugout*, with Jim Prime (Sports Publishing, 2000). That was it for that century.

A year or so after Ted Williams died, and the museum magazine ceased publication, I got hooked on writing briefer items for SABR – initially biographies for SABR's BioProject. It's a group effort to write up biographies of former ballplayers and others associated with the game. They usually run around 2,000-4,000 words and are all posted on the www.sabr.org website, freely available to all. The Rounder Books volume on the 1967 Red Sox team, which was initially published in the 2007 anniversary year, featured the work of more than 60 SABR members, and includes bios of everyone of the team – including coaches and all. It was fun reaching out to some of the players, for more details about their lives growing up and what they have done since the end of their playing days.

I really did get hooked. As of November 2023, I've written 758 bios – most of them of Red Sox players. We published books on the 1967 team, the 1975 team, the first team from back in 1901, the 1912 team from Fenway Park's first year, the 1918 team, one on 1948, and another on Red Sox players on the 1950s. At a certain point, I wondered how many Red Sox bios we had NOT had written – how many players, for instance, would it take to fill in the gaps between the 1912 team and the 1918 team? So I started writing up players who had been "overlooked" by the various books. I enlisted others to help, when I could (some people are not as entranced with writing up Red Sox players. As of November 2023, SABR has biographies of every Red Sox player from the years 1901 through 1987, and when we complete just three more biographies, we will have a biography of every player from 1901 through 1990.

Several years later, Mark Armour and I decided to launch Games Project on SABR, through which members can write up individual game accounts, in historical perspective. The first one I wrote was not a momentous game such as Game Four other 2004 American League Championship Series. It was the game of September 4, 1991. Why that game? I did something I wish my father had done for me – documented the first game he'd taken me to at Fenway Park. So I wrote up my son Emmet's first game. The Red Sox shut out the Angels, 2-0. Was he thrilled? No, he was only 47 days old at the time. But if he ever cares to look it up, the account is there.

I've since written another 280 game accounts, including all 14 postseason games from the year 2004, which will all be referenced in SABR's book on the 2004 Red Sox.

"#9, Bill Nowlin" singling to left field during a charity baseball game at Fenway Park.

There was one other item of note that occurred in 2002. It's when I had my own debut playing baseball at Fenway Park. Brian O'Connor, the banker who had Rounder as one of his accounts, invited me to a charity game to be held there. It was Brian who also got me involved in riding the Pan-Mass Challenge, a two-day 192-mile bicycle ride from Sturbridge out to the tip off Cape Cod to raise money for the Jimmy Fund. Some 25 years later, I still ride the PMC but now I ride one of the shorter routes, in 2023 the 25 miles from Wellesley to Gillette Stadium. The 2023 Pan-Mass Challenge featured more than 6,400 participants and raised $72 million, the single largest donation in the Dana-Farber Cancer Institute's history. Since its founding, the PMC has raised over $900 million.

There was one other time I had taken batting practice at the park, batting against a machine. I rifled a couple of balls, foul, into the left-field seats. But there was a ball I hit that one-hopped the Green Monster, hitting the warning track and bouncing up to hit the wall. This was different. This was a game. Given my admiration for Ted Williams, I wore a #9 jersey and played left field. I don't remember who else was on my team. I don't even remember who won the game. What I do remember is Red Sox broadcaster Ken Coleman serving as PA announcer and introducing me the first time I came up to bat: "Now batting, #9, Bill Nowlin."

First time up, I popped up to the third baseman. Second time up, I popped up to the shortstop. I had fielded one or two groundballs hit to left, but there were no fly balls that I had to try to catch or chase down. Third time up, I was anxious about going 0-for-3 in my big-league ballpark debut. Success! I lined a clean single into left. It wasn't really close to either the shortstop or third base. It was a legitimate single (albeit one hit off a participant such as myself, not off Pedro Martinez.) A couple of batters later, I had rounded the bases and crossed the plate to score. There was no contract proffered, not even an invitation to spring training. But after that day I was able to retire with a lifetime batting average of .333 at Fenway Park.

The 2003 Red Sox

The Red Sox had finished second in 1998 and 1999. As it happens, they finished second five years in a row – in 2000, 2001, 2002, 2003, and 2004. Their record wasn't good enough to make the postseason, though, in 1999, 2000, 2001, or 2002. But it was in 2003.

The 2003 team finished 95-67 for manager Grady Little, his second year at the helm. Three batters with more than 100 RBIs each didn't hurt – David Ortiz (101), Manny Ramirez (104), and Nomar Garciaparra (105). It was Ortiz's first year with the Red Sox. Oddly, no pitcher won more than Derek Lowe's 17 games. Second was Pedro Martinez, with 14. They finished six games behind the Yankees but with two more wins than Seattle in the West and one more than the White Sox in the Central.

During the summer of 2003, I helped organize another memorial for Ted Williams at San Diego's Hall of Champions. Nephew Ted Williams both came – in fact, in all, the event drew 33 members of Ted Williams' extended family. A photograph I took of the assembled family in Balboa Park graces the back cover of my 2018 book *Ted Williams: First Latino in the Baseball Hall of Fame.*[57] Nephew Ted and I later visited the community in Mexico from where ballplayer Ted Williams maternal grandparents came from.

Another Rounder Book - *Ted Williams: First Latino in the Baseball Hall of Fame.*

The Division Series

The Division Series pitted Boston against the Oakland Athletics, the team that had swept them in both 1988 and 1990. And Oakland won the first two games in this best-of-five series.

Game One was a 5-4 A's win in 12 innings. Tim Hudson started against Pedro Martinez. Red Sox second baseman Todd Walker hit a solo homer in the top of the first. In the third, Erubiel Durazo drove in two with a double for Oakland and Miguel Tejada singled in a third run. Varitek's solo homer in the fifth brought Boston within a run. With two outs in the seventh,

Garciaparra singled off Hudson. The next batter, Walker, hit a two-run homer off reliever Ricardo Rincon. Martinez had a 4-3 lead after seven innings and Mike Timlin pitched a scoreless eighth. Boston's Byung-Hyun Kim got an out, then walked a batter and hit the next one. He struck out the fourth batter, then gave way to Alan Embree who gave up a game-tying single to Durazo. In the bottom of the 12th – the game obviously still tied – Derek Lowe walked three batters (the third one intentionally), then saw Ramon Hernandez bunt safely toward third base, winning the game.

In Game Two, a pair of walks, a hit-by-pitch, a passed ball, and an error complicated Tim Wakefield's second inning in which the A's scored five runs on just two hits. The Red Sox got one run off Barry Zito in the third on back-to-back doubles by Doug Mirabelli and Johnny Damon. There were no other runs scored in the game, which thus went in the books as a 5-1 win for Oakland, with them needing to win just one more to win the Division Series. At this point, the Athletics had won 10 postseason games in a row from the Red Sox.

Game Three was at Fenway Park and, like Game One, went into extra innings. Both starters Derek Lowe and Ted Lilly worked seven innings. Lilly allowed one run in the second on a single, three errors, and a fielder's choice. Lowe allowed one run in the top of the sixth on a single, walk, fielder's choice, and two errors on the run-scoring play, which also wound up with the third out of the inning. By the time the game reached the 11th, the pitchers of record were Scott Williamson and Rich Harden. Williamson retired the A's in order. Harden gave up a one-run single to Mirabelli and then a two-run homer to Trot Nixon. Boston 3, Oakland 1. If the A's had put some kind of whammy on the Red Sox, it was over.

Game Four. In the top of the second, Boston's John Burkett walked the first batter and then gave up three consecutive singles, but only one run, before booking three consecutive infield pop flies. In the bottom of the third, Johnny Damon hit a two-run homer off Oakland's Steve Sparks. In the sixth, the Athletics took a 4-2 lead on an RBI triple by Adam Melhuse and a two-run homer by Jermaine Dye. Todd Walker led off the Sox sixth with a solo home run, off reliever Rincon. In the bottom of the eighth, losing

4-3, Garciaparra hit a one-out double off reliever Keith Foulke. Manny Ramirez (now with Boston) singled. David Ortiz doubled to right field, driving them both in and giving the Red Sox a 5-4 lead. Scott Williamson had retired the A's in order in the eighth; he did so again in the ninth.

The series was tied, two wins for each team. Game Five was back in Oakland late the following afternoon. The starting pitchers were Barry Zito and Pedro Martinez. Neither team scored for the first three innings. In the bottom of the fourth, with a runner on first, left fielder Jose Guillen doubled and drove in the first run of the game before being thrown out going for third base. In the top of the sixth, Jason Varitek homered to lead off and, not long afterward, Manny Ramirez hit a three-run homer into the left-field stands. It was 4-1, Red Sox, but the A's got one back right away on an RBI double by Tejada. Their first two batters in the eighth doubled and singled and drove Pedro from the game, but Boston still led by one and the bullpen closed out the inning. In the ninth, the Red Sox got two men on base but did not score. The first two Athletics walked off Williamson. Derek Lowe relieved. A sacrifice bunt advanced both runners. A strikeout was the second out, but a base on balls loaded the bases. Lowe struck out the final batter and the game was over.

The Red Sox had won the series, and were due to face the New York Yankees, who had beaten the Minnesota Twins the day before. In each of their three wins, they had held the Twins to just one run. As in 1999, it was the classic rivals head-to-head again. The Yankees had won four of the five games in 1999. Perhaps this year would be different. Many Red Sox fans insulated themselves with a protective attitude: "Nah, no way. They'll find a way to blow it." But some dared to hope.

The 2003 American League Championship Series

Yankee Stadium – this was still the original Yankee Stadium, opened in 1923 – hosted Game One, with Mike Mussina (17-8, 3.40) facing Tim Wakefield, who was 0-3 in six postseason appearances for the Red Sox, losing each of his three starts. Mussina walked two in the top of the second. Wakefield gave up two singles in the bottom of the second. The first runs came in the fourth, when Manny Ramirez led off with a single and David Ortiz homered. Boston scored twice more in the fifth on solo homers by Todd Walker and by Manny. Wakefield had not allowed a Yankee to reach base since two early singles. Boston boosted its lead to 5-0 on an RBI single by Kevin Millar in the seventh. Wakefield then walked the first two batters, and was replaced by Alan Embree. Jorge Posada doubled for one run and Hideki Matsui's sacrifice fly brought in another. They were the last two runs of the game, a 5-2 Red Sox victory.

The Yankees evened things up in Game Two with a 6-2 win for Andy Pettitte. He had given up three hits in a row to start the second, but only one run. Nick Johnson hit a two-run homer off Lowe in the bottom of the second. Bernie Williams singled in a run in the third. Matsui made it 4-1 with a run-producing single in the fifth. Boston's other run came on a solo homer by Jason Varitek in the top of the sixth. The Yanks added another run in the seventh.

In Game Three, Pedro Martinez pitched against Roger Clemens. This time, Clemens came out on top. The Red Sox did score first, when Manny singled in a pair in the bottom of the first. But the Yankees scored one in the second, one in the third (a Jeter homer), and two in the fourth, the first on a ground-rule double by Matsui, the second while the Sox executed a double play. After putting the first two on base, the Red Sox got a run on a double play in the seventh but they were still shy one run, 4-3, the score at the end of the game.

Game Four was a rematch of Wakefield and Mussina and once again Wake wound up the winner. He gave up one run on five hits and four walks in the seven innings he worked, on two singles and a Jeter double in the top of the fifth. Mussina gave up solo home runs to Todd Walker (again – it was his fifth homer in nine games in the 2003 postseason, after hitting just 13 in the entire regular season) and to Trot Nixon. In the bottom of the seventh, the Red Sox collected a third run on a bases-loaded groundout by pinch-hitter Varitek (batting for Wakefield's usual catcher Doug Mirabelli). It was 3-1, Red Sox. In the top of the ninth, Ruben Sierra hit a solo homer off Scott Williamson, but the game ended a 3-2 Red Sox win.

The Yankees took the series lead in Game Five, with a 4-2 win at Fenway. They got three runs off Derek Lowe in the top of the second after two walks (one intentional) and a single loaded the bases, which were then cleared by a two-run single from Karim Garcia and another single by Alfonso Soriano. Manny Ramirez led off the Boston fourth with a solo home run off starter David Wells. No other runs scored until the eighth. New York got an insurance run after Jason Giambi walked. A one-out single put runners on first and third, and (after Embree took over on the mound) their fourth run scored on a groundout fielded by the pitcher. Todd Walker tripled to lead off the bottom of the eighth; he scored on a groundout but that was it.

View on Boston's Storrow Drive heading back toward Cambridge – 2002.

The Red Sox weren't ready to throw in the towel. They scored nine runs in Game Six, back in New York. Andy Pettitte faced John Burkett. Giambi homered in the Yankees first, with the bases empty. Varitek led off the top of the third with a homer off Pettitte. A walk, a single, a groundout, and another walk loaded the bases. David Ortiz singled to left, driving in two. Kevin Millar singled to center, driving in a fourth run. The Yankees took the lead, driving Burkett from the game with four runs in the bottom of the fourth. Nick Johnson drove in one. Another scored on Aaron Boone's groundout, short to first. Two scored on a double by Soriano. They extended the lead to 6-4 when Posada hit a solo homer off reliever Bronson Arroyo. In the top of the seventh, Garciaparra tripled, and scored on an errant throw in. Manny doubled, then took third on a wild pitch. Ortiz singled in Ramirez and the score was 6-6. Felix Heredia took over from Jose Contreras, who had come in after five. After a wild pitch, a strikeout, and an intentional walk, Johnny Damon walked on four pitches. The Red Sox took a 7-6 lead, adding two more in the top of the ninth on a homer by Nixon.

It all came down to Game Seven. The winner would go to the World Series; the loser would go home. What would history tell cynics of any stripe? What were Red Sox fans inured to? What had Yankees fans come to expect?

The game was another Clemens/Martinez battle. The Red Sox struck early with a two-run Trot Nixon homer in the top of the second followed by a third run after Varitek doubled and a throwing error on a ball Damon hit to third baseman Enrique Wilson. Millar swung at the first pitch in the fourth and homered. It was 4-0, Red Sox. Did Boston fans dare hope? Perhaps, among them, there was a demographic difference dictated by age and experience?

Jason Giambi swung at Pedro's first pitch in the fourth, and homered. The 4-1 score held until the bottom of the seventh when Giambi hit another solo home run off Pedro. Clemens had left after three innings. Pedro had pitched seven full innings, having thrown precisely 100 pitches and left with a 4-2 lead. As he left the mound, he pointed to the heavens, and accepted a hug in the dugout from Nomar.

David Ortiz bumped the lead back up to three runs, swinging at reliever David Wells' first pitch in the bottom of the eighth and driving it over the wall in right field. But – to everyone's surprise – Pedro Martinez came back out to pitch the bottom of eighth. He got the first out, and had Jeter down 0-2, but Jeter doubled on a ball that could have been caught in right. Bernie Williams singled Jeter in. Grady Little came out of the dugout and paid a mound visit. And he left Pedro in the game. Two strikes. Matsui hit a ground-rule double. And then Posada dropped a looping base hit into center field, driving in two runs to tie the score, 5-5. Pedro had had two strikes on every one of the batters but the four consecutive base hits drove him from the game. The inning ended tied, Embree getting the second out and Mike Timlin the third. The Sox got a single in the ninth and a double in the 10th, but no more. While Mariano Rivera was pitching three shutout innings, Timlin shut down the Yankees in order in the ninth and Tim Wakefield came on in the 10th, likewise retiring the Yankees in order. But on his first pitch in the 11th, third base-man Aaron Boone – who had come over to the Yankees from Cincinnati on July 31, homered into the left-field seats and won the game. And the League Championship Series.

There was, naturally, a great deal of second-guessing of Grady Little for not overruling his ace and pulling Pedro from the game. All the analytics showed Martinez was less effective after 100 pitches. There were viable – very solid – bullpen options available. Grady stuck with his starter. Eleven days later, he was no longer employed by the Red Sox.

The Red Sox had found a way to blow it. Hardly anyone blamed Tim Wakefield. Some blamed Little. Most blamed Fate.

This might seem weird to fans of other teams, but for many Red Sox fans, this was just the way it was. One might expect more anger, more bitterness. There was at least some bitterness, but for those of us who had lived through this same sort of thing several times, there was a sort of acceptance. This was just the way it was.

Some took it personally; it was "poor me." Was it the team that was cursed, or was it that "long-suffering Red Sox fan" who was cursed? Each time the Red Sox lost, no doubt quite a number of fans dropped away – switched to other teams, or other sports, or just chose pastimes not so rife with disappointment. My guess is that there were at least a few new fans added after each soul-crushing loss, perhaps attracted to a fascination with this fan base that persisted despite losing and losing and losing.

Those of us who had been Red Sox fans for a long time had long since resigned ourselves to our fate. It was familiar, losing. Yes, we wanted to taste what it was truly like to win it all, but we had no reason to think we were entitled to experience that someday. We didn't give up hope, but there was an acceptance of this recurring pattern. This was just the way it was.

Two days later, for those who cared to watch, most Red Sox fans found themselves rooting – to a degree – for the…Florida Marlins.

And the Marlins beat the Yankees in the 2003 World Series. But one suspects that in the hearts of Red Sox fans, there was but slim satisfaction in the Marlins win. Instead, it was just another year in the books of Red Sox losses. Eighty-five years of them. There were many years in which the team had never really had a chance, but many with excruciating last-minute losses.

This was one of the most difficult ones to stomach. It's one thing to lose to the Big Red Machine. It's something else to get swept by the Athletics, twice in a row. But to lose to the Yankees, to cough up a three-run lead with five outs to go and then see a season end on one pitch, in Enemy Territory, in extra innings. There is no way to count the numbers who swore off the Red Sox after 2003. One suspects there were many.

Give the new Red Sox ownership credit. On page 10 of the *2004 Boston Red Sox Media Guide*, published before the season began, as part of a seven-page mission statement, they declared as their final goal: "TO END THE CURSE OF THE BAMBINO AND WIN A WORLD CHAMPION-SHIP FOR BOSTON, NEW ENGLAND, AND RED SOX NATION."

In the Red Sox dugout, sometime more than 45 minutes before game time.

There had been other things in 2003, even at Fenway Park. In early September, my son and I saw Bruce Springsteen and the E Street Band play to a packed house. Over the years, I've seen a few other concerts there, as well as a couple of Boston Bruins professional hockey games (the first one on January 1, 2010), some soccer including a Liverpool game, pickleball in 2023, some high school and college sports, a film, etc. In February 2016, there was a 140-foot-high ski jump installed as part of Big Air at Fenway. From the 1960s until early in the 21st century, the Kenmore Bowladrome (later Ryan Family Amusements) inhabited the space below what is now Game On! with a 20-lane bowling alley.

Jumping way ahead, I even got my first two COVID-19 vaccinations at Fenway Park in early 2021 when the park opened for thousands to take advantage of the new vaccine.

8

No Better Way to Break a Curse

The 2004 season

Hope springs eternal? Perhaps for some. Perhaps for most, depending on the depths of loyalty and devotion. I was 58 years old when Boone hit his homer. I saw it while sitting in my in-laws' place in Laredo, Texas. I shut off the TV, shut down my disappointments (something I had become more practiced at), and somehow was not as troubled as one might think.

One who still hoped was Kathryn Gemme. She had been waiting a long time – a long, long time. She had seen the Red Sox play back in 1918, when Babe Ruth was still on the team. She was 108 years old when I visited her in 2003 at the Atrium Nursing Center in Middleboro, Massachusetts. I wrote an article about her which appeared in *Red Sox Magazine*: "At 108, Kathryn Gemme's Still Putting On Her Sox."[58] She was a passionate fan who had the nursing home staff wake her up so she could watch West Coast road trips. She was remarkably well-informed, talking about how infrequently Red Sox pitchers would shake off Jason Varitek. Naturally, she was hoping to see the Red Sox win another World Series championship in her lifetime. See more on Kathryn Gemme below.

Under new manager Terry Francona, the Sox remained "competitive" in 2004. They had some new players, thanks to further investment by the new ownership group. Among them were starter Curt Schilling, who became a 20-game winner, something they had lacked in 2003. Schilling finished the 2004 season with a record of 21-6 (3.26). Keith Foulke closed 61 games, and earned 32 saves (exactly double Boston's 16 saves earned by Kim in 2003), with an ERA of 2.17.

The season had a bit more ups and downs to it. The 2003 Red Sox were in first place for 11 days during the course of that season and never further out than the 7 ½ games behind they were for one day in August. They finished 96-67, six games behind the Yankees. The 2004 Red Sox finished 36 games in first place, but also dipped more deeply, spending eight days at 10 or more games behind in the first part of August. They finished more strongly, still in second place but winning 98 games and thus this year were only three behind the first-place Yankees who had, once again, won 101 games.

Very early in the new century, Emmet and I in Box 123
season ticket seats.

The 2004 Division Series

The Sox had the fourth-best record in the league and found themselves facing the Anaheim Angels in the ALDS. The Angels had won the World Series in 2002 (the only one they have won), beating the San Francisco

Giants in seven games. Nine times the Angels have made postseason play, but 2002 was the only time they made it as far as the World Series.

In 2004, they were swept by the Red Sox.

The first two games were in Anaheim. Jarrod Washburn started for the Angels, a lefty who had been 11-8 (4.64), Schilling started for the Red Sox, and pitched the better game. Boston scored once in the first on back-to-back hits by Manny Ramirez and David Ortiz. They drove Washburn from the game in the fourth. Ortiz walked and Kevin Millar homered. The bases were loaded with Red Sox, and one out, when Johnny Damon hit the ball to third. Chone Figgins threw home, but threw wildly, and two runs scored. Scot Shields relieved Washburn and struck out Mark Bellhorn but then Manny hit a three-run homer to center. It was 8-0, Red Sox. The seven runs scored in one inning represented the most any Red Sox team had scored in a postseason inning. Troy Glaus homered off Schilling, leading off the Angels fourth. Neither side scored until the Angels seventh, when Darin Erstad hit a solo homer. With two outs, Schilling fielded a ball, throwing so wildly that batter Garret Anderson wound up on third base. Glaus doubled him home. Schilling departed. The only other run scored came in the top of the eighth, on an RBI bunt by Doug Mientkiewicz. 9-3, Red Sox.

The Red Sox won Game Two by a similar score, 8-3, but it had been a one-run game through the first eight innings. Bartolo Colon issued a bases-loaded walk to Manny Ramirez in the top of the second. Anaheim tied it when Pedro Martinez gave up a walk, single, and then an RBI single to Dallas McPherson. Pedro was far from a lock; he had lost his final four starts of the regular season. And he had given up those five runs in Game Seven of the 2003 ALCS. Two singles and a hit-by-pitch loaded the bases with Angels in the fifth. Vladimir Guerrero singled in two. Boston tied it in the sixth on a two-run homer by Jason Varitek. The Angels never scored again. The Red Sox took a 4-3 lead on a seventh-inning sacrifice fly from Ramirez. Francisco Rodriguez had taken over pitching for Mike Scioscia's Angels. Brendan Donnelly pitched the ninth for Scioscia, and he imploded, giving up four runs on three hits, two intentional walks (both batter scoring), an RBI single by Trot Nixon, and a three-RBI double by Orlando Cabrera, who had taken Garciaparra's place as part of a four-team trade on July 31. Pedro had worked seven innings, given up just three runs, and earned the win.

The Red Sox scored eight more runs in Game Three, helping survive a five-run top of the seventh by the Angels. Bronson Arroyo started for the Red Sox and allowed two runs over the six innings he worked. Kelvim Escobar started for the Angels. The Red Sox scored first, on two hits in the third. Troy Glaus hit a solo homer in the top of the fourth. Boston got three more runs in their half of the fourth. They added a sixth run in the fifth. Anaheim fought back, though, and tied the game, 6-6, in the top of the seventh on a bases-loaded walk by Erstad and then a grand slam by Guerrero. The game remained tied until the bottom of the 10th inning when Damon singled and, two outs later, David Ortiz hit a walkoff home run. Derek Lowe had pitched the 10th; he picked up the win.

The Red Sox had won another postseason series and were once again due to face the New York Yankees. The Yankees had won three of their four Division Series games against the Minnesota Twins. They were shut out, 2-0, in Game One, but then won the next three, two of them in extra innings – Game Two in 12 innings and Game Four in 11.

The 2004 League Championship Series

The Red Sox had lost in five games in 1999 and then suffered the seventh-game extra-inning defeat in 2003; they now faced their rivals in postseason play for the third time in six years. The 2004 Yankees had been 11-8 in regular-season games against the Red Sox. Several of the players were different from the year before, for both teams. The Sox had a new manager in Terry Francona; the Yankees still had Joe Torre. One fan base was still deeply traumatized from losing the 2003 ALCS. And the Yankees fan base was not pleased with having lost the World Series to the Marlins.

Curt Schilling only lasted three innings in Game One. The Yankees scored twice in the bottom of the first and four more times in the third. Matsui had driven in four of those runs, on a double in the first and a bases-loaded double in the third. Schilling had to leave with what looked to be an ankle injury. Starter Mike Mussina actually had a perfect game going through six innings – and an 8-0 lead after Kenny Lofton homered to lead off that inning and Matsui got his fifth RBI of the game on a single. Mussina lost his magic in the top of the seventh. Kevin Millar doubled in two, Trot Nixon singled in one, and then the first batter that reliever Tanyon Sturtze faced – Jason Varitek – hit a two-run homer. Former Red Sox reliever Tom Gordon was now with New York and he started the eighth, leaving after a two-run triple hit by David Ortiz that brought the Red Sox from an 8-0 deficit to within one run, 8-7. Mariano Rivera shut down the threat. Bernie Williams drove in a couple of runs in the bottom of the eighth off Boston's Mike Timlin. Final score, 10-7, Yankees.

Game Two was the lowest-scoring game of the series. The Yankees' Jon Lieber pitched seven innings of shutout ball. New York scored a run off Pedro Martinez in the first before making an out, on a walk to Derek Jeter, Alex Rodriguez being hit by a pitch, and a single to center by Gary Sheffield. They added two more in the sixth on a two-run homer by John Olerud. It was 3-0, New York. The Red Sox only scored once in the game, in the top of the eighth. Nixon singled off Lieber. Varitek doubled, Nixon stopping at third. He scored on a groundout by Cabrera.

After Game Three of the ALCS, it looked like it was just about all over for Boston. Another season, down the drain. Another loss to the hated Yankees. More taunting by Yankees fans, with their sing-song "19-18" chant. To this point in the book, I have provided brief capsules on the various postseason games. I faced the choice here – detail this game, or skip it to spare Red Sox fans all the gore and despair. I could simply dismiss it, maybe urge those readers who wanted to know more to see my writeup of the game on the SABR Games Project site.[59] No, I decided it was better to tell it like it was, how it all unfolded, leaving those who weren't at the game to try and imagine how it might have felt to those of us who were. It makes for a longer account than the other capsules, because the Yankees simply kept scoring and scoring. And scoring. And scoring. But that's what happened. If you don't want to suffer through the carnage, feel free to skip ahead to Game Four.

Game Three was at Fenway Park. Bronson Arroyo started for the Red Sox, and Kevin Brown started for the Yankees. Before the Red Sox came to bat, it was New York 3, Boston 0. Arroyo walked the leadoff batter, Jeter. Second up was Alex Rodriguez, who doubled and picked up his first RBI of the game. After Sheffield flied out, Matsui hit a two-run homer. Bernie Williams singled. After 30 pitches, Arroyo had all of one out. Fortunately, his next pitch was hit for a double play.

Some may not remember it, but the Red Sox actually took a 4-3 lead in the bottom of the second. Nixon homered after Varitek walked. Bill Mueller doubled and Johnny Damon singled. After a wild pitch and a walk, Jeter committed an error on a ball hit by Manny Ramirez as the fourth run scored. The lead only lasted a few minutes. It was the only lead the Red Sox had in any of the first three games.

A-Rod tied it up with a leadoff homer in the third. After a base on balls to Sheffield and a double by Matsui, former Yankee Ramiro Mendoza relieved Arroyo. Bernie Williams singled in a second run. Mendoza then balked and Matsui scored. It was 6-4, New York. The Red Sox were still fighting – something perhaps few remember – and re-tied the score right away, after the Yankees, too, turned to the bullpen. Javier Vazquez loaded the bases with one out. Cabrera doubled to center, driving in two, with the possible go-ahead run cut down at home plate trying to score.

After Mendoza hit the first batter, Francona turned to Curt Leskanic. He got one out, but Sheffield hit a three-run homer. After Matsui doubled, Wakefield relieved Leskanic. With two outs, Ruben Sierra tripled to right and the New York lead was 11-6.

In the fifth, back-to-back doubles hit by Rodriguez and Sheffield made it 13-6.

In the top of the seventh, with two outs and runners on first and third, Alan Embree relieved Wakefield. Matsui singled for his third RBI of the game. Bernie Williams doubled for his second and third RBIs. Jorge Posada doubled and drove in Williams. It was 17-6, Yankees.

Many Red Sox fans stood up for the seventh-inning stretch and never sat down. They left Fenway Park. By way of confession, this author was among them. My friend Roy Cohen and I had gone to the game. We had left our two 13-year-old sons home by themselves. What could go wrong on a Saturday night with two 13-year-olds left alone? With the Yankees leading by 11 runs, leaving seemed like the mature, responsibly parental thing to do. Besides, then we wouldn't have to see the final humiliation.

Varitek hit a two-run homer in the bottom of the seventh. But in the top of the ninth, Matsui picked up his fourth and fifth RBIs of the game, and restored the 11-run Yankees lead. The final score was 19-8.

After Game Three

The Yankees now had a three-games-to-none lead in the ALCS. And a 19-8 defeat was something of a shellacking. This was the team that so often won (if you count 39 pennants and 26 world championships in eight decades as often) against the team that always found a way to lose. Well, at least for the last 86 years.

The Yankees/Red Sox record for championships since 1918 stood at 26-0.

And in all of baseball there had never been a best-of-seven playoff series in which the team which had been down 0-3 had come back to win it all. Not once. Never.

Jackie MacMullan wrote, "So now it's 3-0 and it's over, and everyone knows it, even the resilient Sox players who have never said die all season, and aren't about to start now." [60]

Bob Ryan said he had truly let himself believe this would be the year. But, no, "They are down, 3-0, after last night's rout, and, in this sport, that's an official death sentence."[61]

Tony Massarotti of the *Boston Herald* went all out: "They are doing more than just losing now. They are disgracing the game and embarrassing themselves, and they are doing a disservice to the paying customers who blindly and faithfully stream through their doors. Shame, shame, shame on the Red Sox…What a joke."[62]

"How much more can New Englanders take?" asked Dan Shaughnessy.[63]

I had tickets for Game Four. I had been planning to take my son. I didn't want to expose him to yet another Red Sox elimination. I still hadn't gotten over 1978. Would it be child abuse to subject him to this game? True, he wasn't emotionally invested the way I was. True, the Red Sox might actually win the game and enjoy a bit of a respite. But….

I made a deal with him: "You don't really want to go to tonight's game, do you? I'll tell you what – I'll sell the tickets and we can stay home if you promise to take a trip to Africa with me next summer." He went for it. I drove by the park and sold the tickets outside, for face value. I wish I had taken the name of the person who bought them, so I could include his story in this telling.

Game Four was on Sunday night. It didn't get over until after 1:00 A.M. on Monday morning.

In the meantime, before the game, Kevin Millar had uttered one of the most noted phrases of the 2004 postseason: "Don't let us win tonight!" Red Sox GM Theo Epstein remembered it: "We had just been humiliated. There was a sense of how bad can this get? Once we got in the clubhouse, I was encouraged by how light the mood was with the players. Millar and a few others were optimistic and energetic and a little out of control. Their refrain was, 'Don't let us win. Don't let us win tonight,' and Millar rattled through the whole pitching rotation. Win tonight, then we got Pedro, then we got Schilling. …"[64]

Lowe started for Boston. Alex Rodriguez hit a two-run homer in the top of the third. Through the first four innings, El Duque had given up just one single and walked a couple (Ramirez and Ortiz) back in the first. In the fifth, he walked another two but had two outs when Cabrera singled in the first Red Sox run. He walked Ramirez again, loading the bases. Ortiz singled, driving in two and giving Boston a 3-2 lead. The Yankees wasted no time in responding. Matsui tripled off Lowe and Bernie Williams singled him in off reliever Timlin. They added a go-ahead run on a single by Tony Clark. They held the 4-3 lead until the bottom of the ninth.

Mariano Rivera was on the mound – none other than arguably the greatest closer in the history of the game. He had led all of baseball with 53 saves in the regular season; there were just four that he had blown. Let me repeat: 53-4. Rivera walked Millar on five pitches. Dave Roberts came in to pinch-run for Millar and everyone in the world knew his mission was to try and steal second base, to get into scoring position. He did. Just barely, but he did. Bill Mueller singled to center, tying the game. There was still nobody out. A blown save for Rivera. Mientkiewicz sacrificed, and Mueller took second. Johnny Damon reached on an error by Clark at first base and the Sox had runners on first and third with just one out. Yes, it was OK to hope they could pull out this game. But Rivera struck out Cabrera on three pitches. He pitched to Ramirez and walked him, then pitched to Ortiz, who popped up to second base.

The game went to extra innings. Neither team scored in the 10th or 11th, though the Yankees loaded the bases in the top of the 11th. Curt Leskanic got the third and final out, and gave up just a leadoff single in the top of the 12th. Paul Quantrill came in from the bullpen to pitch to the Red Sox in the bottom of the 12th. Ramirez singled to left, and David Ortiz – Big Papi – hit his second walkoff homer of the 2004 postseason deep into the Yankees bullpen in right field. The Yankees had let the Red Sox win that night, 6-4.

OK, so the Red Sox had won a game. The history still remained: no base-ball team had ever come back from being down three-games-to-none and winning a seven-game postseason series.[65] They'd have to win three more in a row to change history.

Game Five was set for a 5:10 P.M. start, just about 16 hours after Game Four ended. It was Pedro Martinez vs. Mike Mussina. This one lasted even longer than Game Four – five hours and 49 minutes. And 14 innings, not just 12. The Red Sox scored first, in the first, on a single by Ortiz and a bases-loaded walk to Varitek. Bernie Williams homered on Pedro's first pitch of the second. The 2-1 Red Sox lead held through the first five innings. In the sixth, Pedro struggled. Posada and Sierra both singled. With two outs, he hit Miguel Cairo with a pitch. Derek Jeter doubled down the right-field line and cleared the bases, making it 4-2, New York. With Flash Gordon pitching, Ortiz homered to lead off the bottom of the eighth. A walk and a single put runners on first and third with nobody out. Rivera relieved Gordon. Varitek tied the game with a sacrifice fly to center.

By the end of 11 innings, the Red Sox had spooled through five relievers and the Yankees had brought in their sixth. Tim Wakefield pitched the next three innings. Esteban Loaiza worked the last 3⅓ for the Yankees. New York had runners in scoring position in both the 12th and 13th. Ortiz had been caught stealing in the 12th. With Varitek instead of Mirabelli behind the plate, there were three passed balls in the top of the 13th, but no one scored. Loaiza retired the side in the bottom of the 13th, Wakefield retired the side in the top of the 14th. In the bottom of the 14th, Loaiza struck out Mark Belllhorn, then walked Damon, struck out Cabrera, then walked Ramirez. This brought up Ortiz again. He kept fouling off pitches, the count 2-2 after nine pitches. The 10th pitch, he laced into center and won the game. It was his third walkoff hit of the 2004 postsea-son and – remarkably – his second extra-inning walkoff hit on the same calendar day, October 18.

I was glad I had gone to Game Five! So was my friend Saul Wisnia. So were most of the 35,118 others at the ballpark, and many other thousands worldwide.

Game Six – the Bloody Sock Game

After Game Five, the Red Sox had won again. But they were heading to Yankee Stadium for Game Six and, if necessary, Game Seven. The likelihood of any Game Severn was still remote. Repeating the refrain: no team had ever come back from being down three-games-to-none and won a seven-game postseason series.

Game Six became known forever after as the "Bloody Sock Game." After Dr. Bill Morgan performed innovative surgery on Curt Schilling's right ankle to temporarily bind the tendons back in place, the Red Sox pitcher took the mound – not knowing if the procedure might work or for how long. He retired each of the first eight batters he faced, gave up a double, then retired the next batter. In the top of the fourth, Jon Lieber got outs from the first two Red Sox batters but then Millar doubled, took third on a wild pitch, and scored the first run of the game on Varitek's single to center. Cabrera singled and then Mark Bellhorn hit a three-run homer. Now this was getting interesting.

An unfamiliar sort of drama became evident to television viewers, who could all see clear evidence of blood seeping through Schilling's sock. He gave up a couple of singles in the bottom of the fourth, but Red Sox infielders made each of the next three outs. He struck out the first two batters in the fifth, got a groundout, and retired the side in order again in the sixth. In the bottom of the seventh, one Yankee hit the ball hard – a solo home run by Bernie Williams. The Red Sox led 4-1 heading into the bottom of the eighth. Schilling's night was done; Bronson Arroyo took over. Cairo doubled and Jeter singled, and the Yankees added a run. They got no more. Alex Rodriguez was called out for interfering with a play, swatting the ball out of Arroyo's grip as Arroyo was ready to tag him out running to first. Sheffield popped up behind the plate. Keith

Foulke pitched the bottom of the ninth. He walked two, got a popup to third base, and struck out two. The Red Sox won Game Six, 4-2. Now – improbable as it was – the ALCS was tied with three wins apiece. Whichever team won Game Seven would advance to the World Series.

Johnny Damon scored 461 runs in his four seasons with the Red Sox, but may be best remembered in Boston for his grand slam in Game 7 of the 2004 ALCS.

Game Seven was on October 20. Joe Torre entrusted the season to Kevin Brown. Terry Francona gave the game ball to Derek Lowe. Presumably wishing the Yankees hadn't let the Red Sox win on the night of Game Four, Brown gave up a leadoff single to Johnny Damon, who then stole second. With one out, Manny Ramirez singled to left but lost out on a run batted in as Damon was thrown out at the plate. David Ortiz homered a few rows deep into the right-field stands. Lowe set down the Yankees in order. After getting one out, Brown saw Millar single, then walked Mueller and Cabrera to load the bases. Torre called in Javier Vazquez. Damon swung at his first pitch and hit a grand slam into the seats in right field, giving the Red Sox a 6-0 lead.

Jeter singled in a run in the New York third, but Damon then stepped into the box and – again, first-pitch swinging – hit another homer. Now it was 8-1, Red Sox. This was not boding well for the Yankees. At the end of six, it was still 8-1. To pitch the bottom of the second, Francona turned to a surprise relief pitcher – Pedro Martinez. Since 1993, Pedro had served in relief in a total of three regular-season games and once back in Game Five of the 1999 ALDS when he had worked six innings of no-hit relief and got the win to clinch that series. In this deciding game of the 2004 ACLS, he gave up back-to-back doubles to Matsui and Williams and then – after getting one out – an RBI single to Kenny Lofton. One good thing about a seven-run lead is that one can afford to give up a couple of runs. He got outs from the next two batters.

Mark Bellhorn offered a particular bit of punctuation with a leadoff homer off Tom Gordon in the top of the eighth. Mike Timlin relieved Pedro and got a groundout, strikeout, and groundout. In the top of the ninth, Gordon gave up two singles and the dwindling Stadium crowd saw the Red Sox take a 10-3 lead on Cabrera's sacrifice fly. In the bottom of the ninth, all the Yankees needed was seven runs to tie, and eight to ensure that the winner of the first three games of a seven-game series would win out in the end. It didn't happen. Matsui was .404 with 13 RBIs in the 2004 postseason. He singled. Timlin got a couple of outs, walked Lofton, and gave way to Embree, who secured the final out.

The Red Sox had not only made history, defying all odds, but done so against their historic rivals – the Yankees – the team which had snatched the ALCS away from them just the year before.

Kevin Millar had warned them – "don't let us win tonight!" But they had. And then won the next three games, too.

For some Red Sox fans, that might have seemed like redemption enough. Yes, there was the World Series and they'd have to wait another day to find out if they would be facing Houston or St. Louis, but their team had triumphed over the New York Yankees, and in the most improbable of ways. It was supremely satisfying.

There were plenty of heroes to go around. Ortiz had won two elimination games with extra-inning walkoff hits. Schilling had pitched a game with blood seeping from the stitches near his ankle. The leadoff batter in Game Six – Damon – collected six RBIs. Foulke relieved in five ALCS games and allowed just one hit. There were plenty of contributors.

There was a tragedy that night. A huge and boisterous crowd spontaneously surrounded Fenway Park. Many college students from the area flocked to Kenmore Square and crowds grew to an estimated 70,000. Keep in mind that this was just an LCS victory, not a World Series win! But it was a win over the Yankees, and it was an historic win, coming back from being down and out – then winning four games in a row, a loss in any one of them meaning the end of yet another season. The tragedy was the death of 21-year-old Victoria Snelgrove, a student at Emerson College who was shot in the eye with a Boston Police pepper-pellet projectile.[66]

Three days later, the Red Sox had returned to Fenway Park for the 2004 World Series. It had been 18 years since they had been in the World Series. And 86 years since they had won one.

2004 World Series

The St. Louis Cardinals won 105 regular-season games in 2004, and took three of four from the Dodgers, but had to battle the full seven games to win the NLCS over the Houston Astros. They won their first two at home, lost all three on the road, then came back to St. Louis to win Games Six and Seven.

They were, of course, the team which beat the Red Sox in the 1946 World Series and again in the 1967 World Series. Both times, the Series went the full seven games. This one did not, and each game saw progressively fewer runs scored by each team.

Tim Wakefield started Game One for the Red Sox, at Fenway Park. Wake was fresh off the win in Game Five against the Yankees, in which he'd given up just one base hit from the 12th through the 14th innings. Woody Williams was the starter for St. Louis. He had been 11-8 (4.18) during the season. An established veteran, Williams had started and won Game One of both the NLDS and NLCS. In Game Five of the NLCS, he had started and thrown one-hit ball for the first seven innings, but the Astros had shut out the Cards and won the game on a three-run homer in the bottom of the ninth.

Both pitchers were hit hard in Game One. Wakefield got through the first. Leading off for Boston was Johnny Damon. On the 10th pitch of his at-bat, he doubled. Cabrera got hit by a pitch. And then David Ortiz hit a three-run homer, high and deep into the seats past the Pesky Pole in right. Their inning wasn't over yet. Millar doubled, tagged and went to third on a fly ball from Nixon, and scored on a single to left by Bill Mueller.

The Cardinals got one run in the second and one run in the third. The Red Sox got three more. Damon singled in one and drove Williams from the game. Dan Haren let two inherited runners score before closing out the inning. It was 7-2, Red Sox, but this game was far from over. The Cardinals scored three times in the fourth after Wakefield walked the bases loaded with nobody out. After he then walked yet another batter, Francona brought in Arroyo. In the sixth, St. Louis tied it, 7-7, on a two-out single and then back-to-back doubles by Edgar Renteria and Larry Walker (who had homered in the third.) The Red Sox took a 9-7 lead in the seventh, on consecutive singles by Ramirez and Ortiz. Ortiz's RBI was his 19th of the postseason, tying a record at the time.[67] The Cardinals re-tied the game in the top of the eighth, Renteria singling in the first run and the other coming in on an error. Julian Tavarez became the sixth pitcher of the game for St. Louis. As was once written, "The teams were like two slightly punch-drunk fighters, landing blows at will with neither willing to fall down."[68] Working the bottom of the eighth, Tavarez allowed just one hit but it was a two-run homer off the Pesky Pole by Mark Bellhorn. 11-9, Red Sox. Keith Foulke allowed a ground-rule double to left but no more. It was the first World Series game anyone had seen the Red Sox win at Fenway since Game Five in 1986, 18 years earlier to the day.

One might think that committing four errors in Game Two would condemn the Red Sox to defeat, but it did not. They scored their first two runs in the bottom of the first inning off St. Louis starter Matt Morris

(15-10, 4.72). After getting two groundouts, Morris issued back-to-back walks to Manny Ramirez and David Ortiz. Next up was Jason Varitek, who tripled into the center-field triangle in center field.[69] It gave him 16 RBIs in his last 18 games. Curt Schilling was the Red Sox starter. With a ligament still stitched in his right ankle, he allowed all of one run in the six innings he worked. With his second double of the game, Albert Pujols led off the fourth, tagged and went to third on a fly ball to right by Scott Rolen, and then scored on an error by Bill Mueller at third base. Bellhorn hit a two-run double in the bottom of the fourth, giving Boston a 4-1 lead. Two Cards reached base on the top of the sixth, both on infielder errors, but neither scored. After Nixon and Damon had both singled in the sixth, so did Orlando Cabrera and the Red Sox were up, 6-1. Embree relieved Schilling and struck out the side in the seventh. St. Louis picked up one more run in the eighth, off Mike Timlin, on a walk, groundout, single by Pujols, and a sac fly from Scott Rolen. The final was 6-2, Red Sox – their sixth win in succession.

Both teams traveled to St. Louis for Game Three. It was Jeff Suppan vs. Pedro Martinez. Suppan had pitched for the Red Sox twice before, 1995-97 and in 11 games in 2003. He was 12-10 (5.87) for Boston. He'd been the winningest pitcher for the 2004 Cardinals. Three other starters had 15 wins. Suppan was 16-9 (4.16). He had won the game that clinched the Division Series for St. Louis and the one that clinched the League Championship Series. Boston scored first, a solo home run by Manny Ramirez in the top of the first. Pedro loaded the bases on two walks and a single but escaped giving up a run after Ramirez caught Jim Edmonds' fly ball to left and threw out Larry Walker at home plate. Another double play with a runner thrown out at the plate (Suppan, who had singled to lead off) bailed out Pedro in the third. Bill Mueller singled and drove in Nixon to put Boston up 2-0 in the fourth. It improved to 4-0 in the fifth on RBI singles by Ramirez and Mueller. The Cardinals only scored once in the game, in the bottom of the ninth on Larry Walker's solo home run off closer Keith Foulke. The Red Sox won Game Three, 4-1.

This put the Cardinals in a tough position. No team – except the 2004 Red Sox – had ever come back from being down three-games-to-none in a seven-game postseason series.

In Game Four, on the night of a lunar eclipse, the Cardinals pinned their hopes on Jason Marquis, one of their 15-game winners (15-7, 3.71). The first batter Marquis faced was Johnny Damon, who served notice with a leadoff home run. That was the only run the Red Sox needed, as events transpired. Derek Lowe started for the Sox. He threw seven shut-out innings, allowing just three hits and walking just one. Boston added two more runs in the third on a two-run double by Trot Nixon. The Red Sox loaded the bases in the top of the eighth, but failed to add to their lead. The Cardinals got runners into scoring position in both the eighth and ninth, but were unable to score.

Keith Foulke had come on to try to close the game in the bottom of the ninth. Albert Pujols led off with a single. There came two outs. Pujols took second due to defensive indifference. Edgar Renteria stepped into the box. Nearly 20 years later, many Red Sox fans worldwide could recite radio broadcaster Joe Castiglione's final call: "Swing and a ground ball, stabbed by Foulke. He has it, he underhands to first –and the Boston Red Sox are the world champions. For the first time in 86 years, the Red Sox have won baseball's world championship. Can you believe it?"

The Red Sox had won the game, 3-0, and won the World Series, four games to none. They had won each of their last eight postseason games. The final pitcher for the Red Sox in each of the four World Series games was Keith Foulke. And Derek Lowe had been the winning pitcher in each of the clinching games–in the ALDS, the ALCS, and the World Series.

9

Dejection Is Replaced by...Expectation?

After 86 years

Well, I was only 59, but it had been a long wait for both those older and many of those younger. Had it been real? The moment the Red Sox won it, I drove to Kenmore Square, parked a few blocks away, and joined the masses, said to be more than 70,000, who had likewise flocked to Fenway. After the tragedy of the week before, fans were perhaps more restrained and the police better prepared. I do recall a guy climbing up and onto a street lamp – the kind that arc well out over a street, in this case Commonwealth Avenue – climbing out on the arm, and then dropping into the waiting crowd below, as though they were a mosh pit. Tear gas and other measures helped disperse the crowds. Just a few hours later, after returning home for an attempt at sleep, I was back at Fenway (the crowds having mostly departed) in time to see the team buses arrive from Logan Airport and the conquering heroes emerge, waving to the relatively small group assembled.

The next night I got a lot more sleep, but several times over the next two to three weeks, I woke up wondering, "Was it really true? Had the Red Sox really won the World Series?" I didn't literally pinch myself (well, maybe once or twice just for fun) but I needed to talk myself into believing it. "Yes, that really did happen. You are not dreaming this."

Some even lamented, in a way, the passing of an era. "The Red Sox, as we have always known them are gone forever. They never again will be the cuddly team on a near century-long, quixotic quest. They are no longer cursed and they will cease to be America's team once the hangover wears off. The ghosts are purged." That was written by Dan Shaughnessy, who generously ended his column: "Now the men who play at Fenway Park are simply the World Champion Boston Red Sox. The best team in baseball. I guess we'll have to settle for that."[70]

There was a parade, a "rolling rally" parade featuring the ballplayers with even a part of the parade on water on the city's "duck boats" – attracted more than 3,200,000. The population of the City of Boston in the year 2000 was 589,141. The parade thus drew more than five times the population of the entire city.

And there was a trophy tour. The Commissioner's Trophy – the 2004 World Series trophy – traveled to every one of the 351 cities and towns of the Commonwealth of Massachusetts by June 24, 2005, as well as to 13 other states, the District of Columbia, and the Red Sox academy in the Dominican Republic.

For many, the celebrations and commemorations were personal and private. Across much of New England, one could see gravestones which were decorated with Red Sox banners, balloons, caps, or other items bearing the "B" logo – all in memory of dedicated but departed Red Sox fans.[71]

For those still living, the title of Bill Simmons' book captured a related feeling: *Now I Can Die in Peace*.[72]

And as Simmons noted, no longer would Red Sox fans need to be tormented – every time they seemed to have something to celebrate – by the obligatory re-run of TV clips of Bill Buckner in 1986 or, more recently, the Aaron Boone home run from 2003. One could watch these clips now with different emotions. These were historic curiosities. No longer did the accustomed anguish bite and fester.

This may have resonated with Kathryn Gemme. Born in November 1894, she had been 23 when the Red Sox had last won the World Series, in 1918. See my mention of her above, at the beginning of this detailing of the 2004 season. Sometime after my *Red Sox Magazine* story ran, the *Brockton Enterprise* had reported, "the 109-year-old Gemme said she will not leave this earth until the Sox, who last won a World Series in 1918, win the series again."[73]

The day after Game Four of the 2004 World Series, I sent an email to Sharon Gosling, the activities director of the Atrium Nursing Center, saying that I hoped that Kathryn had enjoyed the long-awaited triumph. Sharon wrote back later that day – October 28 – and said, "She is pleased, and now that her goal is met, she is ready to go!! Sad but true she is now talking about death. She turns 110 on Nov. 9th. She says she hopes to see her 110th, then she's ready."[74] Sharon added, "If there was a Game 6, she and I were going, but they had to sweep them and go out in

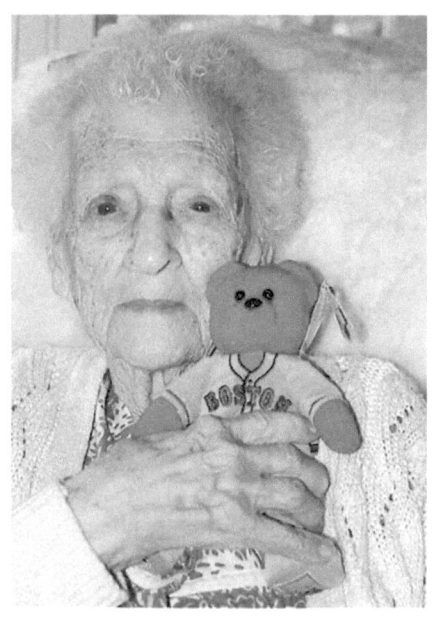

Kathryn Gemme, lifelong dedicated Red Sox fan, age 108.

style!!" Certainly, Kathryn Gemme went out in style. She did see her 110th, and even her 112th, before she died on December 29, 2006 at Nemasket Healthcare in Middleboro. At the time she had been the oldest person in the Commonwealth of Massachusetts and the eighth-oldest in the United States.

The 2005 season

The 2005 season started, of course, with Opening Day ceremonies, which included the raising of the World Championship banner in center field. Needless to say, it was a moment many had wondered if they would ever live to see. Johnny Pesky and Carl Yastrzemski were the ones who pulled the cords that raised the banner on the flagpole in center field. There were – as at every game – ceremonial first pitches thrown. On this day, four champions of Boston-area sports history threw them – Richard Seymour and Tedi Bruschi (New England Patriots), Bill Russell (Boston Celtics), and Bobby Orr (Boston Bruins). I can't remember how this happened – and we never met the four – but there was a pregame run-through before the park was opened to the public and for some reason I was the stand-in for Bobby Orr. I walked to the mound and threw a first pitch. My son Emmet held back, but friends Roy and Ethan Cohen were on the mound as well miming the throws of the others. It was Roy I had gone to ALCS Game Three with, our sons Ethan and Emmet remaining at home. That had been the lowest point of 2004, and now it was all a new day.

The team the Red Sox played that Opening Day of 2005? The New York Yankees, who had to watch all the ceremonies and suffer a degree of abuse – though when Mariano Rivera was introduced, the Fenway faithful let out a spontaneous cheer (which – give him credit – Rivera graciously acknowledged.)

The 2005 postseason

There was no lengthy wait until the Red Sox reached the postseason again. They did so this very next year. They actually finished the 2005 season tied with the New York Yankees for first place in the A.L. East. Both teams had records of 95-67, but the Yankees had won one more game in the 19 they played head-to-head in the regular season (10 wins to Boston's 9). The Yankees played the West Division leaders, the Anaheim Angels, and lost to them in five games. The Red Sox played the Central Division champs, the 99-63 Chicago White Sox.

The 2005 Division Series

Too much winning? The streak the Red Sox had going of eight consecutive postseason wins was snapped in Game One of the ALDS, a somewhat decisive 14-2 White Sox win in Chicago. Boston's Matt Clement (13-6, 4.57) gave up five runs in the first inning alone. He hit two of the first three batters, saw two runs score a few minutes later, and then surrendered a three-run homer to A. J. Pierzynski. Clement also gave up a solo homer to Paul Konerko in the third and a two-run homer to Juan Uribe in the fourth. Scott Podsednik later hit a three-run homer and Pierzynski had a solo home run, too. The only Red Sox runs were both off starter Jose Contreras – on singles by Trot Nixon and Jason Varitek, a run-scoring wild pitch, and then a double by Kevin Millar.

Game Two saw the Red Sox jump out to a 4-0 lead off starter Mark Buehrle. Manny Ramirez drove in two in the first inning. Varitek knocked one in on a bases-loaded single in the third, and Nixon picked up an RBI on a groundout. The Red Sox still led, 4-0, at the game's halfway point, but Boston starter David Wells was hammered for five runs in the bottom of the fifth. Two runs had scored and then second baseman Tadahito Iguchi hit a three-run homer. Neither team scored the rest of the game, and so the White Sox won, 5-4.

The third game in the best-of-five series was held at Fenway Park, Tim Wakefield against Freddy Garcia. Chicago got two in the top of the third on a double by Podsednik and a single by Iguchi. Boston led off the fourth with back-to-back solo home runs by David Ortiz and Manny Ramirez. That naturally thrilled the home crowd, with memories of 2004 still fully in place. The game was tied, 2-2. In the top of the sixth, Konerko hit a two-run homer off Wakefield. Manny Ramirez hit a solo home run to bring Boston back to within one run. Relievers took over for both teams. Only one more run was scored, and it was an insurance run for the White Sox in the top of the ninth. Pierzynski doubled off Mike Timlin, was sacrificed to third, and then scored when Uribe bunted back to the pitcher.

Shades of years past. The Red Sox had been swept in the postseason. Give the White Sox credit. They were a juggernaut. They lost just one game – the first – to the Angels in the ALCS, and that by just one run. They ran the table then, winning the next four over the Angels and then sweeping the Houston Astros, though every game a close one. It was their first World Series win since 1917 – they had had an 88-year wait. It was a nice treat for White Sox fans. North Side fans of the Chicago Cubs would have to wait another 11 years for their deliverance. The year 2016 became the year.

A book that combined both baseball and music

During the year 2007, Rounder Books published a 221-page book that Chuck Burgess and I collaborated on. It spanned my interest in both baseball and music. There are three songs that play at every Fenway Park game – before the game, there is "The Star-Spangled Banner." In the break before the bottom of the seventh inning, there is "Take Me Out to the Ball Game" – played on the organ by Josh Kantor and sung along to by many. Josh has not missed even one home game for 20 years – since 2003. In the last 20 years, in the middle of the eighth inning, the masses sing Neil Diamond's "Sweet Caroline." And they sing it with gusto – even if the Red Sox are losing 12-2, and the opposition just scored five runs in the top of the eighth. It can be a little disconcerting to suddenly see so many people become so irrationally joyful.

But for *real* Red Sox fans, the song they most yearn to hear is the one played after every Red Sox home win at Fenway, a tradition since April 10, 1998—"Dirty Water" by The Standells. If the Sox lose, it doesn't play. If it does, it kicks off a trilogy of songs – "Dirty Water," followed by the Dropkick Murphys' "Tessie," and then Three Dog Night's "Joy to the World."

How did a 1966 song by a California group become such a song? That's the story Chuck and I tell in our *Love That Dirty Water: The Standells and the*

Improbable Red Sox Victory Anthem. There's plenty of history in the book, going back to the first World Series ever played and how the original song "Tessie" – sung by the Royal Rooters in the stands – flustered the Pittsburgh Pirates so much that some of them said years later it may have cost them in the 1903 World Series. "The Star-Spangled Banner" was first played on a regular basis at Fenway Park during the 1918 World Series. More than a decade later, it was designated as the National Anthem.

I first saw The Standells in 1966, opening for The Beatles at Suffolk Downs. That was the year "Dirty Water" rose to #11 on the *Billboard* Hot 100 chart. The lyrics, of course, talk about "lovers, muggers, and thieves" and about "frustrated women" who "have to be in by twelve o'clock." It's a safe bet the Chamber of Commerce or Boston Visitors Bureau would never have commissioned a song about polluted water "down by the banks of the river Charles." But it always resonated well in Boston and one line repeats a couple of times: "Oh, Boston, you're my home!"

We talked to each of The Standells, and any number of others involved – including the sound room folks at Fenway who first started playing the song. And put together a book on the subject that was enjoyable – fascinating at times – to research and write.

A one-day baseball experience in Venezuela

Cashing in some frequent flyer miles, I decided to do two things and took a brief trip to Venezuela in 2005. I spent the first couple of nights in Caracas and went to see a baseball game there. I was impressed to see some of the players step outside the park in uniform and chat with fans. Then I flew to Angels Falls to see the world's highest waterfall. The final stretch of the flight from Ciudad Bolivar to Canaima was in a very small plane that had a loose door to the left of my seat and as the pilot flew, I had to hook my elbow outside the window and keep the pressure on in order to keep the door closed. (I was in a seat belt, but....) The falls were spectacular.

An album with Peter Gammons, George Thorogood, and six Red Sox players

In July 2006, Rounder released an album by Peter Gammons and friends. For those keeping track, it was Rounder 9070. The writeup on Amazon does a very good job of explaining what that was all about:

"With the assistance of a crack band of Boston rockers and some very special guests, celebrated baseball commentator and columnist Peter Gammons (ESPN, The Boston Globe, Sports Illustrated) trades in his typewriter for a Stratocaster and delivers a rousing set of vintage classics, originals, and rock obscurities – all to benefit Theo and Paul Epstein's Foundation to be Named Later, a charity which raises funds and awareness for non-profit agencies serving disadvantaged youth in the Greater Boston area. Gammons's ruggedly soulful vocals and guitar are featured alongside cameos from Red Sox G.M. Theo Epstein, Juliana Hatfield, George Thorogood, Little Feat's Paul Barrere, Kay Hanley, and an all-star chorus consisting of Red Sox players Jonathan Papelbon, Kevin Youkilis, Trot Nixon, Lenny DiNardo and Tim Wakefield, former Red Sox pitcher Bronson Arroyo, and NESN broadcaster Don Orsillo."

I wasn't in the studio. Not sure where I actually was at the time of the sessions, but that would have been fun.

2007 Red Sox – World Champions again

After making the postseason three years in a row, the 2006 Red Sox only finished third, 11 games behind the Yankees. But in 2007, they finished first in the division, two games ahead of the Yankees. The most they were ever out of first place was by one game, and from April 18 on they had first place to themselves.

While not a single one of the 1918 Red Sox was still living in 2004, not only were all the members of the 2004 Red Sox champions still living in 2007, the team still had the same manager and bench coach (Terry

Francona and Brad Mills) and several – though not many – of the same players. Doug Mirabelli, David Ortiz, Manny Ramirez, Curt Schilling, Mike Timlin, Jason Varitek, Tim Wakefield, and Kevin Youkilis were the eight players who overlapped, and might hope to earn a second ring.

The 2007 Division Series

On Labor Day, the team had been up by seven games; they held on to win the East by two. The second-place Yankees played Cleveland in the ALDS and only won Game Three. The Red Sox played the Angels and swept all three games, outscoring them 19-4.

The first game was a shutout for Josh Beckett – who as a Florida Marlin just four years earlier had shut out the Yankees in Game Six of the 2003 World Series. In the bottom of the first, Kevin Youkilis hit a solo homer into the Green Monster seats off John Lackey – later a Red Sox pitcher, and on Boston's 2013 world championship team. In the third, Youk doubled and David Ortiz hit a two-run homer into the right-field grandstand. Manny Ramirez walked, went to second on a wild pitch, and scored on Mike Lowell's single. It was 4-0, all the runs in the game. Indeed, the Red Sox only had one more hit the rest of the way. Beckett went the distance, walking no one, and allowing just four hits – all singles. Luis Tiant had shut out Cincinnati in Game One of the 1975 World Series. No Red Sox pitcher had done it since (and through 2023, none have done it since Beckett.)[75]

In his first year in American baseball, Daisuke Matsuzaka won 15 games for the Red Sox. Staked to a 2-0 lead, thanks to a first-inning bases-loaded single by J. D. Drew off Kelvim Escobar, "Dice-K" gave up three runs. It was the last run of the game for the Angels, but they led 3-2. In the fifth, Dustin Pedroia doubled. After walks to Ortiz (intentional) and Ramirez (not), Lowell hit a sacrifice fly that tied the game. Four Red Sox relievers combined to throw 4⅓ innings of no-hit ball. Three Angels relievers allowed just two hits. They both came in the bottom of the ninth, a leadoff single by Julio Lugo and – after two outs – another intentional walk to Ortiz (the fourth time he had been walked in the game, and a record sixth intentional walk of the game) followed by a three-run walk-off homer far over everything in left field, and off Francisco Rodriguez ("K-Rod") by Manny Ramirez. Jonathan Papelbon got the win in relief.

Game Three was a close one – until it wasn't. Jered Weaver started for the Angels. In the top of the fourth he gave up back-to-back solo home runs to – guess who? – Ortiz and Ramirez. Curt Schilling started for the Sox and threw seven scoreless innings. In the top of the eighth, manager Mike Scioscia used three relievers. Scot Shields walked Lugo. Justin Speier gave up an RBI-double to Pedroia, who took third on the throw to the plate, then scored on a Youkilis sac fly. Ortiz singled, Ramirez walked. Lowell doubled and the Red Sox led 5-0. Darren Oliver came in from the bullpen. Drew hit into a run-producing fielder's choice. Varitek doubled in Lowell. Coco Crisp singled in both Drew and Varitek. The 9-0 lead was enough to win the game. The Angels scored but once, in the bottom of the ninth, off Eric Gagne.

The 2007 League Championship Series

In the meantime, as noted, the Indians beat the Yankees, and thus it was Cleveland vs. Boston in the ALCS. In four of the seven games between the two, one or another team scored 10 or more runs.

This year, it was arguably the Indians who were the underdogs – in that it had been 59 years since they had last won a World Series, back in 1948, beating the Boston Braves. Red Sox fans had only borne two years of frustration.

The Red Sox were the first to score in double digits, winning Game One at Fenway, 10-3. Josh Beckett started for the Red Sox and struck out three batters in the top of the first inning. The third of the four batters he faced was Travis Hafner, who homered, putting the Indians on the board first, 1-0. The Red Sox responded with a tying run right away.

CC Sabathia got the first out but then surrendered three consecutive singles to Youkilis, Ortiz, and Ramirez. Sabathia (who won the Cy Young Award in 2007) struck out the side in the second, but Boston took a 5-1 lead in the third. After a double, sacrifice, walk, and hit by pitch loaded the bases, Ramirez walked, earning his second RBI of the game. Mike Lowell doubled in two, and Varitek knocked in another on a groundout, third to first. Right fielder Bobby Kielty singled in two more to make it 7-1, and Tek doubled in Kielty off reliever Jensen Lewis. In the sixth, Manny accepted another bases-loaded base on balls and Lowell's sacrifice fly drove in the 10th run. Cleveland added a run in the sixth and one in the eighth, but they didn't add up to anything meaningful.

Game Two tilted the other way, Red Sox pitchers giving up 13 runs. Curt Schilling gave up the first five, and the Sox burned through eight pitchers by the time the game was over. Roberto Hernandez started for Cleveland and was actually behind, 3-1, after three innings. Remarkably, the first Red Sox run came on yet another bases-loaded walk to Manny. Lowell singled in two more. Immediately, in the top of the fourth, the Indians re-took the lead on a three-run homer by Jhonny Peralta and added one more on Grady Sizemore's solo homer in the fifth. Boston went ahead, 6-5, on a two-run Ramirez homer and a Lowell solo home run in the fifth. But then the Red Sox stopped scoring. Cleveland made it 6-6 in the top of the sixth, but then they stopped scoring, too, until the 11th inning when the Indians scored seven runs (which we won't burden Boston fans with reading about here) off three different pitchers. The game ended 13-6, Cleveland.

Game Three was at Jacobs Field, Jake Westbrook against Daisuke Matsu-zaka. A two-run Kenny Lofton homer and fifth-inning RBIs for Asdrubal Cabrera and Hafner gave Cleveland a 4-0 lead. Jason Varitek hit a two-run homer in the top of the seventh, for the only Red Sox runs. The six relievers (three for each team) all pitched hitless ball. Cleveland 4, Boston 2.

The Indians won Game Four as well, their third consecutive win, 7-3, scoring all seven runs in the bottom of the fifth in what had been a scoreless game until that point. Starter Tim Wakefield gave up three, and was then relieved by Manny Delcarmen who allowed the two runners he had inherited to score, on a three-run homer by Peralta, and then allowing another run as well. All three Red Sox runs were scored in the top of the sixth on three consecutive solo home runs – by Youkilis, Ortiz, and Ramirez.

Game Five was a Sabathia/Beckett rematch. Youkilis hit a solo homer in the top of the first. The first two Indians got on and then tied the game as one run scored on a double play. A two-out walk to Ortiz in the third was followed by a long single that Ramirez hit off the top of the wall in right field, an inch short of going out. Ortiz scored all the way from first base. In the seventh, the Sox added two runs when Pedroia doubled and Youkilis tripled off Sabathia, Youk then scoring when Ortiz hit a sacrifice fly off reliever Rafael Betancourt. The Red Sox scored three more in the eighth, on just one hit, the runs scoring on passed ball, a base on balls, and a sacrifice fly. Boston 7, Cleveland 1.

The series returned to Boston. Should the Indians win either game, they would advance and the Red Sox season would be over. Neither of the games were close ones.

The Red Sox scored four runs in the first inning of Game Six, on a grand slam which J.D. Drew hit off Roberto Hernandez. It was the third grand slam in Red Sox postseason history.[76] Schilling allowed a leadoff home in the second to Victor Martinez, but his teammates scored six more runs in the third inning. A walk, a walk, and a Drew single produced the first run. Rafael Perez relieved Hernandez. Jacoby Ellsbury singled in a run, and Lugo singled in two more. After a walk, a Youkilis single resulted in Boston's 9th and 10th runs. The Indians got a second run in the seventh; the Red Sox added two more In the eighth. The final was 12-2.

Gave Seven was somewhat nip-and-tuck through the first six innings. Matsuzaka vs. Westbrook. The Sox scored one run in each of the first three innings, and the Indians clawed one back in the fourth and one in the fifth. It was still 3-2 heading into the bottom of the seventh, until

Pedroia hit a two-run homer off Betancourt. In the bottom of the eighth, Red Sox batters put the game beyond reach. Lowell doubled and Drew singled him home. A double and intentional walk loaded the bases but Lugo whiffed for the second out. Pedroia cleared the bases with a double to center and (off Jensen Lewis) Youk homered, Pedroia scoring before him. It was 11-2, Red Sox, and they were the team that went on to the World Series.

The 2007 World Series

The Red Sox faced the red-hot Colorado Rockies. The Rockies had finished the regular season winning 14 of their final 15 games, including a tiebreaker for the Wild Card on October 1, a 9-8 walkoff over San Diego at Coors Field. It was "Rocktober" as they swept the Phillies in the Division Series, then swept the Diamondbacks in the NLCS. All told, Colorado came into their first World Series sporting a record of 21-1 from September 16 through October 15 and with seven consecutive playoff wins. Because the Rockies had swept the opposition aside, and the Red Sox needed the full seven games to beat Cleveland, the Rockies had eight days off. Arguably, the momentum could cool. They were presented a problem similar in some ways to that which had been faced by the 1946 Red Sox, having to try to stay in prime shape while not playing sufficiently challenging opposition.

In Game One, Josh Beckett started for the Red Sox and struck out each of the first three batters he faced, this time (in contrast to Game One of the ALCS) not allowing any intervening home runs. The first batter that Rockies starter Jeff Francis faced was Rookie of the Year Dustin Pedroia, who homered. The second batter he faced was Kevin Youkilis, who doubled to right. A one-out single by Ramirez allowed Youk to score. A two-out double by Drew allowed Manny to score. It was 3-0, Red Sox. Alternating strikeouts and doubles gave the Rockies one run in the top of the second. It was the only run they ever got. But the Red Sox didn't stop scoring. Ortiz doubled in Youkilis for a fourth run. Varitek's bases-loaded ground-rule double made it 6-1 in the fourth inning. Franklin Morales took over pitching for the Rockies in the fifth and he was responsible for seven more runs, all after two outs. There were RBI doubles by Youkilis and Ortiz, an RBI single by Ramirez, a record-setting eighth double by Lowell, and then another single by Drew.[77] Ryan Speier relieved Morales, with the bases still loaded. He walked Lugo, then walked Ellsbury, and then walked Pedroia. He'd faced three batters before manager Clint Hurdle replaced him, and walked each one of them, each time the walk forcing in an inherited baserunner. There was no scoring from that point on, but with a 13-1 final score the Red Sox had taken Game One. Beckett had improved to 4-0 in the 2007 postseason, with a 1.20 ERA. It was the third postseason game in a row that Boston had scored in double digits.

Red Sox pitching held the Rockies to one run in Game Two as well. Schilling gave up that one run pretty quickly. He hit the first Colorado batter – Willy Taveras. An out, single, groundout and error, and then a groundout to first, Schilling covering, let the run cross the plate. Ubaldo Jimenez shut down the Red Sox until they tied it in the fourth on a walk, single, and Varitek's sacrifice fly in the fourth. With two outs in the fifth, he walked Ortiz, gave up a single to Ramirez, and then a double to Mike Lowell. That was all it took for a 2-1 Red Sox win. Hideki Okajima threw 2⅓ perfect innings of relief, striking out four – the first Japanese-born pitcher to appear in a World Series game.

For Game Three – the first one in Denver – the Red Sox scored in double digits again. The starters were Josh Fogg and Daisuke Matsuzaka, then first Japanese-born pitcher to start a World Series game. In the top of the third, seven Boston batters got base hits and four of them picked up runs batted in. Had Manny Ramirez not been thrown out of the plate, there might have been more. Ellsbury led off with a double to left. Pedroia singled. Ortiz doubled, driving in Ellsbury. Manny was walked intentionally. Lowell singled and drove in two. Drew popped up to short. On Varitek's single, Manny tried to score but was out. Lugo walked on four pitches. Matsuzaka then helped his own cause with a two-run single. Ellsbury doubled for the second time in the inning, driving in Lugo.

Franklin Morales replaced Fogg and got the third out. It was 6-0, Red Sox. In the bottom of the sixth, Dice-K walked two and was relieved. Both scored on back-to-back singles off Javier Lopez. The Rockies got to within a run in the bottom of the seventh. Mike Timlin had allowed two singles. Hideki Okajima came in to take over and Matt Holliday hit his first pitch for a three-run homer. Boston 6, Colorado, 5. The Red Sox added three more off Brian Fuentes in the top of the eighth, Ellsbury doubling in one and Pedroia doubling in two. A ninth-inning sacrifice fly by Jason Varitek made it 10-5, the final score.

Rocktober seemed perhaps a thing of the past, but – then again – just three years earlier, the Red Sox had overcome a deficit of 0-3 by winning four postseason games in a row. Game Four was a well-fought one-run game. Boston scored once in the top of the first off Aaron Cook. Ellsbury led off with a two-base hit, took third on Pedroia's groundout, and then scored easily on Ortiz's single to right. In the fifth, Lowell doubled and Varitek singled him in. Red Sox starter Jon Lester meanwhile pitched 5⅔ scoreless innings. Cook's final pitch was to Lowell in the top of the seventh – hit out for a solo home run that gave Boston a 3-0 lead. Manny Delcarmen had taken over for the Red Sox. Brad Hawpe was first up in the Rockies seventh and he homered. Bobby Kielty was first up for the Red Sox in the eighth and he homered off Fuentes, giving the Red Sox a 4-1 lead. It was good for the Red Sox that he had, because in the bottom of the eighth, Garrett Atkins hit a two-run homer off Okajima. That brought the Rockies to within one run, down 4-3. That proved to be the final score. The Red Sox had swept the World Series – again.

After all those years of losing out, often at the last minute – pennants, tiebreakers, and World Series Game Sevens – the Red Sox had swept the World Series in 2004 and again in 2007. They were 8-0 in 21st century world championship play.

I remember telling fellow Red Sox fans – be humble. We waited a long time for the win in 2004 and now we've got two of them in a four-year stretch. Let's not become obnoxious, or boasters. There are other fan-bases who have been waiting a long time, too. Most every Red Sox fan had some sense of what it was like to be a Chicago Cubs fan. They had been waiting even longer, since 1908. Their wait was now pretty much a full 100 years. They supposedly had their curse, too – the Billy Goat Curse. Be that as it may, they had been in seven World Series, and lost every one of them – in 1910, 1918 (to the Red Sox), 1929, 1932, 1935, 1938, 1945 – and then hadn't even made it to a World Series since then. Once an additional round or two of the playoffs was added, they had participated in 1984, 1989, 1993, 2003, and this very year – 2007, when they were swept by the Diamondbacks. The Cubs finally did win a World Series in 2016, after a 108-year wait, in a series that went the full seven games, beating Cleveland. I think it's safe to say that most Red Sox fans were rooting for the Cubs.

But in 2007, it seemed important to wear the mantle well – two-time World Series champions in the current century. There was no need to taunt others – not even fans of another American League franchise about 200 miles south of Boston who had yet to win even once in the 21st century.

The 2008 postseason

The very next year, the Red Sox were back again in postseason play. They finished second in the A.L. East, just two games behind the Tampa Bay Rays. The Sox were in first place for much of April, May, and June, and tied for first on one day in September – the 15th. In the Division Series, the 95-win Red Sox faced the 100-win Los Angeles Angels of Anaheim, who led the A.L. West, finishing 21 games ahead of the second-place Texas Rangers.

Before they got to the postseason, there was the preseason, of course – spring training. And in this case an unusual situation prompted by the team's visit to Japan to open the regular season there in two games against the Oakland Athletics on March 25 and 26 in Tokyo. They won the first one, 6-5 in 10 innings, and lost the second, 5-1. They then returned to the United States and finished spring training with games against the Dodgers on March 28, 29, and 30. The game on the 29th was played at the Los Angeles Coliseum in front of the largest crowd to ever witness a baseball game – 115,300. I didn't go to that game, but I did go to Tokyo to see the two against Oakland at the Tokyo Dome as well as exhibition games the Red Sox played against the Hanshin Tigers and the Yomiuri Giants. It was great fun to see the team play the four games and the different styles of rooting the Japanese teams engendered. I took some time off to visit the tower at St. Luke's Hospital, from which former Red Sox catcher Moe Berg had shot home movies of the Tokyo skyline in 1934, which were later used during World War II to help Gen. Jimmy Doolittle plan the April 1942 bombing raid on Tokyo. I wrote up the visit for *Red Sox Magazine*.[78]

2008 American League Division Series

The Red Sox had had their way with the Angels in postseason play, regardless of what the Angels called themselves. The Red Sox won the final three games of the 1986 ALCS (beating the California Angels), then swept the 2004 ALDS (from the Anaheim Angels) and again the 2007 ALDS (after they had renamed themselves as the Los Angeles Angels of Anaheim). This year, the team from Boston (which had last changed its name 100 years earlier, in 1908) lost one of the ALDS games, but won the other three.

The Red Sox won Game One, in Anaheim. The Angels scored first, one run off Jon Lester, in the bottom of the third inning on a single, error, and a Torii Hunter single. John Lackey had finished his eighth season with the Angels. He had shut out the Sox through five, but in the sixth inning walked Kevin Youkilis and then gave up a homer to left fielder Jason Bay. It remained 2-1, Red Sox, through eight. Boston scored twice more in the top of the ninth. Jed Lowrie singled, was sacrificed to second, and scored on Jacoby Ellsbury's single. Ellsbury then stole second; he had stolen 50 bases during the season (and in 2009 stole a team-record 70.) Ortiz singled him home, and Boston soon won, 4-1.

The Red Sox exploded for four runs in the top of the first inning in Game Two, against Ervin Santana. After a pair of two-out singles, J. D. Drew doubled in David Ortiz and Jason Bay followed with a three-run homer. In the bottom of the first, three consecutive two-out singles off Red Sox starter Matsuzaka produced one run, the third single earning Torii Hunter a run batted in. In Boston's fourth, back-to-back doubles by Alex Cora and Ellsbury gave the Red Sox another run. The Angels got one back in the bottom of the fourth. Two walks and a Hunter single brought the Angels to within two runs, 5-3. They closed the gap to one run, when the Angels' Mike Napoli drew a bases-loaded walk off reliever Justin Masterson. Chone Figgins led off the eighth with a triple, then scored the tying run on Mark Teixeira's sacrifice fly. In the top of the ninth, David Ortiz doubled. Two batters later, J.D. Drew hit a two-run homer. Papelbon closed the game, and the Red Sox won, 7-5.

Back in Boston for Game Three, again the two teams entered the ninth inning tied. The starters were Josh Beckett and Joe Saunders. Figgins doubled, the first batter in the game. Beckett struck out the next two, but a walk and a single loaded the bases. He then walked right fielder Juan Rivera, giving the Angels a 1-0 lead. In the bottom of the second, Saunders loaded the bases, and then saw Ellsbury clear them with a three-run single. Napoli's two-run homer in the top of the third tied the game, 3-3. Both teams scored once in the first – Napoli hit a solo homer off Beckett and Youkilis doubled in Ellsbury. After nine innings, the score remained 4-4. Each team used six pitchers in the course of the game. In the top of the 12th, the Angels took a 5-4 lead when Napoli singled off Javier Lopez, was sacrificed to second, and then scored on a single by Erick Aybar. The Red Sox couldn't score.

Game Four (Lester vs. Lackey) was scoreless for the first four innings. In the bottom of the fifth, Ellsbury came to bat with runners on first and third, grounding out but producing a run. Pedroia then doubled for a second run. In the eighth, Torii Hunter tied it, 2-2, with a two-run single off Justin Masterson. The game entered the bottom of the ninth still tied (despite a leadoff double and a subsequent but fruitless attempt to steal home). With one out, Jason Bay doubled. With two outs, Jed Lowrie singled him home to win the game, and the Division Series for the Red Sox.

2008 American League Championship Series

Despite a pair of blowout losses at Fenway Park, the Red Sox battled the Tampa Bay Rays to Game Seven of the League Championship Series.

Game One saw James Shields and Daisuke Matsuzaka both survive runners on third base in the first inning and both throw four scoreless innings. Boston scored first, on a sacrifice fly from Jed Lowrie in the top of the fifth. In the top of the eighth, they got one more run on a double by Youkilis off reliever J.P. Howell. Tampa Bay never did score, despite four walks and four singles off Matsuzaka. None of the relievers who threw the final two innings let any Rays reach base. Red Sox 2, Rays 0.

Game Two went into extras. Scott Kazmir surrendered a two-run double to Jason Bay in the first, and Josh Beckett gave up a two-run first-inning homer to Evan Longoria. Pedroia homered to lead off the third, but the Rays made it 4-3 on a B. J. Upton homer and then a Carl Crawford single that scored Longoria, who had doubled. Tampa Bay took a 5-3 lead on a fourth-inning leadoff homer by Cliff Floyd. Three Red Sox hit solo homers in the fifth – Pedroia, Youkilis, and Bay. The Rays went ahead, 8-6, on a walk and three base hits. Jason Bay singled in a seventh Red Sox run in the top of the sixth and was at the plate in the eighth when thrown a wild pitch on which Pedroia scored from third. That made it 8-8. The Sox got two on, thanks to walks, in the top of the 11th. Mike Timlin walked the first two Rays batters he faced in the bottom of the 11th, and then an intentional walk after both baserunners had advanced on a groundout. Upton's fly ball to right was deep enough to allow the runner on third to tag and score the winning run. 9-8, Rays.

Game Three in Boston was one of the blowouts. Tampa Bay scored nine runs again. They eked out one run against Jon Lester in the second on a walk, single, passed ball, and groundout, then added four more in the next inning on a three-run homer by Upton and a solo homer by Longoria. The Red Sox scored but once, in the bottom of the seventh on a walk, single, and sacrifice fly. With Paul Byrd pitching for the Red Sox in the eighth, the Rays got three more runs on a homer by Rocco Baldelli. They added a ninth run in the ninth inning, a solo home run by Carlos Pena.

The Rays crushed the Red Sox again in Game Four, starting with three runs in the top of the first off Tim Wakefield, on a two-run homer by Pena and—two pitches later – a solo homer by Longoria. Aybar hit a two-run homer in the third, making it 5-0, Tampa Bay. Andy Sonnanstine started for the Rays. Boston catcher Kevin Cash had homered to lead off the Boston third. Aybar singled in a sixth Rays run in the sixth. In the sixth inning, the Rays scored five more runs. victimizing relievers Masterson and Lopez. By game's end, the final score was 13-4 and the Red Sox had lost three in a row. If they were to return to the World Series, they were going to have to win the next three games.

They did win Game Five. And they won despite the Rays holding a 7-0 lead at the time of the seventh-inning stretch. The starters were Dice-K and Scott Kazmir. The Rays got a two-run homer in the first by Upton and a two-run homer in the third by Carlos Pena followed by a solo home run by Longoria. And then a two-run Upton double in the top of the seventh. How many were left at Fenway after the stretch? Those who wanted to see Grant Balfour relieve Kazmir? Balfour let two Sox get on and then, with two outs, gave up an RBI single to Pedroia and a three-run homer to David Ortiz. Dan Wheeler replaced Balfour and got the third out, but in the bottom of the eighth walked Bay and gave up a two-run homer to J.D. Drew. With two outs, Mark Kotsay doubled to center and Coco Crisp singled him – the tying run – in from second base. With two outs in the bottom of the ninth, Youkilis singled and made it to second on a throwing error, then scored the winning run when Drew singled to right. The Red Sox weren't dead yet.

Game Six saw them even it up, at Tropicana Field, James Shields against Josh Beckett. Upton – again – homered for one run in the Rays' first. Youkilis homered to lead off Boston's second, then drove in another run the next time he came up to bat, in the third. In the fourth, another solo Rays four-bagger tied it, 2-2, thanks to Jason Bartlett. In the Sox sixth, Varitek homered to make it 3-2, Red Sox. Three batters later, Ortiz singled in run number 4. That was the final score, 4-2. The series went to a seventh game.

Joe Maddon entrusted the fate of the Rays to Matt Garza. Terry Francona went with Jon Lester. Garza gave up one run in the first inning, a home run by Dustin Pedroia. It was one of only two hits Garza allowed in seven innings of work. Longoria doubled in one run for the Rays in the fourth. Baldelli singled in one in the fifth. And Aybar homered to lead off the seventh. Tampa Bay won, 3-1, and went on to the World Series – their first.

They won the second game but the Philadelphia Phillies won the other four. The Red Sox had failed to repeat. As it happens, no team has won back-to-back world championships in the current century. The last team to do so was the New York Yankees, in the years 1998, 1999, and 2000. But that was the last millennium.

At the February 2009 Grammy Awards, Rounder artists Alison Krauss and Robert Plant were presented with five Grammy Awards for their 2008 release, *Raising Sand*. I'd been there when the two first met, at the Rock and Roll Hall of Fame in Cleveland at an event honoring Lead Belly (Huddie Ledbetter). They clicked and collaborated on *Raising Sand*, produced by T Bone Burnett. The album earned the exceptionally rare distinction of winning Grammys as both the 2008 Album of the Year and the 2008 Record of the Year. It won three other Grammys, as well: Best Contemporary Folk/Americana Album, Best Pop Collaboration with Vocals, and Best Country Collaboration with Vocals.

The following year, work that I myself had done was nominated for two different Grammy Awards. The project was *My Dusty Road*, a 4-CD boxed set of Woody Guthrie recordings accompanied by a book that Ed Cray and I worked on. The nominations were for Best Historical Album and Best Album Notes. We came up short in both categories, but it was indeed an honor to be nominated (plus you get this very nice medallion on a ribbon that you can wear around your neck.) Seven years later, I earned another nomination for Best Historical Album. The work was *Music of Morocco from the Library of Congress; Recorded by Paul Bowles, 1959*. Rounder itself has received 56 Grammy Awards over our first 49 years.

A travel tangent

During the second week of September 2008, I had the opportunity to visit North Korea. We were told at the time that, since 1953, fewer than 1,000 Americans had been given permission to travel there. I went with Koryo Tours, with whom I later traveled to Mongolia, Turkmenistan, Tajikistan, and a few other travel hotspots. We got to attend the Mass Games that year in Pyongyang, with 100,000 other spectators. And we got to visit the DMZ – the Demilitarized Zone – which separates North and South Korea. A considerable number of tourists visit from South Korea, but rather few from the North. It amused me to see U.S. Marines with their eyes on our small group of maybe 20 or so, observing through binoculars – and to see someone wearing a Boston Red Sox baseball cap! This must have surprised them. Maybe my photo is on file somewhere.

Two years later, I visited Yemen – and am glad I did. It soon became not a safe place to travel and has not been safe for many years now. And in 2013, before the Red Sox season got underway I visited Sudan, which as of this writing in 2023 is a place from which many are fleeing during a civil war there.

The 2009 postseason

The Red Sox did make the postseason three years in a row, doing so again in 2009. They finished second in the A.L. East, eight games behind those recently-mentioned Yankees. The 2009 Red Sox reverted to some of their old ways, swept in three games by the Angels, getting a chance to avenge their losses to Boston in 2004, 2007, and 2008.

Game One was another Lackey/Lester matchup, and Lackey allowed the Red Sox just four hits and one walk in 7⅓ innings. The game was scoreless for four innings, but Torii Hunter hit a three-run homer for the Angels in the bottom of the fifth. The Angels added two more runs in the seventh. They won, 5-0. Enough said about that.

Jered Weaver vs. Josh Beckett in Game Two. Boston scored first with one run in the top of the fourth, Ellsbury led off with a triple, then scored after an out on a single by catcher Victor Martinez. The Angels wasted no time tying the score on a pair of singles and a sacrifice fly by Kendrys Morales. In the bottom of the seventh, the Angels surged ahead on a walk, stolen base, and a single by Maicer Izturis, a hit-by-pitch, and then a two-run triple by Aybar. That was the final score: 4-1 Angels.

The Red Sox hoped to take the next two back home in Boston. They started Clay Buchholz against Scott Kazmir. They kicked off the scoring with a two-run double by Pedroia in the bottom of the third. Victor Martinez then singled in Pedroia. The Angels got one run in the fourth on a solo home run by Morales, but the Red Sox upped the score to 5-1 on a two-run homer by Drew. In the top of the sixth, Buchholz saw the bases get loaded with nobody out. Daniel Bard relieved him, and got Juan Rivera to hit into a double play, but one run scored. 5-2. Rivera singled in two in the top of the eighth off Billy Wagner and Jonathan Papelbon. It was 5-4, but Mike Lowell gave the Red Sox an insurance run with a two-out single in the bottom of the eighth. With two outs and nobody on, the Sox looked good to take the game, but Aybar singled off Papelbon, who then walked Figgins. Bobby Abreu doubled in a run. Hunter was predictably walked intentionally, but Vladimir Guerrero singled in two, giving the Angels a 7-6 lead, which they did not cough up.

The Yankees beat the Angels in a six-game ALCS and then won the 2009 World Series over the Phillies in six games. One might note that the 2009 World Series is the only one the Yankees have won in the 21st century (or third millennium, if you prefer.)

10

Another Decade and Two More Titles

Three years off

The 2010 Red Sox finished in third place, seven games behind Tampa Bay. There was no postseason play for them. The San Francisco Giants won the World Series, beating the Texas Rangers.

During that year, 2010, Ted Williams' nephew Ted Williams and I met in Mexico to visit Valle de Allende, Chihuahua, the village from which the Red Sox Hall of Famer's maternal grandparents had come. We both took part in a "Conferencia Historica" on the Patio Central de la Presidencia Municipal on July 10, 2010 in the city of Hidalgo del Parral. Invited by journalist Ricardo Urquidi Espinoza, we talked of the Hall of Fame ballplayer's background. We also took in a Mexican League baseball game.[79]

The 2011 Red Sox, still managed by Terry Francona, also finished third, again seven games behind the leader in the East, this time that being the Yankees. The Tigers beat in the Yankees, the Rangers beat the Tigers, and the St. Louis Cardinals beat the Rangers in the World Series.

The 2012 Red Sox finished in last place. They had a new manager, Bobby Valentine. The team finished 69-96, a .426 winning percentage – their lowest since 1960. The most any pitcher won was 11 games – a distinction shared by Clay Buchholz and Felix Doubront. They lost 12 of their last 13 games. They finished 26 games out of first place in the A.L. East. The Yankees finished first, but were swept by the Tigers in the second

Visiting Parral, and with Parral cap on, immediately in
front of Ted Williams' nephew – also known as Ted – at
a Mexican League baseball game.

round of the playoffs. The Tigers were, in turn, swept by the Giants in the
World Series.

Somehow the last-place Red Sox managed to sell out every 2012 game
at Fenway Park all season long. Masochists? Perhaps just people who
had planned ahead. Fenway held the record for most consecutive games
sold out, a streak that began on May 15, 2003 and lasted for 820 games,
including postseason games. It's not hard to understand why seasons such
as 2003 and 2004 sold out. And the Red Sox did make the postseason in
2005, 2007, 2008, and 2009. The streak was the longest in U.S. professional sports history and extended through Opening Day 2013. But the
second game of the 2013 season fell about 7,000 short of selling out.

Why would fans keep flocking to Fenway throughout the 2012 season? A
couple of reasons come to mind. Chances are that – knowing seats could
be very hard to come by for the previous nine seasons – fans just bought
tickets well in advance, before the season collapsed in on itself. The 2012
Red Sox actually had a winning record through July – just barely. They
were 53-51, 7 ½ games back, and a game and a half ahead of Toronto.

Their August record, though, was 9-20 and they were then 7-22 through the end of the season, a finish of 16-42.

Another reason – 2012 was the ballpark's 100th anniversary year, too. Fenway Park had opened in 1912. It had seen a lot. It had survived more than one discussion about replacing it, most recently in the stretch from 1999-2001 where there were even models displayed of an envisioned new park, to be constructed across Jersey Street from the current park. The group Save Fenway Park! mobilized. When the Henry-Werner-Lucchino new ownership group arrived in 2002, their thoughts were firmly fixed on to truly saving Fenway Park, not replacing it. For the 100th anniversary game, the Red Sox brought to Boston every former Red Sox player who wished to come. More than 200 former players, coaches, and managers attended, individually introduced while strolling in from under the center-field bleachers. It was my pleasure to watch the game from an upstairs box with Johnny Pesky and Bobby Doerr. The Red Sox have always been particularly good with alumni relations and for nearly 20 years, until her passing, Debbie Matson produced *Diamond Days*, a color magazine which was sent to all alumni. I enjoyed every issue, and writing the occasional article for it.

Fenway's sold-out games streak did indeed end (finishing in last place in 2012 might have had something to do with that), and yet 2013 turned out to be quite a surprise of a year, a year in which many people who did not fully populate the seats soon wished that they had.

I kept busy writing, of course. In 2008, Rounder Books published one of my personal favorite books, *Red Sox Threads*. At 545 pages, it's one of my thicker ones. It was subtitled "Odds and Ends from Red Sox History" and I basically just ran down the story behind any quirky thing that struck me – things like the first Red Sox player of Native American ancestry, the first manager to commit suicide, the first relatives to play for the team, the eight states in which the Red Sox have never played a game, etc. etc. I've kept up the database on which that book is built and I'd guess the word count has grown to become about 20% longer than it was for the book itself.

Bobby Doerr, Bill Nowlin, and Johnny Pesky at June 2010 dedication of "The Teammates" statue by Gate B.

My proclivity for lists – which dates back to childhood, even point-lessly keeping lists of easily-found things like the longest rivers in the world – has paid off in other ways, for instance in my database of Red Sox uniform numbers. They didn't even have numbers on their uni-forms before 1931. But since then, more than 1,500 Red Sox players have been assigned numbers, ranging from 0 to 99. Some are retired, of course, but if you wanted to know who was the first to wear #9 before Ted Williams, you could consult the 2010 book *Red Sox By the Numbers*, which was apparently popular enough that a new edition came out in 2018. The year 2023 was a quite active one, with 39 new num-bers being assigned from Opening Day through the end of the season. And that doesn't even count Norwith Gudiño. It was on June 24th that the Sox assigned #77 to Caleb Hamilton. Just the day before, they had assigned #70 to David Hamilton. In the preceding 122-plus years, there had never been a Hamilton on the Red Sox, but now there were ones added on back-to-back days. Wait – who was Norwith Gudiño? He was a right-handed pitcher from Venezuela, who had been in the minors since 2015, and was brought to the big leagues by Boston on July 22, summoned from the Triple-A Worcester Red Sox but who never appeared in a game.

That's indicative of astonishing roster churn, and doesn't count the many others who already had numbers and were shuttled this way and that throughout the season.

The 2013 Red Sox season

John Farrell was named the new Red Sox manager. The team got off to a strong start, going 18-8 in April. There was a brief stretch in May when they were *not* in first place, but only for one day were they more than two games back. There was a stretch in late July where they were edged out of first place, but not by more than a half-game. From August 1 on, they were in first place, tied or in sole possession. With a record of 16-9 in September, they pulled a bit ahead of the pack and finished 5½ games ahead of second-place Tampa Bay.

The team had gone from worst to first. They faced Tampa Bay in the Division Series. They were 12-7 against the Rays but there were certainly no guarantees. After all, their record in five postseason series from 1988 through 1999 had been 2-18. Yes, they had two World Series championships in 2004 and 2007 but that's no guarantee of anything at all. In 2005, as reigning champions, they were swept in the Division Series. In 2008, as reigning champions, they lost the ALCS and the very next year were again swept in the Division Series. But to have gone from 69 wins in 2012 to 97 wins in 2013, from winning 43% of their games to winning 66% gave a team confidence.

And this was an unusual team. Unlike a collection of ballplayers wearing the same uniform, as they had been in 2012, the 2013 Red Sox were a *team*. They forged an identity early on, as the "Band of Bearded Brothers."

Indeed, after the season, NESN released a film by that very title. There were a few books written on the subject as well.[80]

Monday, April 15 was the sixth and final game of the team's first home-stand of the season. They had swept Tampa Bay on Saturday the 13th, Shane Victorino's walkoff single winning 2-1 in the 10th and then won on the 11:05 A.M. Patriots Day game on the 15th, too. They had led 2-1 through eight, but then saw the Rays tie it in the top of the ninth. With one out in the bottom of the ninth, Pedroia walked and Mike Napoli (now with the Red Sox, after playing for the Angels against them in the postseason of 2007, 2008, and 2009) doubled to left-center for another walkoff win. The game ended a few minutes after 2:00 P.M. Less than an hour later, as they were headed to Cleveland for the next night's game, the Red Sox learned that at 2:49 two bombs had exploded near the finish line of the Boston Marathon. The bombs killed three people and injured more than 260 others, with 16 ultimately losing their legs.

A hunt was on for the bombers. They killed a policeman at M.I.T. in Cambridge but eluded capture for a few days. The city – and much of Greater Boston – was urged to "shelter in place" and only the occasional Dunkin Donuts was open, as much as anything to supply sustenance to more than 1,000 law enforcement personnel engaged in the manhunt.

Four days later, I was on the phone with my ex-wife Yleana, who lived a few miles away in Watertown. We were talking about my bringing our son over to her from where he had been with me in Cambridge. A police-woman had told her it was probably OK, though the night before – just about a mile away from her house – was where the two Tzarnaev broth-ers now suspected in the bombing were stopped by police. One escaped by car, running over his brother in the process. The one who had been shot and then run over did not survive. We had been talking on the phone and she suddenly said, "That sounds like gunshots." The brother who had escaped was captured about three blocks from her house.

After a brief three-day trip to Cleveland, the Red Sox came back to Boston. No one who lived through those several days will ever forget it. And even though the players hailed from all over, with several of them born in other countries, there were bonds formed by going through this experience. The very day after the second bomber was captured, the Red Sox played an afternoon game at Fenway Park. There was time taken to silently remember those who had been killed. David Ortiz took the field and uttered his immediately-famous speech, which included the words, "This is our (expletive) city. And nobody's going to dictate our freedom. Stay strong."

Boston Strong became a motto, for all those in the region.

The 2013 postseason

The Red Sox did finish first in the East. They faced Tampa Bay in the Division Series.

The first game was something of a blowout. Two left-handers squared off, Jon Lester (15-8, 3.75) started for the Red Sox and Matt Moore (17-4, 3.29) for Tampa Bay. Lester had started two games against the Rays in the 2008 ALCS and lost then both – Game Three and Game Seven. In this one, he pitched the first 7⅔ innings allowing just three base hits and two runs. Those two runs had given the Rays a 2-0 lead, the first on a second-inning homer by Sean Rodriguez and the other on a leadoff homer by Ben Zobrist in the top of the fourth. Moore hadn't allowed a hit for the first three innings, though he hit one batter, walked another, and threw a wild pitch. In the bottom of the fourth, Dustin Pedroia led off with a single. David Ortiz hit a ground-rule double to right. After one out, left fielder Jonny Gomes doubled in both baserunners, tying the game. Stephen Drew singled in Gomes. Will Middlebrooks doubled in Drew. And Shane Victorino singled in Middlebrooks. It was 5-2, Red Sox. The Rays didn't score again, but the Red Sox scored seven more times. Jerrod Saltalamacchia doubled in two in the fifth and Ellsbury singled in Salty. Boston added four more runs in the eighth, Victorino singled in one, Napoli drew a bases-loaded walk, Gomes hit into a double play but one that saw a run score, and Saltalamacchia singled in another run. The final was 12-2, Red Sox.

Game Two featured John Lackey for Boston. He had been 1-2 in four postseason starts against the Red Sox while with the Angels. In 2013, his third season with the Red Sox, he'd actually lost more games than he had won (10-13, 3.52). Starting for Tampa Bay was David Price, a three-time All-Star who had won the A.L. Cy Young Award in 2012 with a record of 20-5 and a 2.56 ERA. In 2013, he had been 10-8 (3.33) but led the league with a 5.59 strikeouts/walks ratio. The Red Sox got a quick two runs in the bottom of the first on a sacrifice fly by Pedroia and a solo homer by Ortiz. The Rays got one back in the second, but gave up two more in the third. Ellsbury doubled in one, then scored on a later groundout by Pedroia. Drew drove in a fifth run on a triple in the fourth. James Loney made it 5-3, with a two-run double for Tampa Bay in the fifth, but Pedroia doubled in another Red Sox run. Ortiz led off the bottom of the eighth, homering off Price and knocking him out of the game. It ended 7-4, Red Sox.

The Sox held a 3-0 lead in Game Three at the midpoint, after a single, hit-by-pitch, and groundout gave them one off Alex Cobb in the top of the first, and they added two more in the fifth, one on a wild pitch by Cobb and the other on an Ortiz single to left field. With one swing of the bat, Even Longoria homered off starter Buchholz and tied the game, 3-3. The Rays pushed across a run in the bottom of the eighth on a bases-loaded groundout, but Boston fought back and tied it with a run of their own in the top of the ninth, likewise on a groundout. With two outs in the bottom of the ninth, Jose Lobaton won the game for Tampa Bay with a home run off Koji Uehara – a 5-4 walkoff.

The Rays led in Game Four, but by the slimmest of margins – 1-0 – after six full innings. Neither team scored through the first five. Jake Peavy was pitching for the Red Sox and the Rays run came on a double by Yunel Escobar and then a single by David DeJesus. The Rays used nine pitchers in the game. It was their fifth one – Jake McGee – who started the seventh. To that point, the Red Sox had just three base hits – all singles. After one out, McGee walked pinch-hitter Xander Bogaerts. After two outs, Ellsbury singled and Bogaerts went

Kathy Gould, Fenway Park's first woman usher, began in 1981 and was still working in 2023. I wrote about her for *Diehard* in 2012.

first to third. Joel Peralta replaced McGee. Ellsbury stole second, while Peralta threw a wild pitch on which Bogaerts scored, Ellsbury taking third base, from where he scored on a soft infield single by Victorino. That gave the Red Sox a 2-1 lead. They added one more in the ninth when Fernando Rodney managed to load the bases on two walks and a hit-by-pitch. Chris Archer replaced Rodney and Pedroia lined a sacrifice fly to right field. The final was 3-1, Red Sox. They took on the Tigers in the ALCS.

The 2013 American League Championship Series

Jim Leyland's Tigers had won the Central, then played a five-game Division Series against Oakland.

Detroit's Anibal Sanchez led the league with a 2.57 ERA; his record was 14-8. He came to Fenway Park for Game One and, though he walked six batters in the six innings he pitched, he didn't allow even one base hit. Jon Lester only walked one, but he allowed the only run of the game, in the top of the sixth, on a walk to Miguel Cabrera, a hit-by-pitch, and a single to Jhonny Peralta. Sanchez and three relievers no-hit the Red Sox through eight innings. Daniel Nava broke up the no-hitter with one out in the bottom of the ninth, but the Red Sox were shut out in a one-hitter, 1-0.

Things were looking pretty bleak for Boston in Game Two as well. Clay Buchholz vs. Max Scherzer. The Tigers scored one run early, and then added four more in the top of the sixth on a solo homer by Cabrera, an RBI double by Victor Martinez, and a two-run homer by Alex Avila. It was 5-0, Detroit. With two outs in the bottom of the sixth, Victorino singled and Pedroia doubled and Boston had one run. So it remained until the bottom of the eighth. 5-1. With one out, Middlebrooks doubled. Manager Jim Leyland brought in another pitcher, who walked Ellsbury. Leyland brought in another pitcher who struck out Victorino but then saw Pedroia double, loading the bases. Leyland brought in another pitcher – Joaquin Benoit. Ortiz swung at the first pitch and homered – a grand slam into the Red Sox bullpen. It was more late-inning Ortiz magic and it produced a fan-favorite Fenway photograph of Boston police officer Steve Horgan raising both arms in exultation while Detroit right fielder Torii Hunter's two legs were also vertical in a "V" as he tumbled headfirst into the bullpen. The game was tied. Rick Porcello worked the bottom of the ninth for the Tigers. Gomes reached on a single, taking second on a throwing error, and then third on a wild pitch. On the next pitch, Saltalamacchia singled and Gomes scored the winning run. It was an odd feature of the game that Detroit's six pitchers had each allowed just one run. Add them up and it was Boston 6, Detroit 5.

Game Three was, like Game One, another 1-0 game. This time it was won by the Red Sox. Both starters went deep – Lackey for the Red Sox (6⅔ innings) and Justin Verlander for the Tigers (8 innings), and both allowed but four base hits. The hit that made the difference was a one-out solo home run by Mike Napoli in the top of the seventh. The Tigers left two runners on base in the first inning, two in the seventh, and two in the eighth, but never got one across home plate.

The Tigers evened the series at Comerica Park in Game Four, scoring five runs off Jake Peavy in the second inning and two more in the fourth, before being pulled. The Red Sox got three runs in the game, again one run each off three different pitchers – one in the sixth, one in the seventh, and one in the top of the ninth. 7-3, Detroit.

Sanchez, who had been so strong in Game One, proved mortal in Game Five. Mike Napoli homered off him, leading off the second inning. Gomes reached on an error. Bogaerts doubled. Catcher David Ross then doubled, too, and Ellsbury singled to drive in Bogaerts. In the third inning, Napoli doubled, then went to third on a ball hit back to Sanchez and scored on a wild pitch. 4-0, Red Sox. Detroit scored one run each in the fifth, sixth, and seventh – the first two charged to starter Jon Lester and the third coming in on a double play, charged to reliever Junichi Tazawa. The final was 4-3.

The series came back to Boston for Game Six. Buchholz vs. Scherzer. Neither team scored for the first four innings. The Red Sox got one run in the bottom of the fifth, after two outs, when Bogaerts doubled and Ellsbury singled. After walking Torii Hunter and giving up a single to Miguel Cabrera, Buchholz was pulled in favor of Franklin Morales – who walked Prince Fielder on four pitches and then gave up a two-run single to Victor Martinez. Brandon Workman took over from Morales and got a double play and a strikeout, but Detroit led, 2-1. In the bottom of the seventh, Jonny Gomes doubled off Scherzer who, with one out, walked Bogaerts. Drew Smyly came in to pitch to Ellsbury and might have had a double play but for an error by the shortstop, which let the Red Sox fill the bases. Jose Veras relieved Smyly. On an 0-2 pitch, the Flyin' Hawaiian – Shane Victorino – hit a grand slam. Just like that, the Red Sox had gone from a 2-1 deficit to a 5-2 lead. The Tigers had two more innings in which they could have scored, but never got the ball out of the infield, Craig Breslow retiring the side in order in the eighth and Koji Uehara permitting just a single to shortstop in the ninth.

It was on to the World Series again, though it had been a long six years since the last one.

The 2013 World Series

The Red Sox faced the St. Louis Cardinals again, the team that had beaten them in 1946 and 1967, but who the Red Sox had swept in 2004. Mike Matheny managed them in 2013 and they had to battle; from August 14 on, they never held a lead of more than two games in the N.L. Central — until the final four days. They won the division by three games. The Cards had beaten the Phillies, three games to two, in the NLDS and the Dodgers, four games to two, in the NLCS. They were battle-tested and ready.

Game One was at Fenway, Jon Lester against Adam Wainwright (19-9, 2.94). Those 19 wins led the National League. Mike Napoli came up with the bases loaded in the bottom of the first and two-hopped a ball off the base of the wall in left-center for a bases-clearing double, and the Red Sox had a quick 3-0 lead. The Sox loaded the bases again in the second, adding two more runs on a single by Pedroia and a sacrifice fly by Ortiz. Lester pitched 7⅔ innings, allowing five scattered hits but no runs. The Cardinals called on their fifth pitcher of the game, Kevin Siegrist, in the seventh. His first pitch to David Ortiz was hit for a two-run homer. Boston added another run in the eighth, and entered the ninth with a lead of 8-0. Matt Holliday hit a leadoff home run off Ryan Dempster. The game ended with an 8-1 Red Sox win.

Jon Lester pitched for the Red Sox in Game Two. Rookie Michael Wacha had only appeared in 15 regular-season games, but was 4-1 (2.78). He was unbeaten in three postseason games, winning Game Four of the Division Series and Games Two and Six of the NLCS. He allowed one run in his NLDS start and threw 13⅔ innings of shutout ball in the two NLCS games. He was pretty stingy in this game, too, working six full innings and allowing but two runs. In the fourth, Holliday had tripled and then scored on a groundout hit by Yadier Molina. The two runs the Red Sox scored came on a two-run homer by David Ortiz in the bottom of the sixth. That gave Boston a 2-1 lead, but the Cards responded in the seventh with three runs on a walk, single, and walk, followed by a sacrifice fly that led to two errors – one by the catcher and one by the pitcher – and two runs scoring. A fourth run followed and the Tigers won, 4-2.

The Cardinals won the first game at Busch Stadium. Joe Kelly started for St. Louis and Jake Peavy for Boston. Kelly struck out the first Boston batter, then participated in back-to-back groundouts, 1-3 and 3-1. The first three Cards jumped on Peavy with a classic single, sacrifice bunt, and single (by Holliday) for their first run. Matt Adams and Yadier Molina both singled, too, and St. Louis led, 2-0. For the first three innings, Kelly never saw a ball hit past the infield. Bogaerts led off Boston's fifth with a triple, scoring three batters later when Mike Carp (pinch-hitting for Peavy) grounded into a force play at second base. Boston tied it, 2-2, in the sixth on an RBI single by Daniel Nava. Holliday's two-run double in the St. Louis seventh gave them a 4-2 lead. Nava and Bogaerts both picked up RBIs in the eighth, tying the game again. The Cardinals won it in the bottom of the ninth on an obstruction call. There was a one-out single by Molina, a double by Allen Craig, and then a play on which Jon Jay hit to second base and into a fielder's choice. The throw went home and Molina was out at the plate. Saltalamacchia threw to Middlebrooks at third base, but Craig slid into third, upending Middlebrooks and the throw went down the line. Craig tried to run home, stumbled over Middlebrooks, but even then the throw home seemed to get Craig, too – but the umpires called obstruction on the play and ruled Craig was entitled to come home safely. And thus won the game, 5-4.

The Red Sox evened it up again, in Game Four. The starters were Lance Lynn and Clay Buchholz. The Cards scored first on a single, error, and single in the third inning. In the top of the fifth, Ortiz doubled and the next two batters walked. Bases loaded with nobody out, but the only run came on Stephen Drew's sac fly. It did tie the game, 1-1. In the sixth, Lynn got two outs but then Pedroia singled and Ortiz walked. Matheny brought Seth Maness in to relieve, and he gave up a three-run homer to Jonny Gomes. St. Louis got a second run in the seventh, but a parade of relievers – including John Lackey in the eighth – kept them otherwise scoreless. 4-2, Boston.

The Red Sox scored first in Game Five. Adam Wainwright struck out three Red Sox batters in the first inning but in between the first one and the other two, Pedroia and Ortiz hit back-to-back doubles. In the bottom of the fourth, Holliday hit a solo homer off Jon Lester. It remained 1-1 through six. With one out in the seventh, Bogaerts singled and Drew walked. David Ross then doubled in the go-ahead run. Lester grounded out back to Wainwright. Ellsbury singled and Drew scored, but Ross tried to score, too, and was thrown out at the plate. Lester worked all but the final four outs, those secured by Koji. With that, the Red Sox had won, 3-1.

For Game Six, the two teams returned to Fenway. The starters were the same as in Game Two – Lackey and Wacha. Would the Series go to seven games or could the Red Sox wrap it up in Game Six? Both teams got runners on in the second – the Cardinals had runners on second and third but Lackey struck out Jon Jay, while the Red Sox had runners on first and second and nobody out, but two foul popups and a strikeout ended that. Boston scored first, in the bottom of the third inning, three runs on a bases-loaded double by Shane Victorino. They added three more in the fourth. Drew led off with a homer. With runners on first and third, and two outs, Lance Lynn relieved Wacha. Napoli singled in one. Gomes walked. Victorino singled in their sixth run. Once again, he had driven in four runs in a clinching game, as he had in Game Six of the ACLS. The two hits raised him to a .154 batting average in the 2013 World Series, but they were key hits. And provided enough. Lackey was touched for one run in the seventh. The Red Sox won the game, 6-1, and won the World Series – for the third time in 10 years – in six games.

The 86-year drought between Red Sox world championships had ended in 2004. This win on October 30 was the first time they had won a World Series at home since 1918 – it had been 95 years since the Red Sox had won a World Series at Fenway Park.

David Ortiz hit .688 (11-for-16) in the World Series and was named MVP. With eight walks, he had reached base 19 times in 25 plate appearances for an on-base percentage of .760.

And this team was all the more remarkable because the Red Sox had gone from worst to first – last place in the division in 2012 to first place in 2013 – and all the way to a world championship. What happened the next year? 2014? It was back to worst. They had been 26 games out of first in 2012 and, while one could quibble by comparing 2014 to 2012 and noting they were "only" 25 games out – an improvement of one game in the standings – it wasn't really something that had Red Sox fans bursting with pride.

Whatever they did in 2014, though, probably paled next to the big accomplishment of the year before – they had won three World Series championships in 10 years!

Rounder Records is sold – and more books get written

The final photo of the Founders before the company was moved to Nashville by its new owners in 2013 (Liza Levy).

Ken and Marian and I had sold Rounder Records in April 2010 to Concord Records. There was a three-year interim period while Concord reassured themselves that the deal was a good one, and we all worked together for those three years, with us operating out of a warehouse and office building we owned in Burlington, Massachusetts. Since we were the only building on the street, bizarrely and grandiosely named Commonwealth Executive Drive, I went to town meeting at one point and successfully requested that the street be renamed Rounder Way. (There had always been talk about the company did things "the Rounder Way," so it fit.) Even a full 10 years after we sold the properties and left, one can still find the address on maps: 1 Rounder Way, Burlington, MA 01803.

In 2013, Concord moved everything (except us) to Nashville. We remained involved, to a degree, under a nice arrangement which allowed us to produce a few albums each year and have them released on Rounder. We had a few successes and had the opportunity to work with some new groups, such as the Po' Ramblin' Boys, who played straightforward traditional-style bluegrass. Once the pandemic hit in 2020, things understandably took a different direction.

I did have more time to go to baseball games, and became more active with SABR's publishing program. The first book in the SABR Digital Library (all books available in electronic formats, as well as in paperback) was published in December 2011: *Can He Play? A Look at Baseball Scouts and Their Profession*, edited by Jim Sandoval and myself. The book gathered together articles from 26 different SABR members and launched a series of multi-author collaborative works that provides both an outlet for – over the past dozen years – a few hundred SABR authors and also a nice variety of books (typically 6-8 per year) adding to baseball lore. All these books are completely free to SABR members, a real benefit of membership.[81] I became VP of SABR in 2004 (that memorable year) and then served on the Board for many years.

I had kept writing books and editing books, some about music: *Woody Guthrie: American Radical Patriot* and *The Early Days of Bluegrass* among them. The Early Days project resulted in a 6-CD set and a 203-page book, which were released in 2019. It drew on research that Ken, Marian, and I had done in Rounder's first few years, traveling around the South and trying to locate and interview a number of the early artists who had recorded singles – 78s and 45s – for a number of small, regional record labels. We had released 10 individual albums back then; the music all fit on six compact discs. The Early Days of Bluegrass set was created to help raise funds for the Bluegrass Country Foundation. But most of the books I worked on were about baseball. After the book Jim Prime and I wrote about Ted Williams came out, longtime season ticket holder Lib Dooley (her father went back to the days *before* Fenway Park!) asked me what I was going to do next. She suggested a book on Johnny Pesky. I spent many hours talking with Johnny and in 2004 we all saw *Mr. Red Sox: The Johnny Pesky Story* get published.

I spent a lot of time just hanging around the ballpark talking to people, and was inspired to write a book on the many people who worked there – from VPs and other in the administration to ticket takers to ushers to those working the manual scoreboard, working in the clubhouse, on the grounds crew, in concessions, in media relations, in security, etc. You name it. If they worked at Fenway, I tried to ask what the work was like. I even interviewed a couple of scalpers, who (in their own way) "worked" outside Fenway Park. The book *Fenway Lives* offers 179 different interviews. It was also published in 2004.

Two from 2013 were *521: The Story of Ted Williams' Home Runs* (Rounder Books, 2013) and *New Century, New Team: The 1901 Boston Americans* (SABR, 2013).

Of course, Jim and I had to tell the story of the 2013 season, so the following year came *From The Babe to the Beards*. Allan Wood and I collaborated on a 10th anniversary look at the 2004 team: *Don't Let Us Win Tonight: An Oral History of the 2004 Boston Red Sox's Impossible Playoff Run* (Triumph Books), for which we interviewed most of the players on the 2004 team – and others, such as Dr. Bill Morgan, who did Curt Schilling's surgery. And for SABR, I edited a look at another baseball championship team from Boston, joining 38 other authors in *The Miracle Braves of 1914: Boston's Original Worst-to-First World Series Champions*.

The 2014 and 2015 seasons

Well, it was nice while it lasted. Worst to first…and then right back to worst. The 2012 Red Sox finished in last place in the A.L. East. The 2013 Red Sox were world champions. The 2014 Red Sox finished in last place in the A.L. East. In 2012, the 69-win team finished 26 games behind the first-place Yankees. In 2014, the 71-win team finished 25 games behind the first-place Orioles. There wasn't a single month in which the Red Sox had a winning record, though in April they had been 13-13.

In June, I enjoyed another personal travel experience – again cashing in frequent flyer miles and heading to Fairbanks, Alaska for the Midnight Sun Game. Since the sun never sets in Alaska at the time of the summer solstice, the game started at 10:37 P.M.– and is played without lights. It was a fun experience. I noted at the time that a base on balls in the later innings prompted those running the sound system to play Patsy Cline's country classic "Walking After Midnight." The Goldpanners beat the Lake Erie Monarchs, 13-6. It ended at 1:14 A.M. The day before, I took a quick day trip to Coldfoot, north of the Arctic Circle – just to do it.

The 2014 World Series winners were the San Francisco Giants. The Giants had alternated each year, winning it all in 2010, 2012, and then 2014. This gave them three championships in the 21st century – the same as the Red Sox. Sharing the laurels was perhaps not a bad thing, for keeping Red Sox fans a bit humbler. If a little bragging seemed tempting, one could note that the two teams had only faced each other once in World Series play, and Boston had prevailed. The Giants were, of course, the team the Red Sox had beaten in 1912, when the team was based in New York.

In 2015, the Red Sox finished last again, though "only" 15 games out of first place. The Yankees had earned a Wild Card game against the Astros, but were shut out, 3-0. Ultimately, the Kansas City Royals beat the New York Mets in the World Series. The Royals hadn't won one since 1985. They'd taken the 2014 Series to a seventh game but lost to San Francisco.

Of course, the Mets hadn't won one since 1986 (ahem). But Royals fans had been waiting a year more.

The 2016 postseason

Worst to first was pretty special; it had never happened before in American League history until the 2013 Red Sox did it. And then the 2016 Red Sox did it again!

Yes, in 2016, somehow, the Red Sox were first in the East once more – at the end of another worst-to-first campaign, still under the guiding hand of manager John Farrell. They won 93 games in the regular season, but not the three games they needed to advance to the ALCS. There was, nonetheless, postseason baseball at Fenway Park – for one game.

The Cleveland Indians hosted the Red Sox for the first two games of the Division Series. Their starting pitcher was Trevor Bauer. Boston's starter was Rick Porcello, who had pitched for the Tigers from 2008-2014 and faced all of two Red Sox batters in Game Two of the 2013 ALDS, them both getting hits and walking off with a win. Now he was pitching for Boston and coming off a phenomenal year (22-4, 3.16, the American League's Cy Young Award winner. His 22 wins topped both leagues. Looking ahead, we can see that in the pandemic-abbreviated 2020 season, Bauer won the NL CY Young Award, but in April 2022 he was suspended for allegations of sexual assault and the Dodgers released him at the beginning of 2023.

First to face Bauer was Pedroia, who doubled, later scoring on a double by Hanley Ramirez, but the runner behind Pedroia – Brock Holt – was thrown out at the plate. 1-0, Red Sox, the lone run matched by Cleveland in the second. The Red Sox re-established the lead in the third on a leadoff homer by Andrew Benintendi – but Porcello then gave up three solo homers in the bottom of the third – to Roberto Perez, Jason Kipnis, and Francisco Lindor. There were a couple more homers to come. Red

Sox catcher Sandy Leon hit one to lead off the fifth and Holt hit one to lead off the eighth, but in between Perez had singled off Porcello in the fifth, and scored on a Kipnis single off reliever Drew Pomeranz – it gave them a 5-3 lead and the Holt homer left the score where it ended: 5-4, Cleveland.

In Game Two, the Red Sox didn't score any runs at all. Starter Corey Kluber (who won the Cy Young Award the next year, in 2017) held Boston to just three base hits over the seven innings he worked – singles in the first, fifth, and sixth. The Indians meanwhile built up a 6-0 lead off David Price, who had pitched against Boston for Tampa Bay in 2013. A second-inning three-run homer by right fielder Lonnie Chisenhall was the biggest blow.

The third game was in Boston, Clay Buchholz against Josh Tomlin. After Cleveland batters singled and walked to lead off the fourth, a sacrifice bunt to Buchholz put two runners in scoring position. Tyler Naquin then singled and gave the Indians a 2-0 lead. Xander Bogaerts singled with one out in the Red Sox fifth, then scored on Benintendi's double. Coco Crisp (who had been with the Red Sox from 2006-2008, and had a 2007 ring to show for it) hit a two-run homer off Pomeranz in the top of the sixth. The 4-1 lead was trimmed by a David Ortiz sacrifice fly in the bottom of the sixth, and the Sox crept another run closer in the eighth on a single Hanley Ramirez hit, driving in Mookie Betts. 4-3 was how the game ended and the Red Sox season was over. Swept again.

Cleveland beat the Toronto Blue Jays in a five-game ALCS and then went on to play the Chicago Cubs in the World Series. It was a battle of underdogs, for sure, Cleveland not having won a World Series since 1948 – a 68-year wait – and the Cubs not having won one for more than a century, since 1908, a wait of 108 years. The Cubs won in seven games (three of them decided by one run, and Game Seven in the 10th inning when the Cubs scored twice and the Indians just once), and most Red Sox fans were very happy for them – and their fans.

During a good part of the year, I worked on a history of the BoSox Club. It was founded in 1966-67. during a time that fans were discouraged. The Sox had not done well for years, and lost 90 games in 1966. But –with Dom DiMaggio as its first president – a number of local businessmen formed a "booster club" to try and support the team. Sox PR director Bill Crowley and broadcaster Ken Coleman were involved in the founding. Its first meeting was held in 1967 – and we know what happened that year! Come 2017, as the 50th anniversary of the BoSox Club approached, I was one of the board members and decided to write a history of the club. I reached out to similar clubs supporting a few other teams. The Wahoo Club in Cleveland was one, and Ken Coleman had been a member of that club while working there. But there weren't many of them. The BoSox Club was a pretty venerable one, in the tradition of the Royal Rooters and a few other early Red Sox booster clubs. I ended up writing *The BoSox Club 50 Years*, published by Rounder Books in 2017. It wasn't a bestseller, of course, but it documented a side of Red Sox fandom that had not been written before.

Another personal tangent: If you were to have visited the Hall of Fame any time after September 29, 2016, you might have noticed that I was inducted in the Hall of Fame on that date. No, not the Hall in Cooperstown. The one in Owensboro, Kentucky. Never been there? It's a very nice place. It also happens to be the hometown of major-league umpire Larry Vanover. What hall of fame is in Owensboro? Why, the Bluegrass Music Hall of Fame! Ken and Marian and I ("The Rounders") were inducted on that date, the presentation being made by John Virant – who, while not a founder, joined us years later and became so integral to our ongoing success that we dubbed him the "fourth Rounder") – and Alison Krauss. At one point, in the early 1980s, I had finished my doctorate in political science. By the time I finished it, I was on my way out of teaching and the biggest motivation I had was just so that (a throwback to Bugs Bunny cartoons) maybe some would hail me: "Hey, Doc." I can't say that anyone ever did. But now I was a Hall of Famer.

The 2017 postseason

For the ninth time in the first 17 years of the new century, the Red Sox saw some postseason play. The 93-69 Sox finished first in the East again, just two games ahead of the Yankees. They played the 101-win Houston Astros in the ALDS. The first three games were all lopsided, but the fourth one went down to the wire.

Game One was Houston's Justin Verlander against Boston's Chris Sale. With the Tigers, Verlander had won Rookie of the Year in 2006 and then both the Cy Young and MVP in 2011. He'd placed second in the Cy Young voting just the year before, in 2016. He'd come to the Astros via trade on August 31, 2017 and been 5-0 for them in five September starts, with a 1.06 ERA. Sale had been 74-50 with the White Sox, and was traded to the Red Sox in December 2016. He was 17-8 (3.29) in 2017 and finished second in the Cy Young voting. Sale, though, gave up seven earned runs in five innings, the first two on back-to-back first-inning homers by Alex Bergman and Jose Altuve. Altuve hit another homer off Sale in the fifth, and a third one leading off the bottom of the seventh, off Austin Maddox. Verlander gave up just two runs in six innings. Houston 8, Boston 2.

The second game was the same score, 8-2. Dallas Keuchel was 14-5 (2.90) during the regular season, and an All-Star. Drew Pomeranz's 17 wins tied him with Sale for most of the Red Sox. He finished 17-6 (3.32). With two outs in the first, Altuve singled and his infield partner, shortstop Carlos Correa, homered. Jackie Bradley Jr. singled in a run for the Red Sox in the second, but the Astros got another two in the bottom of the third on a leadoff homer by George Springer and an RBI single by Altuve. It was almost as if Altuve knew what pitches were coming. (Sorry about that; I couldn't resist. See the afterword at the end of this 2017 section.) The Astros got four more in the sixth, taking an 8-1 lead. Bregman hit a sacrifice fly, Correa doubled in two, and Evan Gattis singled in Correa. The Red Sox did add one more run, but not until the ninth. Houston 8, Boston 2.

In Boston on Sunday afternoon, the Red Sox turned the tables in Game Three. Neither starter lasted long at all. Doug Fister was with the Red Sox for just the one year. He'd been with Houston the year before, just for one year. He was 5-9 (.4.88) for Boston, not the sort of stats one associates with a first-place team. The Astros scored three runs off him in the top of the first inning. A single, wild pitch, and a single and Houston had its first run. Altuve grounded out, but Correa hit a two-run homer. This game seemed like it was over before the Red Sox even got to bat. Brad Peacock had been 13-2 (3.00) for the Astros. Maybe they could just go on cruise control? But in the second, two singles and a base on balls, and then a Sandy Leon single gave Boston one run. In the fourth, Hanley Ramirez singled to score a second run and then a 20-year-old third baseman who had just joined the team in late July – Rafael Devers – hit a two-run homer off reliever Francisco Liriano. The Sox took a 4-3 lead. They didn't look back. Four Red Sox relievers kept Houston from scoring after the first inning. And the Red Sox finally blew everything open in the bottom of the seventh, adding six more runs. Hanley Ramirez doubled in two, Devers singled in one, and Jackie Bradley Jr. hit a three-run homer. This one ended Boston 10, Houston 3.

Game Four was a battle. This one started with Porcello against Charlie Morton. The Astros got one run in the first on a ball Altuve hit for a double play. The Red Sox got one on a Bogaerts home run. In the second, Springer drove in Yuli Gurriel, who had led off with a triple. It took a while for the Red Sox to respond, but when Verlander took over from Morton in the bottom of the fifth, the first batter he faced was Benintendi, who homered with a man on. 3-2, Boston. Chris Sale was pitching in relief, and the first batter in the Houston seventh (Bregman) homered to tie it. They took a 4-3 lead later in the inning on a Josh Reddick single. In the top of the ninth, Carlos Beltran doubled in a fifth run. The Red Sox came to bat in the bottom of the ninth, facing elimination. First up was Devers. He hit an inside-the-park home run, to bring the Red Sox within a run. The next three batters, though, all made outs.

A nursery in Chernobyl, Ukraine.

The Red Sox season was done, but I was still glowing from a trip I made to Chernobyl – a one-day visit on August 9, 2017. I wasn't really glowing, of course, and those of us on the roundtrip from Kiev did all wear dosimeters to monitor radiation levels on the day trip. After the Russian invasion of the Ukraine in 2022, I consider myself very fortunate to have had the opportunity to visit that country (and spend a couple of days in neighboring Moldova).

Afterword to 2017

Houston beat the Yankees in the ALCS, and – just four days after they ended the Red Sox season, guess which team most Red Sox fans were suddenly rooting for! The Astros won the first two games by identical 2-1 scores, then dropped three games at Yankee Stadium while being outscored a combined 19-5.

It was a seven-game ALCS in which the home team won every game. The Astros won Game Six, 7-1, and Game Seven, 4-0.

The Astros and Dodgers fought for seven games in the World Series, two of them going into extra innings. The Astros won.

It was their first world championship.

Later, at the end of 2019, it emerged that the Astros had been engaging in sign stealing in 2017. The team was fined a few million dollars, lost some top draft picks, and fired both their GM and manager. Some were incensed, but others knew that there is a very long tradition of sign stealing in baseball. You're not supposed to do it, but in a sense it's the opposing team's responsibility to be smart enough not to let their signs be deciphered.

One other thing about 2017 – I had become very interested in umpires and begun interviewing them in 2015. Larry Gerlach and I edited *The SABR Book of Umpires and Umpiring*, which SABR published in 2017. Any number of them impressed me for any number of reasons. I'd mentioned Tripp Gibson earlier – the banjo-playing ump. I learned that Ted Barrett has a Ph. D. – in theology, no less. And was also a sparring partners for a number of heavyweight boxing champions, such as George Foreman, Evander Holyfield, and Mike Tyson. I don't suppose he was ever intimidated by a manager stomping around and

One of my books on major-league baseball umpires.

gesticulating. Since then, except during the first couple of COVID years, I make a practice of usually stopping by the umpires' room once during each crew's visit to Fenway Park, just to offer greetings and say hello. In 2020, Summer Games Book published another book I myself wrote about umpires, *Working A "Perfect" Game*. Getting to know several of the umpires has given me a number of new perspectives on following baseball.

Umpires D.J. Reyburn and Sam Holbrook in a discussion in the
Press Room at Fenway for Prof. Jeff Gerson's class at the
University of Massachusetts Lowell.

The 2018 postseason

On the 10th anniversary of their 1918 world championship, the Red
Sox won their ninth World Series, and their fourth of the current
century, moving one ahead of the Giants. The manager was Alex Cora,
who had been on the 2007 Red Sox team but had also been manager
A. J. Hinch's bench coach on the 2017 Astros. He was brought to
Boston and helped lead the Red Sox to winning exactly two-thirds of
their games. They finished 108-54, three more wins than they had ever
enjoyed before.

The Yankees won 100 games, but thus finished eight games behind
Boston. It was a Boston vs. New York Division Series, the first time the
two rivals had ever faced each other in Division Series play.

The 2018 American League Division Series

The Red Sox scored early and often enough in Game One, at Fenway Park. The Blue Jays had traded left-hander J. A. Happ to the Yankees near the end of July; Happ had started 11 games for the Yankees and was 7-0 with a 2.69 ERA. He'd given up 10 home runs in those 11 games, and in this game he gave up a three-run homer to J.D. Martinez in the very first inning. Chris Sale was pitching for the Red Sox and five of his first nine outs were strikeouts. In the bottom of the third, Sale got even more of a cushion when Mookie Betts led off with a double and Andrew Benintendi bunted for a single. Manager Aaron Boone called in Chad Green from the bullpen. Sox first baseman Steve Pearce singled and two batters later Xander Bogaerts hit a sacrifice fly. That made it 5-0, Red Sox. Sale struck out three more in the top of the fourth. In the sixth, though, the Yankees got to him for a pair of singles. Cora called on Ryan Brasier. Luke Voit singled in one run. The other runner scored on a groundout by Didi Gregorius. The Yankees loaded the bases but Brandon Workman got the final out. In the seventh, Voit knocked in another and in the top of the ninth Aaron Judge led off with a homer off All-Star closer Craig Kimbrel. The final score was Red Sox 5, Yankees 4.

Game Two went the other way, a 6-2 win for New York, driving Red Sox starter David Price from the game with three early runs – a one-out homer by Judge in the first in the top of the second and a leadoff homer by Gary Sanchez in the second, and two walks followed by an RBI single from Andrew McCutchen. Cora turned to Joe Kelly, formerly with the Cardinals. Boston got one run off starter Masahiro Tanaka when Bogaerts homered in the fourth inning. New York upped the score to 6-1, though, in the seventh when Sanchez hit another home run, a three-run shot high up into the Monster seats just to the left of the center-field flagpole. Ian Kinsler doubled in Mitch Moreland in the bottom of the seventh but that was the only other Red Sox run.

With the series tied at one win apiece, Game Three was played at Yankee Stadium.

Nathan Eovaldi had been traded from the Rays to the Red Sox near the end of July. He'd been 14-3 for the Yankees in 2014, with the best winning percentage in the league, but was just 3-4 for the 2018 Rays and 3-3 for the 2018 Red Sox. In this game, he excelled, throwing seven innings with just one run, on a pair of singles and an RBI groundout in the fourth. By that time, though, the Red Sox already had a 10-0 lead. That isn't what Yankees fans had been hoping to see. Catcher Christian Vazquez singled in Rafael Devers in the second. They got two more runs in the third inning, both coming on outs thanks to three Red Sox singles. When starter Luis Severino loaded the bases with nobody out in the top of the fourth, Boone brought in a pair of relievers (not at the same time!) On four pitches, Lance Lynn walked the first batter he faced, Mookie Betts. Benintendi then doubled, clearing the bases and adding three more runs. Before too long, Chad Green took over from Lynn. Pearce singled for another run and then Brock Holt tripled, once again clearing the bases.

The Red Sox weren't done yet. J.D. Martinez singled in a run off Jonathan Holder in the seventh. With Stephen Tarpley pitching in the eighth, Holt doubled in another run, another scored on a wild pitch, and Betts singled in Holt to make it 14-1. In the top of the ninth, Holt added another two runs on a homer off Austin Romine. Boston 16, New York 1.

One might have mused that the Red Sox should have saved some of those runs for Game Four, but it turned out they didn't need to. CC Sabathia started for New York. His glory years of 2008 and 2009 were well behind him but he had still started 29 games with a very good 3.69 ERA. He was 9-7 in wins and losses. The Red Sox went with Rick Porcello, who had been 17-7 (4.28). Neither team scored in the first two innings. Sabathia hit the first Boston batter of the third, Benintendi. Pearce singled, and Benintendi went first to third, from where he scored on a sacrifice fly by J.D. Martinez. With two outs, second baseman Kinsler doubled in Pearce and third baseman Eduardo Nunez singled in Kinsler.

In the fourth inning, Zack Britton took the mound for the Yankees and Christian Vazquez greeted him with a homer. That gave the Red Sox a 4-0 lead. The Yankees got one run on a sac fly in the fifth, and gave Kimbrel considerable trouble in the bottom of the ninth. Kimbrel walked Judge. Gregorius singled. Stanton struck out, but Kimbrel walked Voit on four pitches and the bases were loaded with just one out. Kimbrel hit third baseman Neil Walker with a pitch and the score became 4-2 with the bases still loaded. Gary Sanchez hit a sacrifice fly to left and it was 4-3. Kimbrel got Gleyber Torres to ground out, third to first, and the Red Sox had won the ALDS.

The 2018 American League Championship Series

In the League Championship Series, it was the Red Sox against the reigning world champion Houston Astros. As noted, Red Sox manager Alex Cora had a ring from 2017 as bench coach for the Astros. He also had one from 2007, with the Red Sox.

Game One was tied 2-2 after the first five innings. Chris Sale pitching for Boston and Justin Verlander for Houston. A two-run single in the second inning had given the Astros their runs. Verlander himself had pretty much given the Red Sox theirs in the fifth. After a leadoff single and a strikeout, he walked the next three batters. Betts grounded to third, for the second out on the throw to the plate, but then Verlander threw a wild pitch and the second run scored. Carlos Correa broke the tie with an RBI single in the sixth. It was a one-run game until the ninth when Brandon Workman was greeted with a homer by Josh Reddick and then, three batters later, a three-run homer by Yuli Gurriel. The final was Houston 7, Boston 2.

Game Two was a bit of a seesaw. Benintendi and Devers each singled in one run off Gerrit Cole in the bottom of the first. Springer tied it with a two-run single off David Price in the top of the second and then Houston took a 4-2 lead on a homer by Marwin Gonzalez in the third. In the bottom of the inning, Boston's Jackie Bradley Jr. came up with the bases loaded and two outs, and doubled halfway up the wall right down the line in left, clearing the bases. Reliever Lance McCullers granted a walk, followed by a strikeout, a wild pitch, a passed ball, another strikeout, and then another passed ball on which Betts scored. That made it 6-4, Boston and provided the decisive run. Each team scored once more, for a 7-5 final, a Red Sox win.

The series shifted to Minute Maid Park for the next three games. Dallas Keuchel vs. Nathan Eovaldi were the pitchers at the start of Game Three. The Red Sox got two runs on three hits in the top of the first and the Astros got one run on three hits in the bottom of the first. The Astros tied it, 2-2, when Bregman doubled in Altuve in the bottom of the fifth. The Red Sox edged back ahead on Steve Pearce's solo home run in the sixth, but then took command in the eighth, adding a fourth run when reliever Roberto Osuna hit Mitch Moreland with a bases-loaded pitch and then on a 1-1 pitch gave up a grand slam to Jackie Bradley Jr. Boston 8, Houston 2.

The Red Sox got eight runs again in Game Four and they were enough for an 8-6 win. There were one or two runs scored in most half-innings and starters Charlie Morton and Rick Porcello were both gone after four innings, with Houston up 4-3. In the fifth, the Sox scored once to tie it but the 'Stros scored again to take a 5-4 lead. In the sixth, Bradley Jr. homered again, for two runs, putting Boston ahead, 6-5. McCullers was back for the seventh inning and this time walked in a seventh run. Both teams scored once in the eighth, but the final was 8-6, Red Sox.

Boston had three more chances to win the ALCS — Game Five in Houston, or either Games Six or Seven back in Boston. Verlander started for the Astros, Price for the Red Sox. First on the board were the Red Sox with a solo home run in the fourth by J.D. Martinez. It was still 1-0 after five innings. In the top of the sixth, Moreland doubled, Kinsler singled, and Rafael Devers hit a three-run home run. Matt Barnes took over from Price with a 4-0 lead heading into the bottom of the seventh. Marwin Gonzalez hit a two-out solo home run, but that was the only scoring in the game after the fourth and with the 4-1 victory, the Red Sox were on their way back to the World Series for the fourth time in 15 years.

2018 World Series

The National League champion Los Angeles Dodgers had finished first in the N.L. West, but just by one game over the Rockies. They played the Atlanta Braves in the Division Series, shutting them out in both the first and second games. They lost Game Three but prevailed in Game Four, then went on to play a full seven-game NLCS against the Milwaukee Brewers. There were three one-run games, one of which took 13 innings, but the Dodgers fought hard and were arguably battle-tested by the time they pulled into Fenway Park for the first game of the 2018 World Series. Just the year before, they had lost the World Series to the Astros in seven games. They hadn't won a World Series since 1988. The Red Sox had been idle for four days.

Game One was at Fenway, Chris Sale (12-4, 2.11) for Boston and Clayton Kershaw for Los Angeles. Sale had won the first game of the Division Series against the Yankees, but had no other postseason decisions. His ERA was 4.11. Kershaw was a three-time Cy Young Award winner. His record in 2018 was 9-5 (2.73). He had won once in each postseason round, but lost Game One of the NLCS. He came into this game with a 2.37 postseason earned run average in 2018. The Red Sox scored first after Mookie Betts singled to lead off, stole second, and then came home on a single to right by Andrew Benintendi. J.D. Martinez later singled in Benintendi. Matt Kemp hit a solo home run off Sale in the top of the second, and the Dodgers tied it in the third on singles by Justin Turner, David Freese, and Manny Machado.

Martinez doubled in a go-ahead run in the bottom of the third. The Dodgers re-tied it on a Machado groundout off Matt Barnes in the fourth, after a walk, single, and wild pitch. In the fifth, Bogaerts knocked in one run while grounding into a force play at second, and then Devers singled in another run, the Red Sox taking a 5-3 lead. A Machado sacrifice fly brought the Dodgers to within one run in the top of the seventh. It was their last run. The Red Sox added three runs on a homer by Eduardo Nunez in the bottom of the seventh. Boston 8, Los Angeles 4.

Game Two featured David Price against Hyun Jin Ryu, who had missed half the season with a severe left groin strain but finished 7-3 with a superb 1.97 ERA. In the Red Sox second, Bogaerts doubled to center and Kinsler singled him home. The Dodgers got two off Price in the top of the fourth, after he loaded the bases with nobody out. A Matt Kemp sac fly produced the first run and a Yasiel Puig single produced the second. After two outs in the bottom of the fifth, Christian Vazquez singled and Betts singled and Benintendi walked. Manager Dave Roberts (of 2004 Red Sox fame) called on reliever Ryan Madson. He walked Steve Pearce to force in the tying run and then yielded a two-run single to J.D. Martinez. It was 4-2, Red Sox, and other than a two-base hit for Betts in the Red Sox seventh, no other batters reached base for either team.

Dodger Stadium was the venue for Game Three. It started at 5:10 P.M. local time and ended at 3:30 A.M. Boston time. It was a seven-hour, 20-minute game that ran 18 innings. Each team used nine pitchers, thus a total of 18 pitchers over the course of 18 innings. The starters were Walker Buehler and Rick Porcello. Porcello gave up one run, in the third inning, on a home run by left fielder Joc Pederson. Buehler never did give up a run, but was replaced after seven innings by Kenley Jansen, who gave up a solo home run to JBJ (Jackie Bradley Jr.). The game remained 1-1 after 12 innings. Brock Holt walked, leading off the 13th. He stole second and then scored after Nunez hit the ball back to pitcher Scott Alexander, but the pitcher's flip to first was off the mark and went into foul territory. Nathan Eovaldi had already thrown a 1-2-3 12th, but in the 13th the Dodgers got a run to re-tie the game, also on a throwing error. Four more scoreless frames followed. Eovaldi stuck with it. In the bottom of the eighteenth, Max Muncy led off. On the 7th pitch of the at-bat, he homered and won the game for the Dodgers.

Rather than be reviled back East, Eovaldi was hailed for throwing six innings of relief and sparing the rest of the staff. The Red Sox had swept back-to-back World Series in 2004 and 2007, but after their 2013 championship failed to result in a sweep, they could afford a loss or two (or even three). Tomorrow was another day – actually, since the game ended after midnight even on the West Coast, Game Four was not tomorrow. It was a little over 17 hours later, also on October 27.

Game Four saw neither team score for the first five innings, Rich Hill pitching for the Dodgers and Eduardo Rodriguez for the Red Sox. In the bottom of the sixth, though, the Dodgers scored four times. A hit-by-pitch, one-out double, and an intentional walk loaded the bases. A groundout to first resulted in a force out at the plate but then a run scored on an error as catcher Vazquez threw wildly to first base. And then Puig hit a three-run homer, making it 4-0, Dodgers. E-Rod left the game. The Red Sox got right back in it in the top of the seventh with a three-run homer of their own, by pinch-hitter Mitch Moreland, batting for reliever Matt Barnes. In the top of the eighth, they tied it on a solo homer by Steve Pearce off Jansen. In the top of the ninth, the Red Sox broke through with five runs. With one out, Holt doubled, then Devers pinch-hit and singled. A walk and a single loaded the bases. Facing the third Dodgers pitcher of the inning, Kenta Maeda, Pearce came up big again, clearing the bases with a double that one-hopped the wall in right-center. Maeda walked Martinez intentionally, but Bogaerts singled to score Pearce before the Sox wrapped it up. Craig Kimbrel was asked to close the game. Staked to a five-run lead, he walked the first batter and served up a gopher ball to Kike Hernandez, but then shut the door and the Red Sox had a three-games-to-one lead in the 2018 World Series.

Game Five was Kershaw vs. Price. First baseman Steve Pearce had only played 50 games for the Red Sox in 2018, having arrived from Toronto via trade at the end of June. He'd batted .279 with seven homers and driven in 26 runs. But now he had knocked in the game-winning run in Game Two and done so again in Game Four. In the top of the first inning, Kershaw got Betts to fly out, then saw Benintendi single. Pearce came up to bat. On the first pitch, he hit a ball into the seats in left-center for a two-run homer. Laying down a marker of his own, the Dodgers' David Freese swung at Price's first pitch and homered. At the end of five, it remained Boston 2, Los Angeles 1. The second batter up in the Red Sox sixth, Mookie Betts homered off Kershaw. The first batter up in the seventh, J.D. Martinez homered off Kershaw. With two outs in the eighth, Pearce came up to bat once more, this time against Pedro Baez. He homered again. Price departed after walking the first Dodger he faced in the bottom of the eighth. Joe Kelly relieved, faced three batters, and struck all three out. Chris Sale took over from Kelly in the bottom of the ninth and he, too, struck out all three batters he faced, all three on swinging third strikes.

The Red Sox thus held on to the 5-1 lead and won the game, and thereby won their fourth World Series of the still-relatively-new century.

It was no surprise that Steve Pearce was named World Series MVP.

11

More Writing About the Red Sox

Sorry, the bug never left me. By this time, I had written or edited quite a lot of books. Earlier in the year, my 500-plus-page biography of former Red Sox owner Tom Yawkey was published as well as another of my books on Ted Williams.[82] Back in 2007, *Ted Williams at War* had offered a detailed look at his stints in the Navy and Marine Corps, which cost him most of five seasons during World War II and then the Korean War, and could have cost him his life. His plane was hit by ground fire over North Korea and he had to crash-land it. It was enveloped in

At home, in Cambridge, next to some of my books, in a photo taken for the *Tufts Alumni Review*.

flame moments after he jumped out of the plane. In 2018, I also saw published *Ted Williams – First Latino in the Baseball Hall of Fame*. That documented his family background on his mother's side of the family, his maternal grandparents coming from Valle de Allende in Mexico.

During the year, I worked on two collaborations, a book I wrote with a Yankees fan – David Fischer – simply called *Red Sox vs. Yankees,* and another book with Jim Prime that featured a look at the 2018 Red Sox outfield, which we thought might be the outfield for years to come: *The Red Sox Killer B's: Baseball's Best Outfield*.

After spending Christmas 2018 in Austin, I cashed in some more frequent flyer miles and took a quick four-day trip to Colombia. It was, after all, a country I'd never visited – and they had baseball. I caught a game at Barranquilla (interestingly, at Estadio Edgar Renteria). Renteria had been with the Cardinals during the 2004 World Series and it was his Game Four groundball that was "stabbed by Foulke" and underhanded to Doug Mientkiewicz for the final out of the World Series, the play that was *not* flubbed and represented the final out which secured the Red Sox their World Series win.

The next two years – 2019 and 2020

The 2019 Red Sox won 84 games, quite a drop from the 108 wins in 2018, and finished third, 19 games behind the New York Yankees in the East. The Yankees swept the Twins the Division Series, but Houston took New York in six games in the ALCS, before losing to the Washington Nationals in the World Series.

There was a special experience in June 2019 when the Red Sox traveled to London, England to play the New York Yankees in the first regular-season major-league games in Europe. Hosted at London Stadium, both games drew over 59,000. They were both Red Sox "home games" – perhaps because Boston is part of (New) England? The games seemed a little other-worldly, in that the scores (both Yankees victories) were 17-13 and 12-8. In the first game, New York scored six runs in the top of the first and Boston scored six runs in the bottom of the first. Neither starter made it through the first inning. I later wrote up both games for SABR's Games Project. Naturally, there were partisans of both teams there, and probably some "locals" who had never seen a real baseball game before. There was indeed a Red Sox UK Supporters Club with a banner and all.

I went to the umpires room before one of the games to say hi to the crew, and got into a conversation with a stadium security man. In chatting about ballgames, he stopped me at one point and asked, "Wait, how many games does each team play?" I replied, "Take a guess." He said, "It sounds like they might play 50 or 60 games!" I let him know it was 162 and that was without spring training or the postseason games. He was pretty astonished.

The Red Sox lost both London games, but a good time was had by most. Later in the year, when the Yankees came to Fenway, the Red Sox swept them – 19-3, 10-5, and 9-5. So there. I'm grateful I got to see the games in London, though, and hope someday to see the Red Sox play in yet another country.

Surely, Red Sox fans were disappointed in the drop from 2018 to 2019, but perhaps even more disappointed that the 2020 team fell to last place. Disappointed, yes, but to the point that not one fan attended a single game in all of 2020? That would have been an extreme reaction. No, there was no boycott. The zero attendance for the 2020 season was because of the COVID-19 pandemic. The season started very late (the Red Sox home opener was on July 24), teams only played a sharply-reduced schedule of 60 games, and all were played to empty ballparks. Cardboard cutouts with photos of fans filled some of the seats.

Alex Cora – who had won rings with Houston in 2017 and the Red Sox in 2018 – was suspended for the 2020 season, for his part in the Astros sign stealing during 2017.

Because I had media credentials, I was able to come to games at Fenway Park and did attend 22 of the 30 home games in 2020, plus two in Buffalo where the Red Sox played the Toronto Blue Jays. (Due to pandemic restrictions, teams were not permitted to cross the border into Canada, so the Jays played their full home season at Buffalo's Sahlen Field.) The press box at Fenway Park, normally bustling with 40-60 people, typically had about five or six of us who came. It's on the fifth floor of Fenway and anyone who wasn't handicapped was (appropriately) not allowed to use elevators, so we walked up and down five floors of ramps. Good exercise. There was (again, very appropriately) no contact with the players, so why did we come? Not even the radio and TV broadcasters came. They worked remotely. One time I asked David Laurila of Fangraphs – seated 9 or 10 feet away – why he came to the games. "Because I can," was his response. It was the same reason I came. It was live baseball. It was Fenway Park.

in between innings at a game at Fenway in the year 2020. Note the cardboard cutouts in the Green Monster Seats.

There was actually *one* person who came to a Red Sox game that year, without credentials but also without a ticket. Wearing – for some reason – an Allen Webster jersey (who knew they ever made them? Webster appeared in all of 19 games for the Red Sox), this gentleman climbed over the wall in left-center field during a game, and had to be removed after disrupting play for about 20 minutes by throwing a couple of things (including a baseball cap) onto the field, shouting, and doing pushups on the platform there. I wrote up the game: "September 20, 2020: Uninvited guest attends Yankees game at Fenway."[83] I never did find out the story behind that story; his name is not provided in public records and the official Boston Police Department report indicates he was taken to a nearby hospital for observation, probably the appropriate response.

Trying to keep busy during the pandemic year, I buried myself in Rounder banjo music for a while and assembled a playlist available on Spotify that I titled "Banjo for Daze." Should anyone wish to give it a listen, please do. And there is a special prize (not yet determined) for anyone who can legitimately claim to have listened all the way through, without stopping. It contains a mere 2,555 tracks and runs just 128 hours and 10 minutes. That's a bit more than 5⅓ days. We did release a lot of music with banjo on Rounder; this isn't all of it.

The 2021 postseason

Cora was back as manager in 2021 and fans began to come back to the parks as well, as health restrictions were gradually loosened. The leagues played a full schedule. Attendance was 1,725,323, the lowest it had been since 1984, but it had officially been 0 the year before.

The Red Sox finished in second place with a record of 92-70 – but so did the Yankees. In head-to-head competition, the Red Sox had won 10 games and the Yankees nine, so a Wild Card Game – a tiebreaker – was played at Fenway Park.

It was like a replay of 1978, likewise at Fenway, after the Red Sox and Yankees had both finished with identical 99-63 records. As we know (see above, if you must), the Red Sox were not the team which won 100 games that season.

Would history repeat itself? Or had, perhaps, the Red Sox broken any curse once and for all in 2004?

To be fair, 1978 was quite a while back – 43 years earlier. There weren't all that many of us who had been at that game, and then at this game. I know Dan Shaughnessy had been there and Yankees sportscaster Suzyn Waldman.

This one featured Nathan Eovaldi, who had been in the spotlight (for those who were still watching in the wee hours of the morning back in Boston) as he threw the six final innings of the 18-inning Game Three of the 1918 World Series. He had a good year in 2021 (11-9, 3.75) and his 32 regular-season starts led the league. He'd gone up against the Yankees six times in 2021, and was 1-2. His last start against them was on September 24, and he'd only lasted 2⅔ innings, banged around for seven runs. In his final start of the season, though, he had thrown six shutout innings against the Orioles on September 29

Gerrit Cole started for the Yankees. Signed to a nine-year contract for $324,000,000, Cole had a very strong year in 2021, with a league-leading 16 wins against 8 losses and a 3.23 ERA. He placed second in Cy Young Award voting (Eovaldi placed fourth).[84]

Boston scored first, in the first, thanks to a two-run homer by Xander Bogaerts. It was nice to have a lead, but of course, the Sox had held a 2-0 lead all the way through the sixth inning in that 1978 game. The 2021 team added a third run, in the third, on a leadoff homer by Kyle Schwarber. OK, that's a bit better.

In the sixth, Anthony Rizzo hit another home run, giving the Yankees one run. Aaron Judge singled, and Cora turned to Ryan Brasier to take over from Eovaldi. Stanton hit a deep single, but Judge tried to score and was thrown out at the plate. It remained 2-1, Red Sox. With one out in the bottom of the sixth, with Luis Severino pitching, Bogaerts walked and Alex Verdugo drove him in. 4-1, Red Sox. They added two more with two out in the seventh after three bases on balls and a two-run single by Verdugo. This game definitely had a different feel from 1978. Not a single player on the 2021 Red Sox team had even been born in 1978; the oldest regular was J.D. Martinez and he was only 33 years old.

New York did score one more run, on Stanton's solo homer in the top of the ninth. That made it 6-2, Red Sox. The Yankees season was over.

For those of who had been present for the "Bucky Dent Game" back in 1978, this one felt like an exorcism. That one had produced so much trauma that winning this game was, in some ways, almost as good as winning another World Series.

In fact, it did get the Red Sox into the ALDS. But not many expected them to get very far. They would have to beat the Tampa Bay Rays, who had won 100 games to Boston's 92. Head-to-head, the 2021 Rays had won 11 of their last 16 games against the Red Sox.

2021 American League Division Series

And the Rays shut out the Red Sox, 5-0, in Game One of the best-of-five Division Series. They scored twice off E-Rod in the first inning at Tropicana and then saw both Nelson Cruz and Randy Arozarena hit solo homers off Nick Pivetta in the third and fifth. Their fifth run came on Arozarena's steal of home plate in the seventh. Shane McClanahan and three relievers held Boston scoreless. It didn't really look like a series that was going to go well for the Red Sox.

Game Two got off to a bit of a hopeful start, though, when the Red Sox scored a couple of runs in the top of the first. The Rays immediately struck back with five runs off Chris Sale in the bottom of the first, including a grand slam by Jordan Luplow. No, this didn't seem a series that was going to go well for the Red Sox. In the third inning, though, they got two solo homers of their own (Bogaerts and Verdugo) and trailed by just one run.

A third solo homer by Kike Hernandez tied it, 5-5, leasing off the fifth and a three-run J.D. Martinez homer later in the inning gave the Red Sox an 8-5 lead. The Rays only got one more run in the game, while the Red Sox added one in the seventh, two in the eighth, and three more in the ninth for a 14-6 win.

Game Three was at Fenway, and it took 13 innings to resolve. Dueling home runs in the first inning gave the Rays a 2-1 lead. The Red Sox went ahead, 3-2, in the third. Kike Hernandez homered to lead off the fifth, and it was 4-2. But the Rays tied it in the eighth and it remained tied through the 12th and into the bottom of the 13th inning. Nick Pivetta struck out seven in the final four innings of relief. Christian Vazquez — who had come into the game as a pinch-hitter in the sixth — hit a two-run homer into the first row of the Green Monster seats in left-center and the Red Sox won the game, 6-4.

The Division Series being a best-of-five series, all the Red Sox needed was to win Game Four and they would win the series. Could this really happen? It had been 17 years since they won the 2004 World Series, but there was still inbred caution against allowing oneself to be overly optimistic.

They did jump out to a 5-0 lead, though, in the third inning. With two outs and two on base, Devers homered into the seats in straightaway center field. Bogaerts followed with a single and Verdugo doubled him home. J.D. Martinez singled and Verdugo scored all the way from first. The Rays weren't ready to quit, though. They scored one run in the fifth and two more in the sixth. In the top of the eighth, they scored two more runs — tying the game, 5-5. A familiar foreboding may have crept into the souls of some Sox fans — but thanks to so many world championships having accumulated, it was now somewhat tempered by the knowledge that should the Rays win the game, there was always another shot in Game Five.

Two Christians led off the bottom of the ninth: Vazquez singled and Christian Arroyo sacrificed him to second. Pinch-hitter Travis Shaw reached on an infield single, Vazquez going to third base. Kike Hernandez hit a sacrifice fly to left-center, deep enough for Vazquez to easily tag and score the winning run. Celebrations ensued. The Red Sox were heading on to the League Championship Series. And they had been able to win the Division Series at home, at Fenway Park.

2021 League Championship Series

Finishing eight games out of first place in the East, who ever expected the Red Sox to be here, prepared to battle the Houston Astros for the American League pennant and the right to play in the 2021 World Series?

Houston won Game One, in Houston, but it was a close one-run game. The Red Sox loaded the bases in the top of the first but did not score. Chris Sale started for the Red Sox and the Astros scored one in the first on a walk, single, wild pitch, and sacrifice fly. The Red Sox scored three runs in the top of the third, and left runners on second and third. In the bottom of the sixth, Jose Altuve tied it up with a two-run homer. Correa homered in the seventh, giving the Astros a 4-3 lead and made it 5-3 when Altuve hit a sac fly in the eighth. Kike Hernandez homered in the top of the ninth, but Boston came up one run short.

The Astros scored five runs again in Game Two, but before they did, the Red Sox already had put nine runs on the scoreboard. The first four came in the first inning when J.D. Martinez hit a grand slam off the Astros' Luis Garcia. The next four came in the second inning when Rafael Devers hit a grand slam off Garcia's replacement, Jake Odorizzi. Another homer happened in the fourth, this one with nobody on base, hit by Kike Hernandez. Nathan Eovaldi had been granted a 9-0 lead with which to work. Houston did score thrice in the fourth, one on a double by Kyle Tucker and two on a single by Yuli Gurriel. Neither team scored again until the bottom of the ninth, when Astros fans perhaps felt a little better when both Gurriel and Jason Castro hit solo homers off Darwinzon Hernandez.

The Red Sox pounded Houston pitching again in Game Three, at Fenway, this time banging in 12 runs. Neither team got a man on in the first, Eduardo Rodriguez retiring three Astros in order and Jose Urquidy retiring three Red Sox in order. E-Rod struck out the side in the top of the second, but Urquidy was chased from the game. A walk, double, and walk loaded the bases for Christian Vazquez, who singled in the first run. A second came in when Arroyo hit into a fielder's choice. Then followed the third Red Sox grand slam of the ALCS, hit by Kyle Schwarber. The Red Sox proceeded to load the bases again but Yimi Garcia managed to secure the final out. Garcia did, however, give up three runs in the third inning on a Vazquez single and Arroyo home run.

Even after the Astros scored three in the fourth, they were still far behind, 9-3. It became 11-3, Boston, when J.D. Martinez homered in the sixth. And just for good measure, Devers homered in the eighth for a 12-3 lead, and win.

The Boston bats then went cold and Houston pitching held the line. There were no more grand slams. The Red Sox had 26 runs on 32 hits in Games One through Three, but then only had 10 hits total in the next three, and progressively diminishing numbers of them at that. A two-run homer for Bogaerts in the bottom of the first inning of Game Four gave the Red Sox a 2-1 lead, but they never scored again, while the Astros tied it, 2-2, in the eighth, then exploded for seven runs in the top of the ninth. Against that onslaught, the Red Sox did get two singles, but struck out three times.

After just getting five hits in Game Four, Boston batsmen only got three in Game Five and two in Game Six. Game Five was 1-0 after five innings; again a fairly-balanced game until the five runs the Astros booked in the top of the sixth off Sale and Brasier. One of the three Red Sox hits was a seventh-inning home run by Devers, but there was nobody on base. The Astros won the game, 9-1.

Leading three games to two, all Houston needed was a win in Game Six and they would return to the World Series. Luis Garcia had a no-hitter going for the first 5⅔ innings. The Astros were leading 1-0, thanks to a run off Eovaldi in the first inning. When Kike Hernandez hit a two-out triple, manager Dusty Baker brough Phil Maton in from the pen. He got Devers to pop up to short. Yordan Alvarez, who'd knocked in the lone run of the game, tripled to lead off Houston's bottom of the sixth. Correa was hit by a pitch. Tucker grounded into a double play, but a run scored and it was Houston 2, Boston 0. The Red Sox only got one other hit in the entire game, a two-out single by Verdugo in the top of the seventh. Tucker came up one more time, in the bottom of the eighth, and put the game away with a three-run homer. The Astros had shut out the Red Sox and it was they who went on to the World Series.

As stated, for many Red Sox fans, though, the fact that they had come from what felt like nowhere to beat the Yankees in the single-game Wild Card was satisfying enough to call the 2021 season a very good one. It was icing on the cake that they had taken the ACLS to just two wins shy of reaching another World Series.

The Atlanta Braves won three of the first four games of the 2021 World Series, and then Game Six to become world champions for 2021.

The 2022 season

The 2022 postseason didn't involve the Red Sox. They returned to the cellar, finishing last and 21 games behind the first-place Yankees. The Yankees beat the Cleveland Guardians in the ALDS, but were swept by the Astros in the ALCS, who did go on to beat the Phillies in a six-game World Series without suggestions of Houston's win being tainted.

I had seen the Red Sox play in the Dominican Republic (a couple of spring training games against Houston in March 2000), in Canada, Japan, and England. And even Buffalo in 2020. This year they played a game in Williamsport, Pennsylvania – the home of the Little League World Series, on the evening of August 21, 2022. Naturally I went there, too, but saw them lose, 5-3 to the Orioles in front of a sold-out Muncy Bank Ballpark, before a crowd of 2,467. The bases were 90 feet apart, not the 60 they would have been were the team playing on a regulation Little League field.

They have yet to play a game in Puerto Rico – exhibition or otherwise – though they have played six games in Cuba (four in 1941, before I was born, and two in 1946, which my parents thoughtlessly did not take me to shortly after my first birthday), as well as games that I could have gotten to myself, but did not, in Nogales, Mexico in 1965 and in the Virgin Islands (one on St. Croix and one on St. Thomas) in 1967.[85]

Another Ted Williams book was published, thanks to Summer Game Books. It is entitled *The Kid Blasts A Winner: Ted Williams' 110 Game-Deciding Home Runs.* Of the 521 home runs he hit over the course of the career, which touched four decades (1939-1960), a full 110 of them provided the run that – at game's end – had made the difference and given the Red Sox a win. The book details each and every one of them.

Speaking of "each and every," as noted above, I did go to each and every Red Sox home game in 2022. It wasn't anything I had planned to do before the season began. I just started going, and kept going. And going. I also went to three road games, two in Baltimore (when the SABR convention was held there, the Red Sox were in town) and the one in Williamsport. It wasn't a real sacrifice. From my desk in the press box, I can get about as much work done there as I can at home – maybe more, in some cases. I would edit articles for SABR, and research others. As we got well into August, it did become something of a self-imposed burden. No one was really keeping track, except me. And, truly, hardly anyone would really care. The 2022 season was by no means a standout season. They did win five more games than they lost; the team was 43-38 at Fenway in 2022. I did tell my son at one point in August that come April 2023 I was going to intentionally skip a game so I didn't have any such "streak" going on.

Then came September 2, the day I almost missed a game. I spent most of the day in a hospital emergency room after I accidentally swallowed a screwdriver! You can imagine there's a story there. Bear with me just a bit. It was a Friday night game; the Sox had won in a walkoff the night before. I had a dentist appointment at 9:00 A.M. at Tufts Dental School. While the dentist was working on me – oops, she dropped a screwdriver in my mouth and I reflexively swallowed it. This was not a 10-inch screwdriver. It was a dental implant screwdriver, maybe about 6mm in length. Easily ingested, but naturally presenting a danger as it – hopefully – progressed on its way throughout my system, with the possibility of getting stuck and tearing something. She immediately took me next door to the ER at the Tufts medical facility for X-rays and observation. I was concerned, but also highly amused. I finally got home at about 6 P.M. Emmet came up with a plan, and we drove over to the ballpark. We got there in about the third inning and he parked next to a hydrant directly across the street from the park, while I went inside for a couple of innings. I made it to the game. Then I went home and rested, returning for more X-rays the following day. I never did find it, but apparently it passed. I hadn't missed a game, and I had a good story, too.

I did go to the first six home games of 2023, but then skipped the April 14 game. I watched it on TV, and that was an odd sensation – watching a game at Fenway Park on TV. The last time I had done that was back in 2021.

The 2023 season

As we approach the 20th anniversary of the 2004 Red Sox World Championship, this team holds – as it did at a similar time in the previous century – the most World Series wins of any team in the 21st century. In addition to the 2004 win, the Red Sox won it again in 2007, 2013, and 2018. No other team has four World Series wins in the current century. That is just what the 1924 Boston Red Sox could have said. As Peter Abraham noted in the April 16, 2023 *Boston Globe*, "There are 4-year-old children who have not been alive for a championship season."

There remains one concern, though, for those still bedeviled by a degree of superstition. Might history repeat itself? Might 2018 prove to be the last Red Sox world championship for the next 86 years? Hopefully, many of us confronted with this daunting question will soon learn it was not.

But am I ready to die in peace? I don't feel that ready to die. It's going to happen eventually, but thankfully the brain hemorrhage didn't get me. There certainly is one thing that provides a sense of peace, though. The Red Sox finally won a World Series in my lifetime – and then did it again. And again. And again.

I don't need 27 of them. Just the ones I've enjoyed in the last 20 years have been a lot. I was glad Cubs fans got to enjoy one, too. If it can't be the Red Sox, then I'd wish well to Mariners fans, and Rockies fans, and Cleveland Guardians fans. And a few other sets of fans. Texas Rangers fans enjoyed their championship in 2023.

There may never be anything like the 2004 Red Sox, though. Yes, Cubs fans had to wait longer between championships, from 1908 to 2016 – 108 years. But, in my lifetime, for Boston to lose two tiebreaker games, to lose four consecutive World Series Game Sevens, to be wiped out by the Yankees in Game Seven of the 2003 ALCS, and then to be down three-games-to-none the very next year, crushed 19-8 in the third of those losses…it really does seem like something that would be tough to top.

Not every Red Sox fan is the same, of course, but in my experience, most Red Sox fans always felt akin to Cubs fans. Even before 2004. That if it couldn't be the Red Sox, it would be nice for the long-suffering Cubs fans to enjoy a World Series win. If it were head-to-head Cubs vs. Red Sox, no question. But if it were the Cubs against any other A.L. team, all things being equal, many – if not the overwhelming majority of – Red Sox fans would have rooted for the Cubs, even if we couldn't have named two players on the team before that hypothetical year's playoffs began.

It has been wonderful to experience four world championships in the past 20 years. If the Red Sox could win 10 of them in the next 10 years, well, that would be fine, too. But if you've a Red Sox fan with a few decades of experience, one is used to losing. Coming up short, or being blown out. Remember, it builds character.

Hope is one thing that characterizes a fan. The 2023 Red Sox didn't seem to have much going for them. Pick a date – say, June 29, my father's 101st birthday – the Red Sox were 40-42 and in last place in the A.L. East, already 15 games out of first. There were injuries galore. They'd been at least 10 games back for a solid month. What was the point of watching Red Sox games? There was nothing at all that was really inspiring any hope — but there was the love of the game. What's the point of watching if one couldn't summon up some sense of hope? Some stopped watching, no doubt, but there have always been fair-weather fans.

There aren't any guarantees in life. Whoever said Red Sox fans were entitled to have a winning season each and every year? We've had more than our share these last 20 years.

But then the Red Sox won eight of their next nine games, and went into the All-Star Break "only" nine games back, hoping that the return of a couple of past heroes from injury would help maintain or build on the recent winning streak. They were nine games behind the division leader but only two games away from making the playoffs as a second wild card team. All it takes is a bit of hope to hold onto (or grasp at) and spirits begin to lift. Yes, some other team will more likely win in the end, but if you love the game and have any reason to hope, it can make following games much more pleasurable.

Well, the 2023 Sox finished last — for the second year in a row. Was history about to repeat itself? Would the Red Sox have won the World Series in another year ending in "18" — and then have begun a drought that might run until 2104? Hopefully, the answer will prove to be "no" — and hopefully we will find that out quite soon.

In the meantime, there will be another Opening Day and new possibilities.

On the set on the film *Eight Men Out* – L to R: Mason Daring, D.B. Sweeney (as Shoeless Joe Jackson), and Bill Nowlin.

Selected Bibliography

Abrams, Roger, *The First World Series and the Baseball Fanatics of 1903* (Boston: Northeastern University Press, 2003)

Boronson, Melinda, *86 Ways to Cope When the Red Sox DON'T Win* (Waltham MA: Brown House Books, 2008)

Boston Globe, *Believe It* (Chicago: Triumph Books, 2004)

Boston Globe, *For Boston: From Worst to First, The improbable Dream of the 2013 Red Sox* (Chicago: Triumph Books, 2013).

Boston Globe. *Livin' the Dream: A Celebration of the World Champion 2013 Boston Red Sox* (Chicago: Triumph Books, 2013)

Boston Globe. *Relentless: 119 Wins and Another Red Sox Championship* (Stevens Point, WI: KCI Sports Publishing, 2018)

Boston Globe, *So Good! The Incredible Championship Season of the 2007 Red Sox* (Chicago: Triumph, 2007)

Boston Herald, *Boston Red Sox, 2004 World Champions* (Champaign IL: Sports Publishing, 2004)

Boston Herald, *Boston Red Sox, 2007 World Series Champions* (Champaign IL: Sports Publishing, 2007)

Boston Red Sox, *Boston Red Sox Media Guide* (Boston: Boston Red Sox, years 1986-2023)

Bradley, Richard, *The Greatest Game: The Yankees, the Red Sox, and the Playoff of '78* (New York: Free Press, 2008)

Browne, Ian, *Dice-K* (Guilford CT: The Lyons Press, 2008)

Browne, Ian, *Idiots Revisited: Catching Up with the Red Sox Who Won the 2004 World Series* (Tilbury House Publishers, 2014)

Burgess, Chuck and Bill Nowlin, *Love That Dirty Water: The Standells and the Improbable Boston Red Sox Anthem* (Burlington MA: Rounder Books, 2007)

Castiglione, Joe with Douglas B. Lyons, *Can You Believe It? 50 Years of Insider Stories with the Boston Red Sox* (Chicago: Triumph Books, 2012)

Corbett, Bernard, *March to the World Series: The 1986 Boston Red Sox* (Boston, Quinlan Press, 1986)

Crehan, Herb. *The Impossible Dream 1967 Red Sox – Birth of Red Sox Nation* (South Orange NJ: Summer Game Books, 2017)

Crehan, Herb, *Red Sox Heroes of Yesteryear* (Cambridge: Rounder Books, 2005)

Crehan, Herb and James W. Ryan, *Lightning in A Bottle* (Boston: Branden, 1992)

Andy Dabilis and Nick Tsiotis, *The 1903 World Series* (Jefferson, North Carolina; McFarland, 2004).

Editors of Major League Baseball, *2013 World Series Champions: Boston Red Sox* (Toronto: Fenn, M&S, 2013)

Femia, Vin, *The Possible Dream* (Worcester MA: Chandler House Press, 2004)

Francona, Terry and Dan Shaughnessy, *Francona: The Red Sox Years* (Boston: Houghton Mifflin Harcourt, 2013)

Frommer, Harvey, *Baseball's Greatest Rivalry* (NY: Atheneum, 1982)

Frommer, Harvey and Frederic J. Frommer, *Red Sox vs. Yankees: The Great Rivalry* (Champaign: Sports Publishing, 2004)

Frost, Mark, *Game Six: Cincinnati, Boston, and the 1975 Word Series: The Triumph of America's Pastime* (NY: Hyperion, 2009)

Funk, Joe, ed. *The Rest is History – Boston Red Sox 2018 World Series Champions* (Chicago: Triumph Books, 2018)

Gammons, Peter, *Beyond the Sixth Game* (Lexington MA: Stephen Greene, 1986)

Golenbock, Peter, *Red Sox Nation* (Chicago: Triumph, 2005)

Gorman, Lou, *One Pitch from Glory* (Champaign: Sports Publishing, 2005)

Hirshberg, Al, *What's the Matter with the Red Sox?* (NY: Dodd, Mead, 1973)

Holley, Michael, *Red Sox Rule* (NY: Harper Entertainment, 2008)

Holmes, Parker. *Yankees vs. Red Sox* (New York: Rosen Publishing, 2014)

Johnson, Bobby, *What Curse?* (NY: iUniverse, 2004)

Longest, A. Knoefel, *Idiot-Syncrasies: How the Red Sox Were Smart Enough to Win the World Series* (Avon MA: Adams Media, 2005)

Martinez, Pedro and Michael Silverman, *Pedro* (Boston and New York: Houghton Mifflin Harcourt, 2015)

Massarotti, Tony, *Dynasty: The Inside Story of How the Red Sox Became a Baseball Powerhouse* (NY: St. Martin's, 2008)

Massarotti, Tony and John Harper, *A Tale of Two Cities: The 2004 Yankees-Red Sox Rivalry and the War for the Pennant* (Guilford CT: Lyons Press, 2005)

Masur, Louis P., *Autumn Glory: Baseball's First World Series* (New York: Hill and Wang, 2003)

McAdam, Sean. *The Franchise: Boston Red Sox A Curated History* (Chicago: Triumph Books, 2022)

McCarney, Tim and Tom Deady, *Surviving Grady* (San Francisco: AiT/Planet Lar, 2004-05)

Montville, Leigh, *Why Not Us?* (NY: Public Affairs, 2004)

Nowlin, Bill, *Curse in the Rearview Mirror* (Black Mesa, 2011)

Nowlin, Bill, ed., *Opening Fenway Park in Style: The 1912 Boston Red Sox* (Phoenix AZ: Society for American Baseball Research, 2012)

Nowlin, Bill, *Pumpsie and Progress: The Red Sox, Race, and Redemption* (Burlington MA: Rounder Books, 2010)

Nowlin, Bill, ed., *Sox Bid Curse Farewell* (SABR 2024)

Nowlin, Bill and David Fischer, *Red Sox vs. Yankees* (Sports Publishing, 2019)

Nowlin, Bill., ed., with Mark Armour, Len Levin, and Allan Wood, *When Boston Still Had the Babe: The 1918 World Champion Red Sox* (Burlington MA: Rounder Books, 2008)

Nowlin, Bill and Jim Prime, *Blood Feud: The Red Sox, The Yankees, and the Struggle of Good versus Evil* (Cambridge: Rounder Books, 2005)

Nowlin, Bill and Jim Prime, *From The Babe to the Beards* (New York: Skyhorse Publishing, 2014).

Nowlin, Bill and Jim Prime, *The Red Sox World Series Encyclopedia* (Burlington MA: Rounder Books, 2008)

Nowlin, Bill and Dan Desrochers, *The 1967 Impossible Dream Red Sox* (Burlington MA: Rounder Books, 2007; republished in an expanded edition by SABR, 2017)

Nowlin, Bill and Cecilia Tan, eds., *'75: The Red Sox Team that Saved Baseball* (Cambridge: Rounder Books, 2005; republished in an expanded edition by SABR, 2015)

O'Nan, Stewart and Stephen King, *Faithful* (NY: Scribner, 2004)

Purciello, Gerard, *The Year They Won* (Weston CT: Brown Barn Books, 2005)

Reynolds, Bill, *Lost Summer: The '67 Red Sox and the Impossible Dream* (NY: Warner Books, 1992)

Reynolds, Bill, *'78: The Boston Red Sox, a Historic Game, and a Divided City* (NAL, 2009)

Ryan, Bob, *When Boston Won the World Series* (Philadelphia: Running Press, 2003)

Shaughnessy, Dan, *The Curse of the Bambino* (NY: Penguin, 1991)

Shaughnessy, Dan, *One Strike Away* (NY: Beaufort, 1987)

Shaughnessy, Dan, *Reversing the Curse* (Boston: Houghton Mifflin, 2004)

Simmons, Bill, *Now I Can Die in Peace* (NY: ESPN Books, 2005)

Soos, Troy, *Before the Curse* (Hyannis, MA: Parnassus Imprints, 1997)

Speier, Alex. *Homegrown: How the Red Sox Built A Champion from the Ground Up* (New York: William Morrow, 2019)

The Sporting News, *Curse Reversed* (St. Louis: Sporting News Books, 2004)

Stout, Glenn, *Fenway 1912: The Birth of a Ballpark, a Championship Season, and Fenway's Remarkable First Year* (Boston and New York: Houghton Mifflin Harcourt, 2012)

Stout, Glenn and Richard Johnson, *Red Sox Century* (Boston: Houghton Mifflin, 2004)

Whalen, Thomas J., *When the Red Sox Ruled: Baseball's First Dynasty, 1912-1918* (Chicago: Ivan R. Dee, 2011)

Wisnia, Saul, *Miracle at Fenway: The Inside Story of the Boston Red Sox 2004 Championship Season* (New York: St. Martin's Griffin, 2014)

Wood, Allan, *1918* (Lincoln: Writers Club Press, 2000)

Wood, Allan and Bill Nowlin, *Don't Let Us Win Tonight – An Oral History of the 2004 Boston Red Sox's Impossible Playoff Run* (Triumph Books, 2014 and 2024)

No author or editor listed:

2007 World Champions: Boston Red Sox. Boston Sweeps Again! (Tinton Falls NJ: 106 Apple Street, 2007)

Most of the games from the 21st century have highlights, if not full games, available on YouTube.com. It can be a valuable source for those looking to better pin down such things as where a home run may have landed or what sort of error a fielder may have committed.

Notes

1. Indeed, one screenplay had to be adapted because of the fact that the Red Sox had finally won it all. The ending for the movie *Fever Pitch* had to be rescripted and shot over. As for myself, I enjoyed being an extra in the film for scenes shot at Fenway Park earlier that summer. I don't think one could make me out in any the crowd scenes. The film was about a rabid Red Sox fan whose team never wins it all. After the Red Sox had indeed won the first three games of the 2004 World Series, the filmmakers realized there was a chance the Red Sox might actually win a World Series this time, and so scrambled to get the two leads – Jimmy Fallon and Drew Barrymore – on a plane and to St. Louis so they could re-shoot the ending to the movie on the field at Busch Stadium. What were the chances the Red Sox would win, despite being up three games to none? After all, no team had ever come back from such a deficit and gone on to win – except the 2004 Red Sox the previous week. But they took a chance, flew the actors out, and shot a new ending. See Whitney Pastorek, "'Fever Pitch' ending is changed after Red Sox win," *Entertainment Weekly*, ew.com, November 12, 2004.

    https://ew.com/article/2004/11/12/fever-pitch-ending-changed-after-red-sox-win/. Accessed June 25, 2023. See also Associated Press, "Red Sox's win throws curve at 'Fever Pitch'," today.com, October 29, 2004. https://www.today.com/popculture/red-soxs-win-throws-curve-fever-pitch-wbna6361156. Accessed June 24, 2023.

    Fever Pitch wasn't the first baseball film in which I was an extra. The first one was *Eight Men Out* (in 1988), for which I even had to get a haircut and be outfitted to wear period clothing. That one came about because of my years in the record business. Mason Daring did the music for director John Sayles films, and the company I founded with two partners – Rounder Records – distributed Mason's

Daring Records. He invited me out to Indianapolis, for scenes shot at the ballpark there. I didn't have any lines. I ended up on the cutting room floor. Just the next year, *Field of Dreams* was shot at Fenway Park. I signed on as an extra and sat two rows behind Kevin Costner and James Earl Jones during scenes of them talking in the stands on the third-base side. You may see my knees in the film, but no more.

I previously had appeared in the 1987 film *The Lion of Africa* with Brian Dennehy and Brooke Adams. In that one, I do appear – for maybe three seconds. I had been in South Africa making arrangements to license some music for Rounder, and on my way home stopped in Kenya to visit Doug Patterson, who was in Machakos and knew of some Kenyan music he wanted Rounder to consider licensing. He picked me up at the airport in Nairobi just after midnight and asked me if I wanted to be in a film. Sure, I said, and after a very few hours sleep, we got to the site where they were shooting next to an open-pit mine. Doug and I – no doubt influenced by our being White – were dressed as mining supervisors, with hard hats and clipboards, and at one point stroll across the screen. There was no recognition of our roles by the Academy. In January 1989, Rounder released *The Nairobi Beat* (Rounder 5030).

Talk about anonymity, Daring Records released a few albums in a series entitled *In the Absence of Man*. The recordings were made with no human beings present. One that I helped with was in the British West Indies. Mason and I took a boat to a small unpopulated island, near Jost Van Dyke, set up a tape recorder, turned it on, and left. We came back a few hours later, and had a recording of nature. One review said, "You could hear the crystal blue ocean ebbs and flows in and around you, far away, the faint roar of the surf on the coral reef added to the atmosphere of the surroundings. Occasionally, a hummingbird flew by the microphones, and goats could be heard on their mid-day walk on the beach. I can almost smell the salt air of the sea." OK, now back to baseball....

2. Author interview with William Nowlin, Sr., in Bill Nowlin, *Fenway Lives* (Cambridge, Massachusetts: Rounder Books, 2004),160.

3. https://follen.org/community/events/christmas-tree-sales/

4. In 1961, the Unitarian and Universalist churches merged.

5. In researching for this book during the year 2023, I learned that Mary Nowlin appears to have lived a long life – until 1998, when she died at age 82 at Grafton State Hospital.

6. Richard Higgins, "Is it Calvinism or realism?" *Boston Globe*, August 14, 1986: 1.

7. Bill Nowlin and Jim Prime, *The Boston Red Sox World Series Encyclopedia [No Longer the World's Shortest Book]* (Burlington, Massachusetts: Rounder Books, 2008).

8. Glenn Stout and Richard A. Johnson, *Red Sox Century* (Boston: Houghton Mifflin, 2000), 38.

9. Lawrence Ritter, *The Glory of Their Times* (New York: Harper, 1992), 27. For one history of this first passionate fan organization, see Peter J. Nash, *Boston's Royal Rooters* (Charleston, South Carolina: Arcadia Publishing, 2005).

10. See, for instance, "Muggsy McGraw speaks his mind," *Buffalo News*, July 21, 1904: 10.

11. "Pres Taylor Challenges," *Boston Globe*, October 11, 1904: 5. Taylor suggested a series of five or more games and said he was content if all the proceeds went to the players. McGraw reportedly never responded.

12. One book dedicated exclusively to these dynasty years is Thomas J. Whalen, *When The Red Sox Ruled* (Chicago: Ivan R. Dee, 2011). The book bears the subtitle "Baseball's First Dynasty, 1912-1918."

13. "Giants Win, 2-1; Devore Snatches Victory in Ninth," *New York Times*, October 11, 1912: 1.

14. Leigh Montville, *The Big Bam* (New York: Doubleday, 2006), 52.

15. "Red Sox are Again World's Champions, Defeating Dodgers," *New York Times*, October 13, 1916: 8.

16. Michael Madden, "Question destiny? Don't even try it," *Boston Globe*, October 27, 1986: 53.

17. Dan Shaughnessy, *The Curse of the Bambino* (New York: Penguin Books, 1991 edition), 19.

18. Shaughnessy, *The Curse of the Bambino*, 209, 210.

19. Mark Armour writes that "Cronin took the unusual step of not just resting players, but allowing several of them to leave the club for several days. He gave many of his star players permission to skip the series in St. Louis, providing them five full days off. Williams, DiMaggio, Doerr, Pesky, Hughson, Ferriss, Harris, and Wagner, along with Cronin himself, headed back to Boston." Mark Armour, *Joe Cronin: A Life in Baseball* (Lincoln: University of Nebraska Press, 2010), 166. See Jack Malaney, "Red Sox Regulars Given Five-Days Rest Before Final Home Tune-Up for Series," *The Sporting News*, September 25, 1946: 4.

20. Associated Press, "Williams, Struck by Pitch, Suffers Bruised Elbow in Exhibition Game," *New York Times*, October 2, 1946: 36.

21. For a full discussion of the subject, see Bill Nowlin, *Mr. Red Sox: The Johnny Pesky Story* (Cambridge, Massachusetts: Rounder Books, 2012), 91-96.

22. For detail on his military service, both in World War II and the Korea War, see Bill Nowlin, *Ted Williams at War* (Rounder Books, 2007).

23. As of this writing at the end of 2023, I hope to wrap up a manuscript with the working title *Ted and Jimmy*, for publication before too long. The book is about Ted Williams, and his key role in helping the Jimmy Fund become one of the most-loved charities in New England.

24. For one account of the tryout, see Glenn Stout, "Tryout and Fallout: Race, Jackie Robinson, and the Red Sox," in Bill Nowlin (ed.), *Pumpsie & Progress: The Red Sox Race, and Redemption* (Burlington, Massachusetts; Rounder Books, 2010), 65-91. This book gathers 15 essays on the subject of race and the Red Sox.

25. I later learned that Ted Williams had – without saying a word – made a point of welcoming Pumpsie Green to the Red Sox, choosing him as his throwing partner before each game, thus demonstrating to all that he was welcoming Pumpsie. There was another whole side to Ted Williams that had never been publicized during his playing days. His mother May Venzor was Mexican-American. He was well aware of the prejudices against Mexicans in his native San Diego and elsewhere back then. For a full discussion of his ethnic roots, see Bill Nowlin, *Ted Williams: First Latino in the Baseball Hall of Fame* (Cambridge, Massachusetts: Rounder Books, 2018).

26. Though I didn't truly meet him, I did encounter Johnny Antonelli, the New York Giants pitcher. He was one of the customers on my newspaper route in Lexington back in the later 1950s. I knew he was a baseball player, but didn't really know much about him and hadn't really been inspired to do any research on him. He was from the "wrong league" – the National League. Antonelli had begun his career with the Boston Braves, which is why he came to live in the area. But before the 1953 season the Braves moved to Milwaukee. Though I was only 8 at the time, I do dimly recall hearing they had moved but it didn't mean much to me. Ours had been a Red Sox-oriented household, perhaps in part because my father had worked at Fenway selling hot dogs. I don't really know how he came to become more Red Sox-oriented. It's not as though he was a rabid fan; that was something that infected Bill Jr. (me).

27. Back in 1956, my family had – through the Follen Church – taken in a Hungarian refugee for a year, Attila Kallai. Thinking back on those days, my parents did some remarkable things that broadened our horizons.

28. https://www.census.gov/library/publications/1969/demo/p60-60.html

29. A quick overview of the timeline of email is available from the *Guardian*: https://www.theguardian.com/technology/2016/mar/07/email-ray-tomlinson-history

30. "Bookies Blanch! Bosox 100-1 at Season's Start," in Bill Nowlin and Dan Desrochers, eds., *The 1967 Impossible Dream Red Sox:"Pandemonium on the Field"* (Phoenix: SABR, 2017), 426.

31. This game and many of the other individual games mentioned are ones that I have written for SABR's Games Project. See this one at https://sabr.org/gamesproj/game/september-16-1965-bostons-dave-morehead-no-hits-cleveland/

32. *Boston Globe*, October 6, 1967: 23.

33. Glenn Stout, "When Defeat is Not a Loss – The 1967 World Series," in *The 1967 Impossible Dream Red Sox:"Pandemonium on the Field,"* 445.

34. For a look at the 1975 Red Sox, see Bill Nowlin and Cecilia Tan, eds., *'75: The Red Sox Team that Saved Baseball* (Phoenix: SABR, 2015).

35. They had not seen each other for nearly 15 years because of the lack of relations between the U.S. and Cuba. U.S. Senator George McGovern made an unofficial trip to Cuba and secured Fidel Castro's permission for the family to come to the U.S. Father and son were reunited in August. For much more of the Luis Tiant story, see *Son of Havana* by Luis Tiant with Saul Wisnia (New York: Diversion, 2019).

36. Peter Gammons, "Weak bench prime cause of Red Sox slump," *Boston Globe*, September 12, 1978: Murray Chass deemed manager Bob Lemon as key for New York. Murray Chass, "Lemon key for Yankees," *Boston Globe*, September 12, 1978: 31.

37. A coin flip on September 12 had determined the locale. The Red Sox won the coin flip, if not the actual game.

38. Peter Gammons, "Yankees have final say again," *Boston Globe*, October 3, 1978: 33.

39. Some of the story is told in more detail in Bill Nowlin, *Vinyl Ventures: My Fifty Years at Rounder Records* (Sheffield UK: Equinox Publishing, 2021), 105-106.

40. Author conversation with George Thorogood on June 21, 2023.

41. Don Cusic, *Baseball and Country Music* (Madison: University of Wisconsin/Popular Press, 2003), 56.

42. Cusic, 56.

43. Bill Nowlin, "The Umpire Band," in Larry R. Gerlach and Bill Nowlin (editors), *The SABR Book of Umpires and Umpiring* (Phoenix: SABR, 2017), 443.

44. Conversation with George Thorogood on June 21, 2023.

45. Michael Madden, "Henderson savors deliverance," *Boston Globe*, October 13, 1986: 41.

46. Larry Whiteside, "It's a title roll for Sox," *Boston Globe*, October 16, 1986: 45.

47. Leigh Montville, "Next – A New York / Boston World Series," *Boston Globe*, October 16, 1986: 1, 45.

48. Bill Nowlin, "Why Was Bill Buckner Still on the Field at the End of Game Six?," in *The 1986 Boston Red Sox: There Was More than Game Six*, ed. Bill Nowlin and Leslie Heaphy (Phoenix: SABR, 2016), 360-361.

49. Less than four years later, as Yleana Martinez and I were hitch-hiking across the Sahara Desert from Algeria to Niger in February 1990, one evening we heard that Nelson Mandela was being freed from prison. On March 17, we both attended a "Welcome home Mandela" concert at Ellis Park in Johannesburg.

50. The COVID-19 pandemic in 2020 put an end to most of my traveling, though I did go to Guyana for a few days at the end of 2021. I've been in touch with two umpires from Uganda, and someday perhaps I will make the time to go visit and see some baseball there. They're written me more than once to let me know I will be welcome.

51. Bill Nowlin, *Vinyl Ventures*, 247.

52. Dan Shaughnessy, "Only the beginning? Well, why not?" *Boston Globe*, September 30, 1998: C3.

53. Shaughnessy, "Only the beginning? Well, why not?"

54. Dan Shaughnessy, "Latest Sox chapter has a sad ending," *Boston Globe*, October 4, 1988: 1.

55. The book on which Henry was working, primarily as photographer, is Walt Hriniak, *A Hitting Clinic – The Walt Hriniak Way* (New York: HarperCollins, 1989).

56. *The Fenway Project* was later republished by SABR and is currently available on the SABR website at www.sabr.org and from booksellers.

57. Bill Nowlin, *Ted Williams: First Latino in the Baseball Hall of Fame* (Cambridge, Massachusetts: Rounder Books, 2018).

58. The article appeared in the Fifth Edition of the 2003 season, on pages 27-31.

59. Bill Nowlin, "Yankees obliterate Red Sox, 19-8, to take commanding lead in ACLS," SABR Games Project, sabr.org, https://sabr.org/gamesproj/game/october-16-2004-yankees-obliterate-red-sox-19-8-to-take-commanding-lead-in-alcs/ .

60. Jackie MacMullan, "Odds are fandom fell into trap," *Boston Globe*,
    October 17, 2004: E1.
61. Bob Ryan, "Even by their standards, this is a new low," *Boston Globe*,
    October 17, 2004: E1.
62. Quoted in Allan Wood and Bill Nowlin, *Don't Let Us Win Tonight* (Chicago:
    Triumph Books, 2014), 103. A new edition is planned for 2024.
63. Dan Shaughnessy, "How Much More Can New Englanders Take?" *Boston
    Globe*, October 17, 2004; 1.
64. Theo Epstein, in Allan Wood and Bill Nowlin, *Don't Let Us Win Tonight*
    (Chicago: Triumph Books, 2014), 108.
65. It had happened in championship ice hockey. In 1942, the Toronto Maple
    Leafs had lost the first three games of the Stanley Cup finals to the Detroit
    Red Wings, but then come back and won the final four. (None of the scores
    was as lopsided as 19-8.) And in 1975, in the NHL Quarterfinals, the
    Pittsburgh Penguins beat the New York Islanders in the first three games but
    the New York team came back and won the next four. In the Semifinals, the
    Islanders again lost the first three games (to the Philadelphia Flyers). They
    won the next three…but not Game Seven. In 2023, the Boston Celtics
    came from an 0-3 deficit in the NBA Eastern Conference Finals and won
    Games Four, Five, and Six, but didn't even come close in Game Seven.
66. For some of the details, see Donovan Slack, "Snelgrove panel rips police,"
    Boston Globe, May 26, 2005. The book *Faithful* by Stewart O'Nan and
    Stephen King is dedicated to "Victoria Snelgrove, Red Sox fan."
67. It was surpassed by David Freese of the Cardinals in 2011, who drove
    in 22.
68. Nowlin and Prime, *The Boston Red Sox World Series Encyclopedia [No Longer
    the World's Shortest Book]*, 237.
69. Varitek hit all of 14 triples in his 16-year major-league career.
70. Dan Shaughnessy, "The feeling is unbelievable," *Boston Globe*, October 29,
    2004: F12.
71. There were many stories published in area newspapers at the time. For
    a summary article, which won a number of awards, see Tom Verducci,
    "Sportsmen of the Year," *Sports Illustrated*, December 6, 2014.
72. Bill Simmons, *Now I Can Die in Peace* (New York: ESPN Books, 2005).
73. Alice C. Elwell, "Kathryn Gemme was 23 the last time the Red Sox won
    the World Series," *Brockton Enterprise*, October 5, 2004.
74. E-mail from Sharon Gosling on October 28, 2004.
75. Four Red Sox pitchers combined on a shutout in Game One of Tampa
    Bay in the 2008 ALCS, Matsuzaka throwing the first seven innings, and

four others (led by John Lackey) combined to shut out the Tigers, 1-0, in Game Three of the 2013 ALCS.

76. Troy O'Leary hit one in Game Five of the Division Series in 1999 (also against Cleveland) and Johnny Damon in Game Seven of the 2004 ALCS against the Yankees. They later added three more – including two in the 2013 ALCS (Game Two by David Ortiz and Game Six by Shane Victorino) and one by Jackie Bradley Jr. in ALCS Game Three in 2018).

77. The eight doubles by one team in one game tied a postseason record set by the Pittsburgh Pirates in Game Seven of the 1925 World Series.

78. I also took advantage of my visit to prompt a special meeting of a dozen or so members of SABR's Tokyo Chapter in a nearby pub. More recently I have written up both the trip and the games at greater length for SABR. See my article "2008 Opening Series Boston Red Sox vs. Oakland Athletics," in Robert K. Fitts, ed., *Nichibei Yakyu: US Tours of Japan, Volume 2: 1960-2019* (SABR: 2023).

79. For more on this, see *Ted Williams: First Latino in the Baseball Hall of Fame*, 194-195.

80. One such book was *From The Babe to the Beards*, written by Bill Nowlin and Jim Prime (Skyhorse Publishing, 2014).

81. For a complete listing of SABR books, a list that is growing each year, see https://sabr.org/ebooks.

82. The Yawkey book is *Tom Yawkey: Patriarch of the Boston Red Sox* (Lincoln and London: University of Nebraska Press, 2018). The Ted Williams book is *Ted Williams: First Latino in the Baseball Hall of Fame* (Cambridge: Rounder Books).

83. One can "Search the Research Collection" at sabr.org, or follow this link: https://sabr.org/gamesproj/game/september-20-2020-uninvited-guest-attends-yankees-game-at-fenway/

84. In 2023, Cole was the unanimous Cy Young Award winner in the American League.

85. Though the Red Sox weren't involved, I have been able to go on two baseball tours of Cuba with the group Cubaball – and even got to visit inside the manual scoreboard in Pinar del Rio, before it was replaced.

www.ingramcontent.com/pod-product-compliance
Lightning Source LLC
Chambersburg PA
CBHW021618120626
46545CB00001B/288